The Rediscovery of Newman : An Oxford Symposium

The
Rediscovery of Newman:
An Oxford Symposium

edited by John Coulson and A. M. Allchin

Sheed and Ward. London and Melbourne

S · P · C · K   London

First published 1967
Sheed & Ward, 33 Maiden Lane, London WC2
Sheed & Ward Pty Ltd, 28 Bourke Street, Melbourne
S.P.C.K., Holy Trinity Church, Marylebone Road, London NW1

Standard book number : 7220 0510 5 (Sheed & Ward)
281 02200 3 (S.P.C.K)

This book is set in 12 pt Linotype Granjon
Made and printed in Great Britain by
William Clowes and Sons Ltd, London and Beccles

Contents

Preface

The first Oxford Newman Symposium was held at Oriel College from the evening of Monday, 28 March, to the afternoon of Friday, 1 April 1966. The conference was sponsored by a Committee consisting of the Rev F. W. Dillistone, Fellow and Chaplain of Oriel College, Mgr H. F. Davis, Recognised Lecturer in the Department of Theology of the University of Birmingham, Father C. S. Dessain of the Birmingham Oratory, David Newsome, Fellow and Senior Tutor of Emmanuel College, Cambridge, Miss Meriol Trevor, David Forrester of Keble College, Oxford, and the organisers, the Rev A. M. Allchin, Pusey House, Oxford, and John Coulson, Downside Centre for Religious Studies. The conference was in a large measure the direct result of the third International Newman Conference held in Luxembourg at Whitsun 1964, which had been attended by a number of members of the sponsoring committee.[1] After that meeting, it had been felt that it was time to organise a similar conference in England, which would do something to explore the distinctive English contribution to Newman studies, to open up new lines of communication between those concerned with Newman in this country and those at work in this field in Europe and America, and to suggest the need for a more systematic inclusion of Newman studies in the regular teaching programmes of British universities. In the words of the Abbé Nicholas Theis, promoter of the Newman Conferences in Luxembourg, it was time 'to bring Newman home'.

Once it was decided to hold the Symposium in Oxford, Oriel immediately suggested itself as the meeting place. The conference

---

[1] For the Luxembourg conferences see the note by Father Boekraad, 'Newman in the Low Countries', p. 193.

gained much by being held in Newman's own college. Dr F. W. Dillistone acted as host throughout the meeting, and was Chairman at most of its sessions. We would like to record the deep sense of gratitude felt by all members of the conference for the skill with which he guided our discussions, and the unfailing courtesy with which he made us welcome in Oriel. Most of those who came from outside Oxford resided in the college, and all the members of the conference were able to take their meals together in hall. We are grateful to the Provost, Mr K. C. Turpin, for his presence with us on the first evening of our meeting, to Dr W. A. Pantin, Fellow of Oriel and Keeper of the University Archives, for his fascinating talk on Newman's life as a fellow of the college, and to Brigadier R. E. Bagnall-Wild, Treasurer, for his assistance in matters of administration.

The essay which stands first in this volume after the Introduction, is the address given by the Archbishop of Canterbury at the opening meeting on the evening of 28 March. On this occasion the full-time members of the conference were joined by a number of distinguished visitors from the University and beyond, among them the Provost of Oriel, the Principal of St Edmund Hall (the Rev Dr J. N. D. Kelly, Chairman of the Archbishop's Commission for Roman Catholic relations), the Apostolic Delegate, Archbishop Hyginus Cardinale, the Archbishop of Birmingham, Mgr G. P. Dwyer, and the Superior of the Birmingham Oratory, Father Geoffrey Wamsley. What the organisers had not been able to foresee was that the Archbishop of Canterbury would be coming to Oxford, only three days after his return from his historic visit to Rome. On the following morning, his Grace celebrated Holy Communion at the University Church of St Mary, and many members of the conference were able to be present on this occasion, which was, as it happened, the centenary day of the death of John Keble on 29 March (Maundy Thursday), 1866.

The conference from the start took place in an atmosphere of great friendship and informality, which deepened as the days passed. Not least important in its development were the opportunities for common prayer. Each morning there was a celebration of Mass in Newman's own rooms (by kind permission of their present occupant, Dr A. G. Weddell), and a celebration of the Holy Communion in the Chancel of the University Church. Thus we were able to worship in the room where Newman had lived during many of his Oxford years, and in the church which he made famous by his parochial and university sermons. We were also able on the last full day of the conference to say Evensong together in Oriel College Chapel.

On Wednesday afternoon, 30 March, the conference made an expedition to Littlemore, where by kind permission of the Vicar, and with the approval of the appropriate ecclesiastical authorities, an ecumenical Service of the Word was held. Based in its general outline on the service in which the Pope and the Archbishop of Canterbury had participated in Rome in the previous week, it included the singing of two of Newman's hymns and the reading of a prayer of intercession from his translation of the *Preces Privatae* of Lancelot Andrews. A brief but deeply moving sermon was preached by the Abbé Nicholas Theis. Recalling his first visit to Littlemore almost thirty years before, he spoke of his life-long love for Newman and for this place; he commented on the changed situation which made it possible for us to gather together in prayer in this church, and to find in our common concern for Newman not a cause of division, but a place of reconciliation, where 'we may meet on common ground, i.e. scriptural holiness'. After the service, the members of the conference took tea at the "College", now restored and maintained by the Fathers of the Birmingham Oratory. They were able to see the excellent guide book to Newman places in Oxford produced jointly by Father Humphrey Crookenden of the Oratory, and the Rev Valentine Fletcher, Vicar of Littlemore, and to hear something of the way in which Littlemore is becoming both a place of pilgrimage, and a place of prayer for Christian unity. We are grateful to Father Crookenden, to Mrs Fletcher, and to the ladies of Littlemore for the arrangements of this afternoon. We wish, also, to take this opportunity to record the indebtedness of all Newman scholars to the continuing generosity of Newman's Oratory at Birmingham, without whose help and concern Newman studies as we know them could not have been developed.

Our gratitude is also due to many others who helped forward the organisation of these days and the preparation of this book; among them Father Michael Hollings, Catholic Chaplain to the University of Oxford, who gave much assistance in the arrangements for worship, Canon Philip Martin, Vicar of the University Church, Miss Meriol Trevor for her transcripts of the discussions, and David Forrester, who as bursar of the conference took the whole weight of its day-to-day administration into his efficient hands. Our debt to him is very great.

From the very beginning, and at every stage, the planning of this conference was a joint Anglican-Roman Catholic operation, and though the Free Church representation in the symposium itself was numerically small, it was, as the records show, weighty and most valuable. In this way, a subject which in the past has been thought to be eminently divisive proved to have unsuspected ecumenical possibilities. Our last word of thanks must therefore go to our publishers, who by agreeing to make this book a joint production, have given a permanent form to an undertaking which in its conception and execution necessarily involved an ecumenical partnership more intimate and thorough-going, than is at present commonly thought possible in this country.

J. C. and A. M. A.

Introduction

John Coulson and
A. M. Allchin

The tide has been turned and a first, immensely important, step has been taken towards the vindication of all the main theological, religious and cultural positions of the former Fellow of Oriel.

This was the verdict of Bishop Butler on the Second Vatican Council, but it might as fittingly stand for the united judgement of this symposium – if we wish to find common elements which, when studied from the differing Christian standpoints, set the agenda for our mutual growth towards unity, then we need go no farther back in history than to Newman. That Newman has a unique part to play in this dialogue may seem merely an arbitrary opinion, however, until we come to see him as essentially a theologian.

In England, for example, Newman studies have tended to be confined to the biographical or literary. In Europe, on the other hand, he has come to be seen not only as one of the foremost theologians of his age, but the one whom it has seemed appropriate to compare with Augustine and Aquinas.

The purpose of this symposium was, therefore, 'to bring Newman home' in more senses than one. Confident that the grounds of former differences need no longer be regarded as sources of estrangement, but rather as opportunities to understand our respective traditions, we decided to hold the symposium at the College and in the University from which Newman 'moved out on to the open sea'.

Put simply, the question which concerned us was – is the study of Newman of limited archaeological interest, or of immediate theological importance? A convincing answer demanded the testimony of many minds. Hence this symposium. It ensured that if Newman could be 'brought home', it would be in company with those who had been the first to show the ecumenical direction of his theological thinking – his European students – and to a welcome which was itself representative of all the main English theological traditions – Anglican, Free Church, and Roman Catholic.

That Newman was a master of the spiritual life and a great apologist for the Roman Church was not in question. At times, as in his *Lectures on Justification*, he writes with a deliberately constructive or ecumenical intention; at others his situation obliges him to be polemical – and in this he was a man of his age. But it is the underlying themes and motives of his work which make him uniquely the pioneer in the recovery of unity. It has, however, needed almost a century of growth towards that unity as well as the specific enactments of the Vatican Council before we can see that he was something more than the author of the *Apologia*.

I

The purpose of the introductory paper by the Archbishop of Canterbury is to suggest why this is so. The Archbishop sees Newman as an outstanding interpreter of the scriptures whose prophetic gifts were exercised under the stimulus of 'occasions'. Like Burke, he worked from concrete challenges and events towards insights of a more general application. And although he largely created and typified the Oxford Movement, he was – in the words of Dr Parker – 'the odd man out'.[1] This was because throughout his life Newman was always in movement and never able to identify himself wholly with positions which were closed to further growth: 'in a higher world it is otherwise, but here below to live is to change, and to be perfect is to have changed often'.[2] The Archbishop emphasises the need to disentangle Newman's thought from its irrelevant associations with the details of Victorian controversy into which he was so often drawn against his will. When we do so we find that what he has to say is of greater relevance to our own needs than to those of his contemporaries. We also see something of the injury done to our understanding of Christian truth when the ice of nineteenth-century religious polemic entered into the souls of its theologians—Evangelical, Tractarian, or into Newman himself.

II

This is a warning which recurs throughout the volume; and it is essential to bear it in mind when we approach the second section

---

[1] Parker, 'Rediscovery of the Fathers in the Seventeenth-century Anglican tradition', p. 43.
[2] *Essay on Development of Christian Doctrine*, 1.7, quoted by Bishop Butler in 'Newman and the Second Vatican Council', p. 239.

of the symposium – on the sources of Newman's power and the development of his theology – since the complexity of Newman's character is unlikely to be neglected by English writers; and it will ever be a source of controversy. David Newsome's paper shows how it was formed by that Evangelical understanding of how the individual is alone before God – it defined and consecrated something in Newman which was surely innate. To acknowledge this quality is a precondition for understanding the roots from which Newman's theology grew, since it is this intense sense of the uniqueness and inwardness of the personal life which helps to make Newman a theologian for our own time. It became one of the master concepts of his theology[1], and it predisposed him to regard the central traditions of the Church of England with a permanently critical eye. But these insights were always threatened by the frosts and mists of religious polemic – they led Newman, like many of his contemporaries, to under-estimate the Reformation[2], and to deny any future to the Anglicanism he had helped to create. The Evangelical movement itself decayed[3], and the political Ultramontane movement in the Roman Church made a massive contribution to the theological ice-age from which we have only just begun to emerge.

Nevertheless, if we are to understand Newman, we must see him as a theologian who was throughout his life in perpetual growth. It was a growth firmly rooted in the Scriptures, and as they are seen through the eyes of the Fathers. How, then, did Newman come to his knowledge of the Fathers? Was it direct, or did it come through reading the Anglican Divines of the seventeenth century? Dr Parker's analysis in the second paper of this section may well be considered to provide a definitive answer: he judges Newman to have come to the Fathers as a by-product of his deepening sense of history, and then to have studied them before reading those Anglican Divines whom the Tractarians considered to be the founding fathers of their view of the Church of England. This conclusion has important consequences—it establishes from the start Newman's position of relative detachment

---

[1] See below, p. xviii, *n.* 3.

[2] Newsome, 'The Evangelical sources of Newman's Power', p. 120; Rupp, 'Newman through Nonconformist eyes', p. 211; Ramsey, 'The ecumenical importance of Newman', p. 7; Cunliffe-Jones, 'Note on the Free Church attitude to Newman', p. 214.

[3] Ramsey, 7; Newsome, 24; Rupp, 198.

from Keble and Pusey – a position further confirmed by the account of his Evangelical origins. 'He looks as much to the future as to the past.'[1]

Yet, at the height of the Oxford Movement, there was a shared intellectual vitality which has been insufficiently recognised; and, in the light of hitherto unpublished material, Father Allchin examines that peculiar ethos of the Oxford Movement in order to assess the part it played in forming certain aspects of Newman's approach to theology. It was as an influence wholly constructive, deriving as it did from that peculiar union of feeling and thought which is the characteristic of the English Romantic movement; and the Tractarians, Newman included, developed in a climate of opinion in which Wordsworth and Coleridge were among the chief formative influences. By means of an analysis of Pusey's unpublished lectures on *Types and Prophecies*, which Newman attended, Father Allchin illustrates this way of conceiving symbols[2] and sacraments, and the view of the Church to which it gave rise as wholly expressive of the given character of Christianity: 'For Christ dwelleth in the Church, and it visibly exhibits Him.'[3] Far from abandoning this view after 1845, Newman developed it in a new, if colder, climate.

The growth of these insights received assistance from an unexpected quarter – from the prevailing traditions of British philosophy, deriving as they did from the empiricism of David Hume. It is the purpose of Professor Cameron's paper to argue that this empiricist tradition saved Newman from attempting to build his theology upon the questionable but then superficially attractive arguments, such as those from design, which were to be challenged so successfully later in the century. 'Empiricism is an experience that has to be lived through if we are to grasp the mentality of the modern educated man'[4], and that Newman lived through this experience helps to explain something of his appeal to us today.

In a note, Father Derek Holmes shows that Newman's philosophical scepticism extended to his historical method – far from permitting his theory of development to be used to dismiss incon-

[1] Parker, 48.
[2] Allchin, 'The theological vision of the Oxford Movement', p. 70; Coulson, 'Newman's idea of the Church – his final view, its origins and influence', p. 126.
[3] Pusey quoted by Allchin, 73.
[4] Cameron, 'Newman and the Empiricist Tradition', p. 95; see also p. 90.

venient facts, Newman was prepared for the logical possibility of
its empirical refutation. Yet while Newman's scepticism preserved
him from that optimistic addiction to philosophical systems which
ravaged theology elsewhere, its chief contribution was to enable
him to make a proper space for theology[1], and to place its foundation where they must always rest – upon scripture and tradition.
Newman's strength arises from this limitation – he is ever, as
philosopher and theologian, the champion of Revealed Religion;
and what theology gained thereby is the subject of the next paper
by Father Stephen Dessain.

It describes the Evangelical origins of Newman's teaching on
the Indwelling of Christ in the believer – its application to religion in the *Parochial Sermons*, and ecumenically in the *Lectures
on Justification*. Once Christians cease to be 'in bondage to their
feelings'[2], they can appreciate 'the ecclesial nature of the divine
Gift, which is not a private grace, but establishes a common
fellowship'.[3]

In this paper Newman's ecumenical significance becomes strik-
ingly apparent, not only because he throws a reconciling light
upon those questions which divided Western Christendom at the
Reformation, but also because – in his emphasis upon our 'organic
participation in the risen life of Christ'[4] – he comes close to the
tradition of Eastern Orthodoxy concerning the Resurrection. The
paper concludes by showing to what extent the Latin West has
recovered this tradition.

Is Newman here a mystic or a theologian, a devotional or a
theological writer? His life and work question the validity of this
antithesis. Apart from the given structure of sacramental dogma,
the experience of the individual becomes shallow and self-centred;
but without that inner experience, tradition must become ossified
into a system of meaningless acts. And the purpose of the final
paper in this section is to show how Newman's developing idea
of the Church as the indwelling presence of Christ was brought to
bear upon the problems facing the Roman Catholic Church after
the decisions of the First Vatican Council of 1870. By means of a
detailed study of the manuscript of the Preface to the reissue of

---

[1] Cameron, pp. 82 and 94; Cunliffe-Jones, p. 214.
[2] Desain, 'The biblical basis of Newman's ecumenical theology', p. 116, and
the related discussion of Sabatier by Dupuy, 'Newman's influence in France',
pp. 154f.
[3] Dessain, p. 109.
[4] C. C. J. Webb quoted by Dessain, p. 117.

the old *Lectures on the Prophetical Office of the Church* (usually referred to as the Preface to the 1877 edition of the *Via Media*), John Coulson shows how Newman's sense of the Church, which derived from his Anglican background, was incompatible with the fashionable Ultramontane view of the Church as confined to its political, sociological, or juridical structure. Instead, by returning to the three offices of Christ as prophet, priest, and King, Newman showed that the Church must itself perform all three offices or functions if it were to be fully itself, and that of these, theology must be restored to its preeminence as 'the regulating function'[1] – a view which, although at variance with much official thinking at the time, is now confirmed by the *Constitution on the Church* of the Second Vatican Council.

Anglicans may well feel that something of the heart of their own tradition has here become revived within the Church of Rome itself, viz, that the idea of the Church is not merely institutional but is akin to the sacramental and symbolic conceptions of a Coleridge, a Maurice, or a Pusey. And if this is so, what happens when the Church denies this multiplicity of functions; or to put the question as it was raised in the discussion by Professor Rupp, what happens when the Church sins? Does the sin of persisting in disunity, for example, make for a withdrawal of grace? That this survey of the sources of Newman's power obliged us to ask such fundamental questions, helps to confirm that claim for Newman's importance on which this symposium rests.

III

To claim that Newman is uniquely important, however, it is essential to show how his influence as a theologian has been felt, not only in the various parts of the Roman Church, but in the chief Christian bodies. Such a survey of Newman's influence, to which this, the third part of the book is devoted, is bound to be selective; but it was concerned to answer two questions in particular; can we trace a common pattern in Newman's influence upon traditions and countries so various; and how has it come about that a writer who has so little of the apparatus of the 'professional' theologian has come increasingly to be recognised as one of the greatest and most formative Catholic theologians of recent times? Should we,

[1] Coulson, p. 143.

for example, revise our understanding of how theology ought to be studied?

It is fitting that this section should begin with a contribution from a French scholar, Father Dupuy, since France has given so much, not only to the development of European theology, but to Newman studies in particular. In tracing the growth of French appreciation of Newman, Father Dupuy outlines a pattern which will be found to apply to Europe as a whole: that interest at first concentrates on Newman as a person and, therefore, as a devotional writer. His relevance is then seen to the more general discussion about the development of Christian doctrine and the function of 'tradition' within the Church. It is at this point that Newman begins to be taken seriously as a theologian; but the modernist crisis intervenes, and the narrow Thomism of the schools is temporarily reasserted. It is not until the study of theology is seen to require a diversity of approaches and disciplines that Newman is valued in his own right as a theologian. This influence upon our own times is then seen to be as potentially formative as that of the greatest thinkers of the Christian tradition.

This may seem a bold claim, but the ensuing papers provide significant testimony from highly diverse sources. Dr Becker from East Germany gives massive evidence of the quality and quantity of attention which Newman has received in Germany during the last hundred years. Since the war his influence has been particularly creative, and Father Becker writes movingly of how Newman studies were revived amidst the ruins of Cologne in 1945 and of their bearing upon the new climate of opinion in German Catholicism. Not least among the achievements of this period has been the regular publication of the volumes of *Newman-Studien*. This renaissance of Newman studies has had a marked influence upon the Second Vatican Council and has affected Karl Rahner[1] in particular in his work for the renovation of the Catholic theological tradition. Dr Boekraad's note brings supporting testimony from the Low Countries. Again we see how studies have gradually moved from the biographical to the theological, and how Newman must be seen in his own light if his thought is to be fully understood.

Of particular interest is the testimony furnished by Professor Gordon Rupp, to which a corroborating note has been added by

---

[1] Becker, 'Newman's influence in Germany', p. 186.

Dr Cunliffe-Jones. In the course of an illuminating comparison between Newman and Luther, Professor Rupp suggests that in what is common to two such disparate men we may find 'evidence for an ecumenical norm, a core of unity, stemming from our unity in Baptism, from which in our time a dialogue might well begin'.[1] Having traced the emergence of an appreciation of Newman by the Free Churches from amidst the narrowness of Victorian polemic, his paper concludes with this advice: 'On the Continent let Hans Kung talk it out with Karl Barth, but in England let us begin with Newman and not the Bishop of Woolwich.'[2]

This point of view is confirmed quite independently by one of that pioneer generation of Newman scholars who have borne the burden and the heat of the day—Mgr H. Francis Davis—whose paper concludes this section. From the standpoint of the first Roman Catholic ever to be appointed to be a full-time member of a department of theology in a British university, Mgr Davis shows how Newman's work is relevant to the difficulties to which theology is currently exposed from the logical analysts on the one hand and from the 'secular' theologians on the other. He reminds us of the very nerve of Newman's teaching – that it is an analysis of our moral experience which implies a capacity for that unique relationship between 'our own soul and the God who made it', which Newman variously describes as 'the echo of a person speaking to me', 'the echo of the living Word', and 'the essential principle and sanction of Religion in the mind'. It is significant that this description of man's relation to God is referred to by almost all the contributors[3] as one of Newman's leading ideas.

But, today, when we speak of the love of Christ or of the presence of Christ dwelling within our hearts, to what extent can we assume our account to be intelligible to others? The discussion in the symposium made it quite clear that it is not merely the objections of philosophers, but the puzzlements of the present generation of Christians that prompt us to ask this question. And although we do not have to accept the charge that nothing in reality corresponds to such expressions, we must be prepared not

[1] Rupp, p. 212.
[2] Rupp, p. 212.
[3] It is that expressed by Newman in 'Sermons on the Subject of the Day', 38 and repeated in the *Apologia* (Oxford ed. 108). Newsome, pp. 21 and 28; Cameron, p. 88; Rupp, pp. 209f; Davis, p. 227; Butler, p. 246.

only to respond to a more rigorous questioning of our terms but indeed to invite it.

What seems accepted is that our starting-point is where Newman placed it – in our personal awareness of moral commitment.[1] And it was here in the symposium that the contributions of such eminent European scholars as Dr Boekraad, Professor Nédoncelle, and Dr Walgrave were particularly valuable.

The theological changes now taking place in Europe and America arise in part from changes in self-awareness, and from a developing understanding of what is involved when we speak of our lives as personal. This is not to imply that theology ought merely to reflect the current philosophy of man: the gospel fulfils human aspirations, but it also brings a judgement. Yet, as Pope John xxiii reminded the Church, we need to listen as well as to speak, in order to hear what God is saying through the events of our time. The attempts by theologians to develop a contemporary Christian anthropology are concerned to free man from the rationalist and subjectivist strait-jackets of his recent past, in order that he may rediscover the unity and social character of the human person – and of the Church. If, as Dr Walgrave pointed out, we accept Newman's 'the whole man moves', and 'paper logic is but the record', then as man moves, so must the Church; and to understand the dialogue of conscience within man is to understand 'tradition' as the dialogue of conscience within the Church[2], whose development 'adds a perfection to the living reality'.[3] Although Newman starts from the heart speaking to the heart in the dialogue of conscience, he places this within the context of the Church as the means appointed by Christ 'to show us how to come to him'.[4]

Newman's understanding of the Church was at once personal and sacramental rather than sociological and political; and it was from the Fathers and from his friends in the Oxford Movement that he gained this sacramental vision of which, in its expression, the key terms are idea[5], image[6], development, and tradition.[7]

[1] Davis, 'Newman's influence in England', p. 231.
[2] Dupuy, p. 173.
[3] Butler, 4. For how far Newman was prepared to go in this matter, see Coulson, p. 138.
[4] *Parochial and Plain Sermons* vii, quoted by Coulson, p. 130.
[5] Coulson, pp. 126ff; Davis, pp. 229ff; Butler, p. 239.
[6] Allchin, p. 72.
[7] Dupuy, pp. 172f; Butler, p. 238.

And it is this dimension of our common faith that so many who have been outside the Catholic tradition are beginning once again to investigate. Thus Professor Rupp speaks of the need to gain a better understanding of the circumference as well as of the centre of Christian experience[1], and Dr Cunliffe-Jones says that 'we ought to recognise that all Christian believers are committed to some belief of infallibility', and he recommends that we 'explore together the different, if overlapping places, where we find it'.[2]

IV

Heart speaks to heart; but, as Bishop Butler makes clear in the concluding paper, *cor ad cor loquitur* cannot be restricted in its application to the heart of the religious man speaking to his God, but it also refers to the heart of God speaking to the heart of his Church and ultimately 'to the hearts of all men of good will'.[3]

Newman has frequently been referred to as the invisible peritus at the Second Vatican Council, which has itself been described as Newman come true. And it is fitting that a symposium which opens with a striking reassessment of Newman from the Anglican standpoint by the Archbishop of Canterbury should conclude with an assessment of the Vatican Council from Newman's point of view and by one, moreover, who was a leading contributor to its deliberations.

It may be said that the Council was the means by which the Church as a whole was at last brought to accept the demands of historical development. In it the Church was enabled to 'turn her eyes and desires outwards from a somewhat unhealthy introspection to the challenges and needs of a world tremendously alive and in a phase of incalculably swift evolution'[4], and thus the essential positions of Newman were vindicated.[5]

The scholars from such diverse backgrounds who came together in this meeting, the first Symposium on Newman to be held in his university, came to a similar conclusion. They also discovered how much they had lost by pursuing their theological studies in isola-

[1] Rupp, p. 212.
[2] Cunliffe-Jones, p. 215.
[3] Butler, p. 246.
[4] Butler, p. 240.
[5] In the words already quoted at the beginning of this Introduction. See Butler, p. 245.

tion from each other, and how much they had to gain from a deeper dialogue. Amongst themselves, and with students in other disciplines, it would seem that theology can only grow in relevance to our times if it ceases to feed upon itself.

Somewhat paradoxically we find that the price of remaining isolated and disunited is that each tradition becomes subjected to factors extraneous to its life and purpose, so that Christian thinking and action become too passively the reflections of fashions and moods in the world of philosophy and politics. The harm done to religion by the polemic of the nineteenth century, with its political undertones, is a case in point.

Unity raises its own problems, however. It could restore to the Church a power of self-determination greater than that which it possessed before the Reformation. In theory this should enable the Church to serve the world more effectively by being more itself. In practice, however, such unity would be tolerable only if it fulfilled, and did not destroy, our moral freedom.[1] And Newman's particular value for the future may arise from the thorough and painful examination he was obliged to make of the relation of freedom and authority within the Church.[2] Yet Christ has prayed that we should be one even as he and the Father are one, and to experience the unity engendered even on the modest scale of this symposium is to learn that ecumenism is not a hobby of enthusiasts: it is a necessary witness to the gravity of our persisting in disunity. Thus, when from their respective positions the Archbishop of Canterbury and Bishop Butler show us that we can learn from Newman not only what are the most profitable subjects to choose for our ecumenical investigation, but how they should be approached, we should perhaps recall Newman's own words on another and equally serious occasion:

Put not from you what you have here found; regard it not as a mere matter of present controversy . . . Wrap not yourself round in the associations of years past, nor determine that to be truth which you wish to be so, nor make an idol of cherished anticipations. Time is short, eternity is long.

[1] Allchin, p. 74.
[2] Coulson, pp. 141f.

Part 1

The significance of Newman today

The significance
of Newman today

A. M. Ramsey

I first heard of Newman as a schoolboy, when we were told by the sixth-form master that if we were to write Latin we must look to Cicero and if we were to write English we must look to Newman. Newman was the writer of English to whom one must aspire. No wonder. Newman could write sentences:

> The year is worn out; spring, summer, autumn, each in turn, have brought their gifts and done their utmost, but they are over and the end is come.

And Newman could write periods:

> Hence it is that it is almost a definition of a gentleman to say that he is one who never inflicts pain. . . . He has his eyes on all his company; he is tender towards the bashful, gentle towards the distant, merciful towards the absurd; he can recollect to whom he is speaking; he guards against unseasonable allusions or topics which may irritate; he is seldom prominent in conversation, and never wearisome. He makes light of favours while he does them, and seems to be receiving when he is conferring. He never speaks of himself except when compelled, never defends himself by a mere retort, he has no ears for slander or gossip, is scrupulous in imputing motives to those who interfere with him, and interprets everything for the best. He is never mean or little in his disputes; never takes unfair advantage; never mistakes personalities or sharp sayings for arguments, or insinuates evil which he dare not say out. From a long-sighted prudence, he observes the maxim of the ancient sage

that we should ever conduct ourselves towards our enemy as if he were one day to be our friend. He has too much good sense to be affronted at insults; he is too well employed to remember injuries and too indolent to bear malice. He is patient, forbearing and resigned, on philosophical principles; he submits to pain because it is inevitable, to bereavement because it is irreparable, and to death because it is his destiny. If he engages in controversy of any kind, his disciplined intellect preserves him from the blundering discourtesy of better, though less educated minds; who like blunt weapons tear and hack instead of cutting clean, who re-state the point in argument, waste their strength on trifles, misconceive their adversary and leave the question more involved than they find it. He may be right or wrong in his opinion, but he is too clear-headed to be unjust; he is as simple as he is forcible, and as brief as he is decisive.[1]

Now it is strange to read a passage like that (I note in passing the biblical undertone both of the sentiments and of some of the language) and then to realise that Newman did not set himself to write as a painter sets himself to paint or a sculptor sets himself to carve, or as a poet sets himself to write poems. It was only duty, he tells us, that forced him to write, that dragged him to put his thought into words. And here I refer to Newman's theory of poetry. He expounded it in his essay, *Poetry with Reference to Aristotle's Poetics*. Newman repudiates Aristotle's theory that poetry means the creation of poems; that poetry is a species of making things. No, says Newman: poetry means an intuitive sensitivity to the world around and all that is in it. But a man may be a poet without writing anything at all. The poet is one who contemplates, and it is the power of contemplating that defines the poet. I quote:

> The poet's habit of mind leads him to contemplation rather than to communication with others. If a poet communicates to others, and not infrequently they have done so, his doing so, and his power to do so, is not part of the poetic gift; it is something perhaps incidental or accidental but it is not the role of the poet at all.[2]

---

[1] J. H. Newman, *The Idea of a University* London 1925, 208.
[2] J. H. Newman, *Poetry with Reference to Aristotle's Poetics* in *Essays, Critical and Historical*, vol. 1 (1907), 24.

Does this theory of poetry held by Newman somehow go with his view of the essence of religion? The Christian is for the greater part of his time by himself, and when he is in solitude that is his real state.[1] I could quote a good many sentences from different works which say the same thing. How far is there a correspondence between Newman's view of poetry as contemplation and Newman's perception of religion? Again, how far did Newman describe himself correctly when he spoke, as he so often did, of the effort and the duty which alone compelled him to write and forced words from him? Perhaps the answer is this: that while indeed Newman's idea of poetry as the contemplation of everything went with that sensitivity which was so deeply a part of his character, nonetheless, when words came into existence, his sensitive perception went out to them, and the *contemplare omnia* in the end could not help applying to words including his own words. I have a feeling that while Newman for many years had this reluctance to write and while for the most part he wrote either because circumstances compelled him to produce pamphlets or duty compelled him to produce sermons, he did win through in the end to an enjoyment of his own writings, perhaps from the time of the *Apologia* onwards. It is possible then to see Newman as one who finds himself joyfully the man of letters in the way that he had never quite done before. Yet for the most part what Newman says of himself is true, and one must trust him. He wrote because duty compelled him; and he wrote pamphlets and sermons.

Pamphlets. Yes. Newman's great works for the most part are pamphlets written in order to debate a particular point in an immediate contemporary situation about which he was sensitive. *The Prophetical Office of the Church* was written in order to demonstrate that both the Roman Catholic and the Protestant theory of the Church were misleading and there was a third theory which was true. *Lectures on Justification* was written to demonstrate that what he believed to be Luther's doctrine of Justification and its counterpart in contemporary Evangelicalism were very misleading and that there was a more excellent way. *The Idea of Development* was written in order to demonstrate that there is an answer to the contrast between the Church as it was once and the Church as it now is. *The Apologia* was written through pain at a terrible personal predicament. Great master-

---

[1] *Parochial and Plain Sermons*, vol. VII (1907), 69.

pieces, but all of them in origin pamphlets. And I quote Lord Coleridge: 'J.H.N., like Burke, always makes a pamphlet a thing of permanent value.' And then, going back to Burke, one remembers John Morley's description of Burke's writings: 'In the midst of discussion of things local and accidental, he takes us into the region of lasting wisdom.' And just because some of Newman's greatest works were pamphlets with a local contemporary and incidental reference, their value to humanity may be other from and greater than the value that Newman himself believed them to have.

I want to test this possibility in relation to two of Newman's greatest writings in his Tractarian period. *The Prophetical Office of the Church*: Newman wrote this as an exposition of the Anglican *Via Media*. He came to feel that the *Via Media* which he had thus expounded was a thing existing on paper rather than in fact, and he abandoned it. Yet, though Newman abandoned it, the belief in this *Via Media* described by him persisted, and subsequent Anglican expositions, with scholarly differences according to the settings in which they have been written, have often been near to the thesis of Newman's *Prophetical Office*. I find a good deal of similarity to it, for instance, in Bishop Gore's exposition of the Anglican position in his work *The Holy Spirit and the Church*, though the anti-Roman polemic in Bishop Gore is not nearly so vehement as it was in Newman's work. But Newman was concerned with the ideal of the Scriptural Church. Where today can we find the counterpart of the ideal of the Scriptural Church? Do we find it in Canterbury or do we find it in Rome? With that question Newman tormented himself. When he edited the work again in a subsequent decade he explains that he feels he made the mistake of thinking solely in terms of the teaching office of the Church and now sees the need to pay attention to other functions of the Church as well. He says: 'Christianity is at once a philosophy, a political power, and a religious rite.' But reading the work now I would say that its greatest value does not lie in the polemics which prompted Newman to write it or in the aspects of it which appealed to him most and worried him most both then and subsequently, but lies rather in the inclusion within the work of some moving descriptions of the nature of the teaching of Christ in the Gospels and the relation of the teaching of the Apostles to the teaching of Christ. Those passages have a value lasting far beyond the polemical interest of the book.

I take another of Newman's Tractarian writings: *Lectures on Justification*. This was a polemic against what Newman thought to be Luther's doctrine, and he supposed Luther's doctrine to be the same as the more stale and decayed forms of Evangelical teaching in England. It is perhaps the most typically Tractarian of all his works, expounding what became a typically Tractarian thesis. Newman was ignorant of Luther, in fact his picture of Luther's teaching is something of a caricature, and Newman's work, alas, begat the habit of caricaturing Luther which lasted on in Anglican divinity until very recent times. Yet within the work there is a positive theme transcending the particular controversy with which the book was concerned, and coming to a head in the final chapter *On Preaching the Gospel*. Justification by faith, if it is faith in Christ, is a principle and not a 'thing in itself'.

> True faith is what may be called colourless – like air or water. It is but the medium through which the soul sees Christ, and the soul as little contemplates it as the eye can see the air. When men, then, are led to holding it in their hands, as it were, ... they are obliged to thicken and colour it, so that it may be touched and seen. They rather aim at experiences, as they are called, within them, than at Him who is without them.
>
> As God's grace solicits our faith, so His holiness stirs our fear, and His glory kindles our love. Others may say of us 'here is faith' and 'there is conscientiousness', and 'there is love', but we can only say 'this is God's grace' and 'that is His holiness' and 'that is His glory'.[1]

The permanent value of the work is its testimony, not only against dogmatic Evangelicalism, but against every form of religious 'spikiness' which contemplates the media of salvation rather than its author and giver.

These are some instances of how the polemical interest of some of Newman's writings is very much less than their permanent value which is somehow upon a different plane. What is it that is so compelling? I believe it is a sensitivity to the language and thought of the New Testament, a sensitivity which compels Newman to understand St Paul alongside St John and the Synoptic Gospels. If that is true of some of Newman's polemical treatises it is no less true of his sermons. In the *Parochial and Plain Sermons*

---

[1] *Lectures on Justification* (1890), 336 and 337.

there is a wonderful nearness to the New Testament, not least to the Gospels. A striking tribute was paid to Newman by William Sanday, the New Testament scholar. Sanday was discussing the qualities needed for the writing of a modern life of Christ and how rare these qualities are, and he said: 'What is wanted is a Newman, with science and adequate knowledge. No-one has ever touched the Gospels with so much innate kinship of spirit as he.'[1] Newman's nearness to the New Testament appears in his grasp of its many-hued contrasts – the mysteriousness of Revelation and the homeliness of the Word made Flesh: the greatness of Divine Sovereignty, Grace and Election, and of men's freedom, responsibility, and dignity; the other worldliness of Christianity – here we have no continuing city – and the belief that every fragment of nature, every moment of time has Divine significance: and above all the insistence that Christianity is the life of those who are called to be saints and that holiness is the way both to truth and to unity.

I am not surprised when I hear it said that the spiritual renewal of the Roman Catholic Church will mean the recapturing of something of the spirit of John Henry Newman. I believe too that the renewal of the Anglican Church will involve the recapturing of something of the spirit of John Henry Newman, and by that I mean not the recapturing of Tractarianism in its particular polemical theses, but rather the recapturing of that spirit of scriptural holiness which pervades his writings from first to last. It was the perception of that which caused Pusey to write only a fortnight after the great grief of 1846, 'As each by God's grace grows in holiness, each Church will recognise more and more the presence of God's Holy Spirit in the other.'

The significance for today of John Henry Newman is that he brings that home to us.

---

[1] William Sanday, *Outlines of the Life of Christ* London 1905, 240.

Part II

The sources of Newman's power

1
The evangelical sources of Newman's power

David Newsome

No one could accuse John Henry Newman of being unduly reticent about the details of his spiritual development or the state of his religious opinions at various stages of his life. Yet the fact remains that he vouchsafed least information about the event which would appear to require the fullest elucidation – the circumstances of his first conversion – when, at the age of fifteen, he passed from nominal Christianity to the consciousness of being in a state of grace. Newman himself acknowledged the experience to have been decisive. Nearly fifty years later he testified to its authenticity, declaring himself to be more certain that he had received a genuine call 'than that I have hands and feet'.[1]

He supplied a few more clues as to its nature, although the details are rather bare. The conversion occurred when he was low in spirits – left at school during the holidays, with his friends away – conscious of being smitten by God, for the family bank had been forced to suspend payments and disaster seemed imminent.[2] This at once suggests a similarity to Henry Manning's conversion, which coincided with the collapse of the firm of Manning and Anderdon in 1831. Manning was cast out alone without prospects in the City at the age of twenty-three, in just that state of mind to fall easy victim to the Calvinist blandishments of the saintly Miss Bevan.[3] Newman's monitor (to use the accepted phrase) was quite

[1] J. H. Newman, *Apologia pro vita sua* London 1913, 108.
[2] Maisie Ward, *Young Mr Newman* London 1948, 25, suggests that the events were linked. This is discussed briefly in L. Bouyer, *Newman. His Life and Spirituality* London 1958, 10.
[3] Shane Leslie, *Henry Edward Manning. His Life and Labours* London 1921, 35–42.

as saintly and Calvinistic, if somewhat less alluring – his pious schoolmaster, Walter Mayers, whom Father Bouyer has represented as being frequently discountenanced by his pupil's precociousness in dialectic. By force of character, rather than by any great learning, and with the aid of several useful books, Mayers wrought 'the great change'. Newman tells us what he read: a book of William Romaine's, though the title escaped him after the passage of years – at any rate, a different *genre* from the works of Tom Paine, Hume and Voltaire, which had previously excited him. From Romaine he acquired conviction in the doctrine of final perseverance, which he came subsequently to abandon at about the age of twenty-one. Thence he passed to Thomas Scott, a convert to Calvinism (of rather milder disposition than the craggy Romaine), whose unworldliness, allied to a 'minutely practical character', so affected Newman that he described Scott in the *Apologia* as the writer 'who made a deeper impression on my mind than any other, and to whom (humanly speaking) I almost owe my soul'.[1]

The conversion was no blinding flash of vision, like St Paul on the road to Damascus. Nevertheless, his independent spirit was subdued; there was a sense of confrontation: God and the individual soul, the awareness of 'two and two only supreme and luminously self-evident beings, myself and my Creator.'[2] Newman did not doubt that the experience was real – 'providing a chain between God and the soul. . . . I know I am right. How do you know it? I know I know. How? I know I know I know etc. etc.'[3] So individual an experience was it, he later admitted, that he could only write of it with great diffidence, falling into the conventional language of books. The reality for him – nothing violent, a sense of 'returning to, renewing of, principles, under the power of the Holy Spirit, which I had *already* felt, and in a measure acted on, when young'[4] – was so altogether different from anything he had ever read that "normal Evangelicals" expressed doubt as to whether he had really been converted at all.[5] Finally, the experience was essentially doctrinal:

[1] *Apologia*, 108.
[2] *Apologia*, 108.
[3] H. Tristram (ed.), *John Henry Newman. Autobiographical Writings* New York 1957, 150.
[4] Tristram, 172.
[5] Tristram, 79.

I fell under the influence of a definite Creed, and received into my intellect impressions of dogma, which, through God's mercy, have never been effaced or obscured.[1]

This is a conflation of the leading statements which Newman made about his Evangelical origins. He had been brought up a Christian; he had revealed, until his adolescence at any rate, what good Christians would have saluted as an encouraging disposition. The Evangelicalism, however, was not indigenous to the family, despite his mother's distant Huguenot origins[2], and his father firmly disapproved. He described his son's 'enthusiasm' as a 'disease of the mind', the inevitable result of carrying one's religion too far. He prophesied that he would grow out of it in time.[3]

At this point, however, we must be sure of our terms. The word "Evangelical" is a misleading one, and had little meaning as a party label at that time. Church parties there were; variants and offshoots for the most part of the traditional distinction between Calvinists and Arminians, which harked back to the faction fights of the early seventeenth century. Disconnected and spontaneous eruptions of gospel-preachers since the middle years of the eighteenth century, a phenomenon labelled retrospectively the Evangelical Revival, had brought a new religious group into being, branded by unsympathetic contemporaries as "enthusiasts". Generally speaking, all Methodists would qualify for this label, were they Arminian or Calvinist. But there were "enthusiasts" within the Establishment too, and these might also belong to either the Calvinist or the Arminian schools. It would be gratifying to be able to say that the groups became more well defined, more homogeneous, as the new century got under way. Alas, it is not so. A clear enough line, constituting a minimal respect for the church order of the Establishment and subscription to the Thirty-nine Articles, divided Anglican Evangelicals from dissenters, although one cannot always discern it from their theology. A much more

---

[1] *Apologia*, 107.

[2] She bore the Huguenot name of Fourdrinier, and her family had taken refuge in England on the revocation of the Edict of Nantes. Dr John Walsh has shown that many of the Evangelical pioneers of the eighteenth century sprang from such families. See his essay on 'The Origins of the Evangelical Revival', G. V. Bennett and J. D. Walsh (eds.), *Essays in Modern English Church History, in memory of Norman Sykes* London 1966, 157.

[3] Tristram, 179.

fluid division was arising among the Anglican Evangelicals themselves during the second and third decades of the nineteenth century, chiefly again on the issue of church order, although also on
the extent to which they were prepared to accept Calvin's teaching
on predestination.

It is no new discovery that the Clapham Sect sought to render
Evangelicalism respectable, to free it from the taint of irregularity
and low-breeding, so that it could the more easily indoctrinate,
pervade, and eventually control the whole Establishment. Such,
too, was the aim of the Venns, of Simeon, the Ryders, the Sum-
ners, and of Daniel Wilson. By the 1820s this trend became so
marked that there is some danger of confusing the language of
the members of this group, not with that of the dissenters, but
with the sombre sacramentalism of High Churchmen. They were
speaking of the Law as well as the Gospel; they were enjoining
respect for the liturgy, and frowned at too much talk of personal
conversion and "illumination". Yet Evangelicals they remained,
for they adhered to the fundamentals. It was their children, like
Samuel, Robert, and Henry Wilberforce, Henry Manning and
George Dudley Ryder, who crossed into the rival camp, not really
noticing until the banners were unfurled at Oxford that they had
changed their sides. At the same time, the more radical element
in the Evangelical party tended to become more strident in tone,
more militant in tactics and more adventist in preaching. It became more contemptuous of church order, and found a new organ
for its views in *The Record* and a new platform at Exeter Hall.[1]
It should be observed that when Newman became an Evangelical,
he belonged for a short while to the Calvinist wing of the party.
He had read Romaine, while the sons of William Wilberforce
had been warned off him.[2] It is interesting to speculate on how
Newman would have shaped at Exeter Hall.

But what of the fundamentals? Gospel-preaching undoubtedly
came first. 'When I first began to desire and seek ... wisdom',
Thomas Scott wrote in *The Force of Truth*, 'I set out with the
assurance, that it was to be found in the holy scriptures, and no-

---

[1] On this whole subject, two theses in the Cambridge University Library
should be consulted: J. D. Walsh, 'The Yorkshire Evangelicals in the Eighteenth
Century', 1956; and H. Willmer, 'Evangelicalism 1785–1835' (Hulsean Prize
Essay for 1962).

[2] See Samuel Wilberforce, Deposit. c. 186. Diary entry for 27 September 1831.
Bodleian Library, Oxford.

where else; they alone being able to make us wise unto salvation.'[1] All Evangelicals would have said "Amen" to that. Through the Word, and through the preaching of the Word, the saving work of the Spirit largely operated. This fundamental scripturalism lies behind all Evangelical theology which is, as the word implies, primarily soteriological. Evangelicals had a passion for souls; a deep sense of the total depravity of man, against which they preached the Cross and the Atonement.

Some were out-and-out solifidians. Faith alone justifies. Sinful man has no inherent righteousness. All comes from without— from Christ. Hence they either denied the regenerative power of baptism utterly, or – if on the right wing of the party, like Wilberforce – admitted the possibility of regeneration, with the reminder that the privilege could be forfeited by sin. There must, in any case, occur "the great change", the sense of personal conversion, whereby justification was truly effected.[2] Thus we find Newman in 1820 trying to reconcile the two views, setting out his own ideas in his diary:

> I will not directly assert that regeneration is not the usual attendant on baptism, if you object to it; but I will put it in this way, and if that tenet does not follow as a consequence, I will not press it. I say then, that it is *absolutely necessary* for *every* one to undergo a *total change* in his heart and affections, *before* he can enter into the kingdom of heaven. This you will agree with me is a scriptural doctrine; the question *then* is, Do we, when children receive this change in baptism. For myself I can answer that I did not; and that, when God afterwards in his mercy created me anew, no one can say it was only *reforming*. I know and am sure that before I was blind, but now I see.[3]

The total change must take place in 'the heart and affections'. On this point we find agreement among all Evangelicals. Their religion is essentially of the heart. This could lead to two facets which made their opponents uneasy. In the first place, as Golightly expressed it to Newman in 1831 when explaining why he felt out of sympathy with current Evangelical trends:

> they appear to me, many of them, to make their *feelings* the

---

[1] Thomas Scott, *The Force of Truth. An authentic Narrative* London 1821, 75.
[2] A. M. Wilberforce, *Private Papers of William Wilberforce* London 1897, 242.
[3] Tristram, 165.

test of their growth in grace. Where this is the case intercourse is impossible, or at all events very disagreeable.[1]

Secondly, this reliance upon the heart led to some confusion about the nature of justifying faith. Did right action and right belief always go together? If so, which came first during the process of justification? Newman mocked this dilemma mercilessly in a famous passage of *Loss and Gain*, when Charles Reding put the cat among the pigeons at the Evangelical tea-party in Freeborn's lodgings. What is the relationship between faith and love? In the course of discussion, it was discovered that Luther and Melanchthon were in disagreement.

> 'I think,' said No. 4, in a slow, smooth, sustained voice, which contrasted with the animation which had suddenly inspired the conversation, 'that the con-tro-ver-sy, ahem, may be easily arranged. It is a question of words between Luther and Melanchthon. Luther says, ahem, "faith is *without* love," meaning, "faith without love justifies." Melanchthon, on the other hand, says, ahem, "faith is *with* love," meaning, "faith justifies with love." Now both are true; for, ahem, faith-without-love *justifies*, yet faith justifies *not-without-love*.' There was a pause, while both parties digested this explanation.

This brought up the question of conditions.

> 'There are no conditions,' said No. 3; 'all must come from the heart. We believe with the heart, we love from the heart, we obey with the heart; not because we are obliged, but because we have a new nature.' 'Is there no obligation to obey?' said Charles, surprised. 'No obligation to the regenerate,' answered No. 3; 'they are above obligations; they are in a new state.' 'But surely Christians are under a law,' said Charles. 'Certainly not,' said No. 2; 'the law is done away in Christ.' 'Take care,' said No. 1; 'that borders on Antinomianism.' 'Not at all,' said Freeborn; 'an Antinomian actually holds that he may break the law; a spiritual believer only holds that he is not bound to keep it.'[2]

There is one further common attribute of Evangelicalism which may be briefly mentioned before returning to Newman's own ex-

---

[1] R. W. Greaves, 'Golightly and Newman, 1824–1845', *Journal of Ecclesiastical History* IX, London 1958, 216.

[2] J. H. Newman, *Loss and Gain* London 1848, 138–9.

perience. This is the distinction universally made, although differently understood, between "real" and "nominal" Christians, a
terminology popularised by Joseph Milner in his *History of the
Church of Christ*, the design of which, explained unashamedly in
the Introduction, was to separate the sheep from the goats and to
focus the attention of the reader 'on the life of true evangelical
piety within the Church'.[1] A similar distinction appears in both
Henry Venn's *Essay on the Prophecy of Zacharias* and Wilberforce's best-seller, *A Practical View*, published in 1797. The Calvinist sense of this distinction is obvious. The Elect, the members
of the Church Invisible, are a body apart from the unregenerate
who profess and call themselves Christian. But neither Milner nor
Wilberforce was a Calvinist. Both understood "real" Christians
to be those who were born anew in the Spirit; but Wilberforce's
main purpose was to draw the very practical conclusion that those
so favoured were marked off from all others by the possession of
the quality of "seriousness". It was this quality – a peculiar
earnestness which showed in one's bearing and demeanour – which
gave to Evangelicalism its spirit of dedication and its fire of zeal,
and also established a kind of mint-mark whereby the faithful
could be immediately discerned.

In a famous passage in one of his journals, Newman reflected in
1823 on Pusey's qualifications for admission into the charmed
circle. 'I walked with Pusey to-day; indeed, I had had several con-
versations with him on religion, since I last mentioned him. Thank
God, how can I doubt his seriousness? His very eagerness to talk
of the Scriptures seems to prove it.'[2] A month later he had learned
from Pusey (a revealing discovery for him, one cannot doubt)
that it is possible to be "serious" while not a member of the party.
'Pusey is Thine, O Lord', he admits. '. . . Yet I fear he is preju-
diced against thy children.'[3] A year later, he was in disagreement
with Hawkins over this spirit of exclusiveness.

Had a conversation with Hawkins on real and nominal Christianity, in fact on conversion [his diary records]. He admitted
there was a line, but he put it much lower than I should. The
majority, he said, of my congregation would not be touched by

[1] J. D. Walsh, 'Joseph Milner's Evangelical Church History', *Journal of Ecclesiastical History* x, London 1959, 176–7.
[2] Tristram, 190.
[3] Tristram, 191.

my preaching; for they would be conscious to themselves of not doing *enough*, not of doing *nothing*. May I get light, as I proceed.[1]

All these principles, then, Newman readily accepted. But we are bound to be more specific. Newman himself bids us to be so, when he identifies his mentors; most particularly when he presents us with the astounding statement about Thomas Scott, whose writings were both the vehicle of the Spirit and the inspiration behind Newman's early ministry. If we turn to *The Force of Truth*, first published in 1779, the relevance of the book to Newman's own position in 1816 is immediately striking. Scott confesses that he was in his sixteenth year (the same age as Newman) when the first conviction of his innate sinfulness came home to him. He, too, had to reckon with a stubborn spirit, inclined to sophisticated learning and clever paradox. The process of conversion was very gradual – like Newman's, no illumination; only the growing realisation, through three years of continuous study which took him via Socinianism and Arminianism into Calvinist truth, that Christ's words to Nicodemus were instructions to every individual soul. He must be born again – 'born of the Spirit'.[2] The final act, when it came, was a personal confrontation between the individual soul and its Creator.

> A certain person once said of me, that I was like a stone rolling down a hill, which could neither be stopped nor turned: this witness was true; but these things, which are impossible with man, are easy with God. I am evidently both stopped and turned; man, I am persuaded, could not have done it; but this hath God wrought, and I am not more a wonder to others than to myself. . . . So that the Lord having made me willing in the day of his power, I was forced to confess: 'O Lord, thou art stronger than I, and hast prevailed.'[3]

He would have been at peace, content to live a quiet life with his books, but God pressed upon him the burden of holiness. He would have stayed where he was, content with his own superficial justification of his professed position, but God called him to the realisa-

---

[1] Tristram, 201.
[2] Scott, 40–41.
[3] Scott, 64.

tion that life is growth, and that one is moved by the Spirit to fulfil what has been ordained for the Elect.[1]

If Newman had never acknowledged his debt to Scott, a reading of *The Force of Truth* would still have revealed the close parallel between the religious experiences of these two men. In time, Newman came to doubt the practical advice of Scott. He thought him too unreal; his system was not well adapted to the work of a parish priest.[2] But the power of the book sank deep into his memory. It is, for instance, revealing that when Newman was called to make another pilgrimage, from Anglicanism to Rome, he not only followed Scott's advice to the letter ('I sat down very coolly to search for the truth, I proceeded very gradually, and with *extreme caution*[3]), he not only communicated to the world the process whereby supposition became conviction, announcing his Catholicism in the *Essay on Development*, as Scott had done his Calvinism in *The Force of Truth*, but he also held in his mind, perhaps unconsciously, both the substance and indeed the actual phraseology of Scott's moving peroration when he came to write the memorable closing words of his last Anglican publication. 'And now, dear Reader, time is short, eternity is long.'[4] Thus had Scott concluded *The Force of Truth*:

Time, how short! eternity, how long! life how precarious and vanishing! death, how certain! ... Be not a *Felix*, saying to thy serious apprehensions about thy soul, – 'Go thy way at this time, when I have a convenient season I will call for thee;' lest death come before that season: and be not an *Agrippa*, almost persuaded to be a *Christian*. ... I say agree but with me in these reasonable requests, and we shall at length agree in all things; – in many, in this world; – in all, when we hear the Son of God address us in these rejoicing words, – 'Come ye blessed of my Father, inherit the kingdom prepared for you from the foundation of the world!'[5]

No other Evangelical writer had such a lasting influence on Newman. He read Beveridge and Doddridge; testified to the debt he

[1] Compare *Apologia*, 109. 'For years I used almost as a proverb what I considered to be the scope and issue of his doctrine, "Holiness before peace", and "Growth (is) the only evidence of Life".'
[2] Tristram, 79.   [3] Scott, 71.
[4] J. H. Newman, *An Essay on the Development of Christian Doctrine* London 1845, 453.
[5] Scott, 90–91.

2*

owed to Joseph Milner in bringing him to the Fathers. But Milner
never made any deep impression. Milner was a Lutheran, not a
Calvinist, and Newman – according to Dr Brilioth[1] – had a poor
understanding of the writings of the German reformer. So, too,
for that matter, had the Milners, both Joseph and Isaac, as James
Stephen rather acidly pointed out, recalling their joint ineptitude
at mastering the German tongue.[2] It is doubtful, also, whether
Newman could have long endured Joseph Milner's 'revulsion
against profane philosophy'[3], since he himself admitted in his
autobiographical memoir that he was wont to treat the authors of
Greek and Latin antiquity as 'inspired moralists and prophets of
truth'.[4]

Newman's first conversion endued him with 'formed religious
convictions' which lasted for the rest of his life. What exactly does
this mean? Is Brilioth right in suggesting that it branded him
with the 'ineradicable' stamp of Calvinism, binding him to a life-
long acquiescence in the doctrine of the predestination to salvation
of the few, and fostering 'in him that fundamental individualism
which no school or party or Church could change'?[5] Or should we
follow Henri Bremond's 'verbal arabesques' (as Father Bouyer put
it) on the motif of *l'autocentrisme*, and admit that Newman's
sense of conversion merely confirmed him in his consciousness of
solitariness, or uniqueness, and made of him even more of an
egoist and misfit than nature had itself contrived? In some respects, Bremond is nearer the mark than Brilioth, and Father
Bouyer does not entirely succeed in his attempt to expose Bremond's
sleight of hand, so that 'the enchanter' might become a mere 'con-
jurer'.[6]

[1] Y. Brilioth, *The Anglican Revival. Studies in the Oxford Movement* London
1925, 35, 282.
[2] James Stephen, *Essays in Ecclesiastical Biography* II, London 1907, 235.
[3] Walsh, *Joseph Milner*, 178.
[4] Tristram, 82.
[5] Y. Brilioth, *Evangelicalism and the Oxford Movement* London 1934, 24.
[6] Bouyer, 22–3. 'That there was in Newman a strong notion of self, of in-
dependence, of self-reliance cannot be denied, but to confuse this basic characteristic with his religious experience is to condemn oneself *a priori* to a misunderstanding of the latter.
How, then, did it come about that this 'self', so adamant in its nature, was
suddenly projected into the 'self' of that Other and became wholly obedient to
Him? That no doubt is the crux, the mysterious element, in this conversion.'
For further discussion of Bremond, see Dupuy. 'Newman's influence in
France', pp. 167f. below.

Newman's sense of isolation and aloofness is no figment of Bremond's imagination. No one has described it better than Henry Scott Holland, when he wrote of Newman's 'spiritual fastidiousness, that makes him conscious always of the personal element itself, to a degree that weakens action'.[1] It may be recalled how Copleston once saw Newman sitting alone, and sought to comfort him by reminding him that 'Nunquam minus solus, quam cum solus'.[2] But he was teaching Minerva wisdom. Newman had known this since boyhood, ever since the days when, musing over 'the Arabian Tales', he let his imagination take over. 'I thought life to be a dream, or I an Angel, and all this world a deception, my fellow-angels by a playful device concealing themselves from me, and deceiving me with the semblance of a material world.'[3]

The same image, expressed more theologically, appears again and again in Newman's sermons. In 1843, preaching on 'Our Lord's Last Supper and his First', he bids his congregation to prepare themselves for judgement. 'Earth must fade away from our eyes, and we must anticipate the great and solemn truth, which we shall not fully understand until we stand before God in judgement, that to us there are but two beings in the whole world, God and ourselves.'[4] Ten years earlier, preaching on the 'Immortality of the Soul', Newman declares:

> To understand that we have souls, is to feel our separation from things visible, our independence of them, our distinct existence in ourselves, our individuality, our power of acting for ourselves this way or that way, our accountableness for what we do. These are the great truths which lie wrapped up indeed even in a child's mind, and which God's grace can unfold there in spite of the influence of the external world.[5]

In 1836 he devoted a whole sermon to the subject, entitled 'The Individuality of the Soul'. This contains that glorious passage in which Newman pictures a populous town, seen – as it were – from above by a detached observer.

> What is the truth? Why, that every being in that great concourse is his own centre, and all things about him are but

[1] H. Scott Holland, *A Bundle of Memories* London 1914, 114–15.
[2] *Apologia*, 118.
[3] *Apologia*, 105–6.
[4] J. H. Newman, *Sermons bearing on Subjects of the Day* London 1918, 38.
[5] J. H. Newman, *Parochial and Plain Sermons* i, London 1868, 19.

shades. . . . No one outside of him can really touch him, can touch his soul, his immortality; he must live with himself for ever. He has a depth within him unfathomable, an infinite abyss of existence. . . . A multitude is a collection of individual souls.[1]

Now this is not necessarily Calvinism. It has, if you like, an im-plicit Protestantism, for it recognises no mediator between God and the individual soul. But what it really is, is Newmanism. As the 1833 sermon shows, it is Newman recalling the great truth which he had apprehended as a child. As he himself testifies, his conversion caused to be 'unfolded' a truth that was already there; it gave doctrinal structure to what the mind had already grasped. This rescued Newman – forever – from liberalism; for this in-dividualism could have been a mighty tool against the Church had it not been consecrated. But the individualism itself was neither crushed nor created by the conversion. We may go further. Con-version may, indeed, mean a new birth, even as Nicodemus was born again of the Spirit. But this is imagery, and could, in this context, be deceptive imagery. Nearer the mark is the metaphor, which Newman actually uses – 'before I was blind, now I see.' Conversion does not create a new personality. By offering a vision of the rightful goal, it gives direction to a personality already formed. The point may be further illustrated by reference to Henry Manning. His Calvinist conversion did not turn him into an individualist. What it did was to direct the talents of an in-flexible and proud young man, who might otherwise have become a great statesman, into the service of the Church. Manning re-tained to the end the sense of personal direction, the feeling that God was calling him by name[2], but he was never tempted towards the spiritual fastidiousness which gave to Newman his peculiar genius and charm (if it also to some extent explained why he was obliged so often to 'stand all the day idle'). It is indeed a most re-markable circumstance that the Roman Catholic Church gained two of its greatest servants in modern history from the ranks of Calvinist Evangelicalism.

What endured of this Evangelical experience? Much was aban-doned by Newman during the 1820s. He came to distrust "en-thusiasm", the perilous reliance on "feelings", the tendency to

[1] *Parochial and Plain Sermons* IV, 82–3.
[2] e.g., the letter to Mrs W. G. Ward in 1865 (quoted in W. Ward, *Ten Personal Studies* London 1908, 270).

antinomianism and the playing-down of the role of baptism. By
1834 he had sternly rejected solifidianism.[1] The writings of the
Fathers and Bishop Butler, together with the personal influence
of Froude and Keble, drew him to the heart of the sacramental
system. A lingering relic of Evangelicalism – the receptionist understanding of the Eucharist – disappeared by 1837.[2] Evangelical
scripturalism caused him more and more offence, not only because it exhibited an improper appreciation of the role of the
ecclesia docens, but because it betrayed an incipient rationalism.
In Tract 73, Evangelicals and latitudinarians are lumped together
as rationalists[3]; private judgment is the quintessential absurdity
of 'popular Protestantism', as Newman portrays it in his *Lectures
on the Prophetical Office*, and he is always cocking a disapproving
eye at the ruin of German Protestantism mainly for this reason.[4]

It would, indeed, profit us little to take this catalogue further,
or to assume that by eliminating the discarded doctrines, we shall
find the answer to our question in the residue. It is not, of course,
as simple as that. Are we to suppose that Newman lost his "seriousness" when he joined Keble and his friends, or when he became
a Roman Catholic? Seriousness and enthusiasm were both expressions of love, and the Evangelicals had acquired a conventional technique – effusive piety and spontaneous ejaculations of
wonder and joy – for conveying these emotions. This was not for
Newman. He was as little suited to it temperamentally as he was
to the silly extravagances of his fellow-Oratorian, F. W. Faber.
Newman sought a different mode of expressing love; and he
found in the High Church tradition, as represented by Keble, and
in the temper of Tractarianism as it developed, exactly the right
emotional *milieu* for his particular tastes and talents. It should not
be forgotten that Tractarianism was as much a 'religion of the
heart' as nineteenth-century Evangelicalism.[5] But whereas the
Evangelicals wore their hearts upon their sleeves (it mattered to
be recognised as "serious"), Keble and his friends concealed their
emotions, lest by advertising them they should seem to cheapen

---

[1] *Parochial and Plain Sermons* II, 310. See also Lecture x in the *Lectures on
Justification* London 1838.
[2] A. Härdelin, *The Tractarian Understanding of the Eucharist* Uppsala 1965,
132–3.
[3] A. Härdelin, 30, esp. *n.* 24.
[4] J. H. Newman, *Lectures on the Prophetical Office of the Church* London
1837, 25.
[5] Owen Chadwick, *The Mind of the Oxford Movement* London 1960, 12.

the objects of their love. There was nothing cold about the doctrine of reserve. The word betokens, it is true, discipline, austerity, and restraint. Precious things must be guarded, even hidden from irreverent eyes. In the simplest elements and objects – water, bread, and wine – the sacramental mysteries are concealed; the most sacred truths are best expressed in an art-form, like poetry, that allows recondite imagery and veiled allusions; even a holy book, like Law's *Serious Call*, had best be kept hidden in a drawer.[1] All for one reason – love. The deeper the love, the more intense the reverence. This is why Keble singled out Spenser as his favourite poet, because of his 'shrinking delicacy'.[2]

In a letter to James Stephen, dated 15 March 1835, Newman revealed how far he had travelled in his understanding of the proper expression of religious emotion. He wrote of the declension of the Evangelicals as a party from the great days of Scott, Milner, and Venn. He then deplored their coarse technique:

> Yet what I shrink from, even in their greatest fidelity, is their rudeness, irreverence, and almost profaneness. . . . I conjecture you will consider this in me fastidiousness in education. I cannot think it so – i.e, it ought not to be so, it need not be so. The poorest and humblest ought to shrink from the irreverence necessarily involved in pulpit addresses, which speak of the adorable works and sufferings of Christ, with the familiarity and absence of awe with which we speak about our friends. Zaccheus did not intrude himself on our Lord – the woman that was a sinner silently bedewed His feet. Which of us is less refined than 'a tax-gatherer or a harlot'?[3]

We may pass from emotional religiosity to two other Evangelical attributes: first, the tendency to make feeling a test of growth in grace. Newman repudiated this in one sense – delusions about conversion. Nevertheless, he remained convinced that there was a real connection between right ethos and a true faith. In a sermon on 'Saving Knowledge', preached in 1835, he quoted St John – 'Hereby do we know that we know Him, if we keep His commandments' – and commented on the text: 'Obedience is the test

---

[1] G. Prevost (ed.), *The Autobiography of Isaac Williams* London 1892, 28.

[2] J. Keble, *Occasional Papers and Reviews* London 1877, 103.

[3] Birmingham Oratory. Box 119, no. 133. This is quoted at length in my article 'Justification and Sanctification: Newman and the Evangelicals', *Journal of Theological Studies* N.S. xv, Oxford 1964, 49–50.

of Faith.'[1] Earlier, in 1828, in correspondence with Blanco White, he challenged the other 'to give me some account of the connection of speculative error with bad ἦθος – e.g, *in what is a consistent Socinian a worse man than an orthodox believer?* I think him to be worse, but I wish my mind clear on the subject.'[2]

Secondly, a rather obvious example – the quest for holiness. Whence came the pietistic element in Newman, the austere severity, the terrifying demands which he imposed upon his congregations to fit themselves for heaven? Once he discarded the doctrine of final perseverance, he posed the question – how, then, does weak and irreligious man acquire the habits of mind and spiritual disposition which would both render him qualified for heaven and, indeed, make heaven endurable for him? There followed the great series of sermons on the subject of sanctification, many of which appeared in his first published volume of sermons. When Samuel Wilberforce protested at their harshness, he received the grim rejoinder: 'We *require* the "Law's stern fires". We need a continual Ash Wednesday.'[3] Here again, the compulsive urge to attain holiness is of Evangelical origin, derived – as has been seen – from Thomas Scott, but the medium and the theological context have completely changed.

In these respects, then, certain Evangelical attributes were carried by Newman into a rival tradition, and because none of these qualities were alien to that tradition, they were accordingly transformed. But there remains the question, did there survive any features of his Evangelical experience which Newman could not have derived from any other source, and which imbued him therefore with some peculiar and very personal power? Newman himself answered this question as follows: he acquired from his conversion conviction of the truth of four doctrines – the Trinity, the Incarnation, Predestination, and 'the Lutheran "apprehension of Christ" '. The first three, being Catholic doctrines, never faded away. The Lutheran teaching on justification by faith alone, because from the beginning imperfectly understood in its relation to

---

[1] *Parochial and Plain Sermons* II, 153.

[2] From a private collection of papers, owned by Miss Irene Wilberforce, at 2, York House, Church St, Kensington. This subject was also discussed by Froude in July 1827. See 'On the Connection between a right Faith and right Practice; on the ἦθος of Heresy' in *Remains* I, 114–19.

[3] From a private collection of letters, owned by the late Dr Octavia Wilberforce, shortly to be transferred to the Bodleian Library, Oxford. It is dated 10 March 1835. See also Dessain, p. 119 below.

the other three, he abandoned as he became better acquainted with true Catholic doctrine.[1] Calvinist theology had no permanent influence upon him, he stated in the *Apologia*, except for the acute consciousness of 'the fact of heaven and hell, divine favour and divine wrath, of the justified and the unjustified'.[2] F. J. A. Hort, after reading the *Apologia*, put it a different way.

> Two things specially struck me [he wrote to his friend, John Ellerton]; the unquestioning assumption that there is one absolutely and exclusively Divine system in all things; especially one Church so entirely right that all other bodies must be entirely wrong, and the complete permanence of his Calvinistic religion, changing nothing but its form when it passed most naturally into Romanism, and placing him throughout in a position where the vision of pure truth as distinguished from edification, i.e, religious expediency, was a simple impossibility.[3]

Calvinism, then, had left a residue of love of dogma and system, together with a tendency to simplify religious truth by viewing good and evil, truth and error, the blessed and the damned, in stark antithesis.

This is not entirely fair to Newman, for in the same passage in the *Apologia* in which he describes his lasting impression of divine favour and divine wrath, he praises the Catholic system which shades and softens 'the awful antagonism between good and evil'. But the criticism has a certain validity. Newman never lost, for instance, his Evangelical apprehension of the gulf between real and nominal Christians. In 1825, while contemplating the state of mind of his fellow ordinands, he dissociated himself from the Calvinist understanding of that distinction. 'When I looked round to-day, I could hope and trust that none were altogether destitute of divine influence, and, tho' there was a difference of spirituality, yet all might be in some degree spiritual.' A year earlier he had conceded that 'the *onus probandi* lay with those who asserted an individual to be a real Christian; and now I think it lies with those who deny it'.[4] Nevertheless, some thirteen years later in 1838, he

---

[1] Tristram, 81.
[2] *Apologia*, 109.
[3] A. F. Hort, *Life and Letters of Fenton John Anthony Hort* II, London 1896, 35–6.
[4] Tristram, 206.

preached a sermon on 'Sincerity and Hypocrisy' in which the old Evangelical distinction is very clearly enunciated.

> Great, then, is the difference between sincere and insincere Christians, however like their words may be to each other. . . . Thus the two parties look like each other. But the word of God discriminates one from the other by this test, – that Christ dwells in the conscience of one, not of the other; that the one opens his heart to God, the other does not; the one views Almighty God only as an accidental guest, the other as head and owner of all that he is.[1]

Father Henry Tristram, in an interesting essay on 'With Newman at Prayer', suggests that this same distinction is drawn in the characters of Sheffield and Charles Reding in *Loss and Gain*.[2]

Brilioth, as is well known, developed at some length the thesis that the sermons of both Newman and Manning reveal a high content of Calvinism, especially the distinction between the Church Invisible, the body of the Elect, and the visible Church, which exists – as Newman expounded in a sermon of 1838 – for the sake of the Elect.[3] 'To spend and be spent upon the many called for the sake of the chosen few, is the office of Christian teachers and witnesses.'[4] A year earlier, Newman had again returned to the image of 'the few who happen still to be on their trial' as opposed to 'the many who sleep in the Lord'.[5] True it is, however – and here Newman is quite orthodox – that the members of the Church Invisible 'who are still on earth cannot be ascertained by mortal eye'.[6] It is not coincidence, surely, that both Newman and Manning, whose religious awakening was so similar, should have returned so often to this theme. Nor is it irrelevant. The realisation that there are, at any one time, a chosen few whose lot it is to proclaim forgotten truths to a slothful generation, and who very often suffer in this life for the sake of the very truths that they proclaim – this is a part of the Calvinist dynamic. Perhaps it is the motive power behind all who would feel themselves called to be prophets. Newman felt this intensely. We have only

---

[1] *Parochial and Plain Sermons* v, 234.
[2] H. Tristram (ed.), *John Henry Newman: Centenary Essays* London 1945, 107.
[3] Brilioth, *The Anglican Revival*, ch. xiii.
[4] *Parochial and Plain Sermons* iv, 154.
[5] *Parochial and Plain Sermons* iv, 172.
[6] *Parochial and Plain Sermons* iv, 173.

to recall the memorable passage in the *Apologia*, describing his home thoughts from abroad (the consciousness of 'a work to do in England') to feel the force of this impression: 'Deliverance is wrought, not by the many but by the few, not by bodies but by persons.'[1]

Many are called, but few are chosen. Those whom God chooses, he also guides. 'Keep Thou my feet; I do not wish to see the distant scene.' Even if one does get a glimpse of the ultimate goal, one cannot move until God directs. This is how Newman felt. Again a famous passage of the *Apologia* is called to mind:

> All the logic in the world would not have made me move faster towards Rome than I did; as well might you say that I have arrived at the end of my journey, because I see the village church before me, as venture to assert that the miles, over which my soul had to pass before it got to Rome, could be annihilated, even though I had had some far clearer vision than I then had, that Rome was my ultimate destination. Great acts take time.[2]

But *why* do great acts take time? Not, as the passage tells us, because the head, or the mind, needs convincing through 'paper logic'. God does not speak to the head; he appeals to the heart: *Cor ad cor loquitur*. Herein lies the essence of Newman's understanding of the relationship between faith and reason, developed in his great series of University Sermons, and receiving its final expression in the *Grammar of Assent*. Why did Newman feel this so strongly? — so strongly, in fact, that the heart occupies the central place in his whole theology. Part of the answer must surely lie in the fact that his first 'formed religious convictions' came about through the agency of a religion of the heart. This conviction was never discarded, but rather developed or grew, from the moment he experienced the sensation of *coram Deo* to the time that he came to select his cardinalatial motto.

Moreover, the Evangelistic technique is a matter of heart speaking to heart. The conscience is touched by 'the appeal to the whole man'. As Wilfrid Ward observed, 'these appeals are the work of the personal influence of the great preacher or Christian writer'[3];

[1] *Apologia*, 135.
[2] *Apologia*, 264–5.
[3] W. Ward, *Last Lectures* London 1918, 108.

and he reminds us of the passage in Newman's letters on the Tamworth Reading Room, where the approach to the head, by scientific argument, is scorned contemptuously, in words that every good Evangelical would have applauded:

> Science has so little of a religious tendency; deductions have no power of persuasion. The heart is commonly reached, not through the reason, but through the imagination, by means of direct impressions, by the testimony of facts and events, by history, by description. Persons influence us, voices melt us, looks subdue us, deeds inflame us. Many a man will live and die upon a dogma: no man will be a martyr for a conclusion.[1]

The heart is reached, he writes, 'by the testimony of facts and events'. What an opening for Henri Bremond! In the course of his notorious chapter, entitled 'Presages', he writes, 'there are no such things as insignificant events'[2], and proceeds to show how Newman was a master at interpreting the insignificant as meaningful in a personal context. This cannot be denied. Bremond points to the intricate explanations of the débâcle of Newman's academic pretensions in the Oxford Schools, to the extraordinary analysis of providential minutiae during his illness in Sicily and to the morbid personal reflections which attended every death of anybody near to him. Examples abound. Sir Geoffrey Faber slightly glossed the passage in the 'Autobiographical Memoir' about the motto in the window of Oriel Hall (*Pie repone te*[3]) to represent Newman as interpreting it as 'clearly intended for a direct message to him'.[4] Then there is Newman's odd uneasiness about the number seven, his professed belief that seven years constituted 'the term of *contubernium* with my friends'[5], and his singular calculations as to the number of the Elect.[6] This mental process, this seeking for providences, was, of course, a marked Evangelical characteristic. The point should not, however, be pressed too far. Belief in providences, just like the quest for holiness and the tendency to identify

[1] J. H. Newman, *Discussion and Arguments on Various Subjects* London 1872, 293.
[2] H. Bremond, *The Mystery of Newman* London 1907, 295.
[3] Tristram, 61.
[4] G. Faber, *Oxford Apostles. A Character Study of the Oxford Movement* London 1933, 67.
[5] C. S. Dessain (ed.), *The Letters and Diaries of John Henry Newman* XIII, London 1963, 120.
[6] W. Ward, *The Life of John Henry Cardinal Newman* II, London 1912, 343-4.

right faith and right practice, was not the exclusive property of this school; and we have already seen that Newman's sense of the unreality of the material world and his appreciation of the realm of things unseen were ingrained characteristics, sharpened and directed, but not created, by his first conversion.

In sum, then, it comes to this. Evangelicalism was a powerful force in the making of John Henry Newman; but every attempt to illustrate this by pointing to particular attributes brings to mind a host of qualifications, the most important of all being the fact that so much of what lay on the surface of Evangelicalism, Newman was later to find hidden in the deepest recesses of other traditions. In the end, we have to admit that Newman was unique – his thoughts and his talents too diverse and too personal to permit any one party, or Church for that matter, to claim him exclusively as their own. If Newman had had to answer this question himself, he would perhaps have replied that his soul was made clean by Thomas Scott that it might be prepared for paradise by St Philip. In this, as in other respects, he is disconcertingly elusive; and our safest conclusion is to take heed to the judicious warning of Wilfrid Ward – 'like the slave of Midas, it has been said, he often whispered his secrets to the reeds'.[1]

[1] Ward, *Last Lectures*, 21.

2
The rediscovery of the Fathers in the seventeenth-century Anglican tradition

Thomas M. Parker

It is almost inevitable that a paper on this subject should begin from the most famous of Newman's literary dedications – that to Martin Joseph Routh of the *Prophetical Office of the Church* in 1837. Let me recall the wording:

> TO MARTIN JOSEPH ROUTH, D.D.
> PRESIDENT OF MAGDALEN COLLEGE,
> WHO HAS BEEN PRESERVED
> TO REPORT TO A FORGETFUL GENERATION
> WHAT WAS THE THEOLOGY OF THEIR FATHERS
> THIS VOLUME IS INSCRIBED.[1]

There is perhaps a little ambiguity about whom Newman primarily intends by the phrase 'their Fathers'. Is it the Fathers of the early Church, or is it the Caroline Divines, or both? Newman's letter of Epiphany 1837, asking the famous President of Magdalen's permission, suggests that it is the classic Anglican theologians he has primarily in mind, for he says, after explaining the purpose of his book 'in illustration of the *Via Media*,'

> I cannot venture to hope that there is nothing in my volume of private and questionable opinion; but I have tried, as far as may

[1] R. D. Middleton, *Dr. Routh* London 1938, 139.

be, to follow the line of doctrine marked out by our great divines, of whom perhaps I have chiefly followed, Bramhall, then Laud, Hammond, Field, Stillingfleet, Beveridge, and others of the same school.[1]

It is interesting too, to find that J. Hamilton Gray records in his *Autobiography* that he undertook to obtain for the Swedish Archbishop of Uppsala an impartial statement from Routh of Tractarian views. Although no details are given, it would seem that his conversation with the President turned largely upon the Tractarians' agreement or disagreement with the standard doctrine of the Elizabethan period and that Routh was most sympathetic to them when they agreed with these.[2] It is strange, if so, that Newman should seek to gain Routh's approbation by referring to a series of Anglican writers only one of whom, Richard Field (1561–1616), could by any stretch of imagination be called an Elizabethan and whose major work, *Of the Church*, was first published in 1606. Gray may be speaking loosely or have misunderstood Routh, and in any case all the evidence suggests that the President's interests lay more in the seventeenth century than in the sixteenth. As is well known, he had in 1823 edited Burnet's *History of His Own Time*, with a second edition in 1833 – the traditional year of the beginning of the Oxford Movement – and as late as 1852 he published once again that part of Burnet which covered James II's reign, partly because of his interest in the dealings of that king with his own college. Moreover, as Burgon puts it, Routh had 'wondrous little respect' for the Whig bishop.

When the Bishop speaks of himself, 'Here comes P.P., clerk of this parish!' he would say, ejaculating to himself afterwards, 'Rogue!' ... 'Why is it uncle,' once asked his nephew, John Routh, 'that you are always working at Burnet, whom you are always attacking?' To whom the President, 'A good question, sir! Because I know the man to be a liar—and I am determined to prove him so; ...'[3]

The repugnance may have been largely on political grounds. Routh's political opinions, although eclectic, were basically Tory, and he was believed in earlier life to have held 'a kind of theoreti-

[1] Middleton, 139.
[2] Middleton, 143.
[3] Burgon, *Lives of Twelve Good Men* I, London 1888, 63.

cal Jacobitism'; Burnet was pre-eminently a Whig.[1] But Burnet
was also the historian of the English Reformation, who excused
the faults of Henry VIII by comparing him with Jehu, who, though
'grossly insincere', destroyed 'the idolatry of Baal'. He apologised
for the timorousness of Cranmer by comparing him (rather oddly)
with Athanasius and Cyril of Alexandria – for, whatever their
faults, neither Athanasius nor Cyril was timid.[2] However strong
his dislike of Romanism, it is difficult to believe that Dr Routh
did not see the Anglican tradition through the eyes of the Carolines rather than those of the Reformers, or that Burnet's view of
the Reformation would be very much more welcome to him than
was his political attitude. To the Elizabethans he may well have
been more favourably inclined, especially to Hooker, but there is
nothing to indicate that the publication of Froude's *Remains*, with
their attacks upon the Reformers, shocked Routh as it did many
others; certainly he retained his sympathy for the Tractarians to
the end of his life. As Dean Church says of the *Tract 90* controversy

> To one who, like Dr Routh of Magdalen, had gone below the
> surface and was acquainted with the questions debated by those
> divines [the great Church of England writers], there was noth-
> ing startling in what so alarmed his brethren, whether he agreed
> with it or not; and to him the indiscriminate charge of Popery
> meant nothing. But Dr Routh stood alone among his brother
> Heads in his knowledge of what English theology was. To most
> of them it was an unexplored and misty region; some of the
> ablest, under the influence of Dr Whateley's vigorous and scorn-
> ful discipline, had learned to slight it. But there it was. Whether
> it was read or not, its great names were pronounced with honour
> and quoted on occasion. From Hooker to Van Mildert, there
> was an unbroken thread of common principles, giving con-
> tinuity to a line of Church teachers.[3]

And here we reach the crux of the matter. For classic Anglican
theology in this sense was patristic through and through. The Reformers had appealed to the Fathers, but usually in the way of
proof texts often gathered from catenae, for, as Professor Green-

[1] Middleton, 148.
[2] Gilbert Burnet, *The History of the Reformation of the Church of England* 1
(ed. Pocock), Oxford 1865, 16.
[3] R. W. Church, *The Oxford Movement* London 1891, 264.

slade has pointed out[8], it was only slowly during the sixteenth century that anything like full printed editions of the Fathers became
available. It was the later Anglicans who read the Fathers for
their own sakes and became more and more impregnated by their
spirit. It is noteworthy that all the divines cited by Newman in
his letter to Routh were renowned for patristic knowledge –
although, indeed, it would be difficult to find any divines of the
tradition to which Newman appealed who were without knowledge of the Fathers. Newman's whole position in *The Prophetical
Office* was that Anglicanism in its classic expression was neither
Papist nor Protestant and that its divines rested their case upon
Christian antiquity.

The question primarily before us, however, is how Newman
came to know the Fathers? Was it by way of the Carolines or
more directly? Here a passage from the *Autobiographical Memoir,*
written for Ambrose St John in 1874 and, after St John's death,
given in 1885 to Anne Mozley in revised form, is specific. After
speaking of his early Calvinism, and of his father's warning
against Lutheranism shortly before his election to Oriel, Newman
goes on to describe the influences which drew him from Evangelicalism:

> One additional feature in Mr. Newman's mind shall be noticed
> which seemed to intimate from the first that the ethical char-
> acter of Evangelical Religion could not lastingly be im-
> printed upon it. This was his great attraction to what may be
> called the literature of Religion, whether the writings of [the]
> Classics, or the works of the Fathers. As to the Greek and Latin
> authors, poets and philosophers, Aeschylus, Pindar, Herodotus,
> Virgil and Horace, or again Aristotle and Cicero, he had from
> the first made much of them, as the Holy Fathers did, as being
> in a certain sense inspired moralists and prophets of truths
> greater than they knew; ... And as to those Fathers themselves,
> much more did he ever delight, and even from a date earlier
> than his ordination, to find himself brought into their company.

Newman goes on to speak of the only obvious alternative to the
Evangelicalism of his youth being Arminianism:

> A cold Arminian doctrine, the first stage of Liberalism, was
> the characteristic aspect, both of the high and dry Anglicans

[1] S. L. Greenslade, *The English Reformers and the Fathers of the Church: an
Inaugural Lecture* Oxford 1960, 12–13.

of that day and of the Oriel divines. There was great reason then to expect that on Newman's leaving the crags and precipices of Luther and Calvin, he would take refuge in the flats of Tillotson and Barrow, Jortin and Paley. It cannot be said that this was altogether a miscalculation; but the Ancient Fathers saved him from the danger that threatened him. An imaginative devotion to them and to their times had been the permanent effect upon him of reading at School an account of them and extracts from their works in Joseph Milner's Church History, and even when he now and then allowed himself as in 1825 in criticisms of them, the first centuries were his *beau idéal* of Christianity. Even then what he composed was more or less directed towards that period and, however his time might be occupied, or his mood devotional, he never was unwilling to undertake any work, of which they were to be the staple.[1]

He goes on to list what he actually did. An argument for strict Sabbath observance, derived from Chrysostom and the Fathers, in 1823; in 1826 a life of Apollonius and the *Essay on Miracles*; in 1826 a plan to write a history of the first three centuries of Christianity for the *Encyclopaedia Metropolitana*; in 1827 a defence of infant baptism from patristic testimonies supplied by Wall – a year in which he also asked Pusey to buy him in Germany as many volumes of the Fathers as possible. 'And in 1828 he began systematically to read them.'[2]

If one compares this with what is said in the *Apologia* (written of course ten years earlier) the account is substantially the same, although less detailed. Let me quote from it:

Now, I come to two other works, which produced a deep impression on me in the same Autumn of 1816, when I was fifteen years old, each contrary to each, and planting in me the seeds of an intellectual inconsistency which disabled me for a long course of years. I read Joseph Milner's Church History, and was nothing short of enamoured of the long extracts from St. Augustine, St. Ambrose, and the other Fathers which I found there. I read them as being the religion of the primitive Christians; but simultaneously with Milner I read Newton on the

[1] H. Tristram, *John Henry Newman. Autobiographical Writings* London and New York 1956, 82–3.
[2] Tristram, 84.

Prophecies, and in consequence became most firmly convinced that the Pope was the Antichrist predicted by Daniel, St. Paul and St. John.[1]

Later,[2] in a famous passage, he refers to his reading of Butler's *Analogy*, to which he attributes his grasp of the principle of a visible Church with authority, but from which, clearly, he can have gained little specifically patristic. Further on Newman refers to one particular aspect of his intellectual relations with Whately, who in 1827 accused him of Arianising because he looked favourably upon the notion (originally due to Petavius)[3], that pre-Nicene Christian theology was quasi-Arian and contrasted the Athanasian Creed with the Nicene.

> My criticisms were to the effect that some of the verses of the former Creed were unnecessarily scientific. This is a specimen of a certain disdain for Antiquity which had been growing on me now for several years. It showed itself in some flippant language against the Fathers in the Encyclopaedia Metropolitana, about whom I knew little at the time, except what I had learnt as a boy from Joseph Milner.[4]

Then finally comes his account of what might be called his definitive conversion to patristic theology.

> There is one remaining source of my opinions to be mentioned, and that far from the least important. In proportion as I moved out of the shadow of that liberalism which had hung over my course, my early devotion towards the Fathers returned; and in the Long Vacation of 1828 I set about to read them chronologically, beginning with St. Ignatius and St. Justin. About 1830 a proposal was made to me by Mr. Hugh Rose, who with Mr. Lyall (afterwards Dean of Canterbury) was providing writers for a Theological Library, to furnish them with a History of the Principal Councils, I accepted it, and at once set to work on the Council of Nicaea. It was to launch myself on an ocean with

---

[1] J. H. Newman, *Apologia pro vita sua* London 1890, 6–7.
[2] *Apologia*, 10.
[3] Newman had not then read Bishop Bull's *Defensio*, which attacked Petavious's case and was probably not aware of its origin – another sign that he came late to the study of the seventeenth-century Anglicans.
[4] *Apologia*, 14.

currents innumerable; and I was drifted back first to the ante-Nicene history, and then to the Church of Alexandria.[1]

This of course was the genesis of the *Arians of the First Century*. Newman goes on to explain how the work he did for this changed his outlook.

> I do not know when I first learnt to consider that Antiquity was the true exponent of the doctrines of Christianity and the basis of the Church of England; but I take it for granted that the works of Bishop Bull, which at the time I read, were my chief introduction to this principle. The course of reading, which I pursued in the composition of my volume, was directly adapted to develope it in my mind.[2]

Unfortunately the *Autobiographical Memoir* after 1827 concerns itself almost wholly with the disputes in Oriel under Provost Hawkins, who then succeeded Copleston, on the tutorship issue, which ended in Newman's being refused any further pupils by Hawkins in the summer of 1830, although a reference to the views of Origen upon the value pastorally of secular education by the clergy, serves to show that the Fathers were still in his mind.[3]

A *Journal* reference of 27 February 1827 confirms that his plan of reading the Fathers systematically did not spring from the invitation to write on the Councils. Indeed the date of beginning, 1828, is two years before the request from Rose and Lyall.

> Lloyd is the new Bishop of Oxford. He is very kind and takes great interest in my plan of reading the Fathers; but he says that our theological systems do not agree. They agree more than when I was in class with him, but I do not tell him so, I deeply feel his kindness.[4]

The passage is interesting in that it does not appear that Lloyd *suggested* the plan to Newman, and his account of his attendance at Lloyd's lectures in 1823 and 1824 would make it seem that patristics entered little into them. The books used in what would now be called a class rather than a lecture – a class of eight, four from Christ Church and four Fellows of Oriel, Jelf, Ottley, Pusey, and Newman himself, to begin with – were biblical or apologetic. Lloyd rallied Newman on his Evangelicalism and tried to 'chaff'

---

[1] *Apologia*, 25–6.
[2] *Apologia*, 26.
[3] Tristram, 91.
[4] Tristram, 210.

him out of it.[1] It would seem that Lloyd at most *approved* a plan of patristic reading Newman had adopted out of his own head – a fact which confirms his own asseveration that it was his reading of Milner at school which first turned his mind to the early Church. (Milner, it is worth noting, was an Evangelical and, considering Newman's upbringing, we must conclude that otherwise Newman would never have read him as a schoolboy.)

It is worth noting that an influence, on the face of it very different from that of Milner's, must have been a big factor in turning his mind towards the patristic age, namely that of Gibbon. Together with Locke, Gibbon was Newman's reading during the long vacation of 1818, the second of his Oxford career. At first sight so incongruous, the influence of Gibbon upon Newman is often underrated. Yet it was considerable. Attracted partly by the style, the future master of English prose was fascinated no less by Gibbon's mastery of history and was to declare in the *Essay on Development* that Gibbon was the only English writer with any claim to be considered an ecclesiastical historian – a statement which might well have puzzled the great iconoclast and opponent of Christianity had he still been alive![2] It seems, indeed, clear that Newman's interest in the Fathers was in a sense first of all a by-product of that interest in history which developed early and continued all his life, stimulated as it was bound to be, by a classical training which, in the nature of things, could not be divorced from history.

How strong was Newman's sense of historical responsibility can be seen from the letter in which he replied to Dr Jenkyn's request in the summer of 1830 that he would collaborate in a projected ecclesiastical history – the request out of which eventually grew his *Arians of the Fourth Century*.

> I hardly know what answer to make to your inquiry without knowing more of particulars. For instance, what I feel most clear about is this; I could never undertake to write on any subject which admits of being treated thoroughly lightly. I think it is the fault of the day.... An Ecclesiastical History for example, whether long or short, ought to be derived from original sources, and not be compiled from the standard authorities.[3]

[1] Tristram, 70–71.
[2] R. D. Middleton, *Newman at Oxford* London 1950, 26.
[3] Maisie Ward, *Young Mr Newman* London 1948, 182. Wilfrid Ward, *Life of John Henry Cardinal Newman* I, London 1912, 46.

A year later he writes to Hurrell Froude:

> My work opens a grand and most interesting field to me; but how I shall ever be able to make one assertion, much less to write one page, I cannot tell. I shall confine myself to hypotheticals; your 'if' is a great philosopher as well as peacemaker.[1]

It seems clear from all this that Newman's patristic interests, derived in the first instance from his reading of Milner as a schoolboy, developed through a general interest in history, stimulated by Gibbon and perhaps by a vague knowledge of the rise of the von Ranke school, with its search for history *wie es eigentlich gewesen ist*, and an increasing concern (especially after Hawkins's University Sermon of 31 May 1818 on Tradition, which, as he tells us, made a deep impression upon him, as he listened to it as an undergraduate) with the historical development of Christianity.[2]

> He does not go one step, I think, beyond the high Anglican doctrine, nay he does not reach it; but he does his work thoroughly, and his view was in him original, and his subject was a novel one at the time. He lays down a proposition, self-evident as soon as stated, to those who have at all examined the structure of Scripture, viz. that the sacred text was never intended to teach doctrine, but only to prove it, and that, if we would learn doctrine, we must have recourse to the formularies of the Church; for instance to the Catechism, and to the Creeds. He considers that, after learning from them the doctrines of Christianity, the inquirer must verify them by Scripture. This view, most true in its outline, most fruitful in its consequences, opened upon me a large field of thought. Dr. Whateley held it too. One of its effects was to strike at the roots of the principle on which the Bible Society was set up. I belonged to its Oxford Association; it became a matter of time when I should withdraw my name from its subscription-list, though I did not do so at once.[3]

Tradition implies history, and another sign of how deeply Newman's deepening historical sense reacted upon his theology and

---

[1] M. Ward, 183; W. Ward, 46.
[2] Middleton, *Newman at Oxford*, 33.
[3] *Apologia*, 9–10.

made the transcendentalist view of revelation held by the Evangelicals, to whose company he had belonged, more impossible to hold, is noted by himself, arising from the doctrine of 'concurring and converging probabilities' learned from Butler. This forced him to see that degrees of probability were relative, leading us to entertain about 'a professed fact' a belief ranging, 'as the case might be', from certitude to mere opinion.[1] He goes on:

> Considerations such as these throw a new light on the subject of Miracles, and they seem to have led me to reconsider the view which I had taken of them in my Essay in 1825–6. I do not know what was the date of this change in me, nor of the train of ideas on which it was founded. That there had been already great miracles, as those of Scripture, as the Resurrection, was a fact establishing the principle that the laws of nature had sometimes been suspended by their Divine Author, and since what had happened once might happen again, a certain probability, at least no kind of improbability, was attached to the idea taken in itself, of miraculous intervention in later times, and miraculous accounts were to be regarded in connexion with the verisimilitude, scope, instrument, character, testimony, and circumstances, with which they presented themselves to us; and, according to the final result of those various considerations, it was our duty to be sure, or to believe, or to opine, or to surmise, or to tolerate, or to reject, or to denounce. The main difference between my Essay on Miracles in 1826 and my Essay in 1842 is this: that in 1826 I considered that miracles were sharply divided into two classes, those which were to be received, and those which were to be rejected; whereas in 1842 I saw that they were to be regarded according to their greater or less probability, which was in some cases sufficient to create certitude about them, in other cases only belief or opinion.[2]

Here is the historical principle applied to a matter which Newman the Evangelical had hitherto approached upon an *a priori* basis: biblical miracles, because recorded in inspired writings, were beyond question; ecclesiastical miracles, because they depended upon non-inspired testimony, and moreover, were asso-

---

[1] *Apologia*, 21–2.
[2] *Apologia*, 21–2.

ciated with a Christianity already, according to Protestant dogma, becoming superstitious, were to be rejected *en bloc.*

The conclusion to which all this evidence seems to me inevitably to lead is this. If one trusts Newman's own account of the development of his theology – and I see no reason to doubt it – he approached the Anglican divines by way of the Fathers and not *vice versa.* No doubt he must have been aware, at least after he came to Oxford, of the patristic tradition in classic Anglican teaching. All the evidence would suggest that before this time his theological reading lay almost exclusively in Evangelical books; the indications he gives of his youthful reading in the *Apologia* suggests this strongly. Walter Mayers of Pembroke, Oxford, under whose influence he fell in the autumn of 1816, when he was fifteen, put books in his hands 'all of the school of Calvin'[1], and although Calvin himself paid a great deal of attention to the Fathers, his eighteenth-century followers commonly did not.[2] All the authors Newman specifically mentions are of this type, Thomas Scott, Daniel Wilson, Romaine. The one exception is William Law, no Calvinist, but equally not a patristic scholar. It is curious to reflect that had Newman read John Wesley he might well have caught Wesley's lifelong devotion to some at least of the Fathers, first acquired at Oxford. But Anglican Evangelicals, Calvinists almost to a man and opposed on principle to the Methodist schism, were suspicious of Wesley as both an Arminian and a schismatic.

It was of course, as Newman says, from an Evangelical writer, Joseph Milner, that he first became attracted to the Fathers – but this was because Milner's book was historical, not theological or devotional. There seems no evidence at all that Newman had read the Carolines before he became involved in the Oxford Movement. Among non-Evangelical Anglicans his reading was in Paley and Butler and William Law.

Can one pinpoint the period at which he began to read the Anglican divines of the patristic tradition? Not exactly perhaps, but the *Apologia* seems to me to give particulars which match exactly the other evidence considered. Speaking of his confidence in his position in 1833, Newman says, after telling of his firm belief in dogma ever since the age of fifteen:

[1] *Apologia,* 4.
[2] *Apologia,* 4–6.

2. Secondly, I was confident in the truth of a certain definite religious teaching, based upon this foundation of dogma, viz. that there was a visible Church, with sacraments and rites which are the channels of invisible grace. I thought that this was the doctrine of Scripture, of the early Church, and of the Anglican Church. Here again I have not changed in opinion; I am as certain now [1864] on this point as I was in 1833, and have never ceased to be certain. In 1834 and the following years I put this ecclesiastical doctrine on a broader basis, after reading Laud, Bramhall and Stillingfleet and other Anglican divines on the one hand, and after prosecuting the study of the Fathers on the other; but the doctrine of 1833 was strengthened in me, not changed. When I began the Tracts for the Times I rested the main doctrine, of which I am speaking, upon Scripture, on the Anglican Prayer Book, and on St. Ignatius's Epistles.[1]

Two points are to be noted here:

1. Newman speaks of 'reading' Laud and the others, but of 'prosecuting' the study of the Fathers. In such an exact writer of prose a distinction must be intended. The former was a new field of knowledge, the latter the continuation of a course of study which we know he had begun seriously in 1828. The inference is that before 1834 he knew little of the seventeenth-century Anglican authors.

2. He says in so many words that in the *Tracts*, begun in 1833, he rested his case upon Scripture, the Prayer Book, and St Ignatius of Antioch, – a statement easily verifiable. In other words he derived his own Tractarian teaching, not from earlier Anglican theology, but from Scripture, the Prayer Book and the Fathers. It was later that he found support for his views in the Anglicans of the *grand siècle*. This, one finds, is exactly the impression conveyed by Dean Church's account of the early *Tracts*:

> They were short papers, in many cases mere short notes, on the great questions which had suddenly sprung into such interest, and were felt to be full of momentous consequence, – the true and essential nature of the Christian Church, its relation to the primitive ages, its authority and its polity and government, the current objections to its claims in England, to its

---

[1] *Apologia*, 49–50.

doctrines and its services, the length of the prayers, the Burial
Service, the proposed alterations in the Liturgy, the neglect of
discipline, the sins and corruptions of each branch of Christendom. The same topics were enforced and illustrated again and
again as the series went on; and *then* [ital. mine] there came
extracts from English divines, like Bishop Beveridge, Bishop
Wilson, and Bishop Cosin, and under the title 'Records of the
Church' translations from the early Fathers, Ignatius, Justin,
Irenaeus, and others.[1]

Then follows significantly:

Mr. Palmer contributed to one of those papers, and later on
Mr. Perceval wrote two or three; but for the most part these
early Tracts were written by Mr. Newman, though Mr. Keble
and one or two others also helped.[2]

Had it been otherwise, and Newman not the principal author of
the early *Tracts*, the appeal to the Carolines might have come
earlier than it did. But Newman did not yet know them. This is
not surprising, for of all the leaders of the Oxford Movement, he
was the odd man out – the convert from Evangelicalism. Both
Keble and Pusey came from the non-Evangelical tradition. Pusey
has left it on record that he derived his religion from his mother.

I was educated on the teaching of the Prayer Book ... the doctrine of the Real Presence, I learnt from my mother's explanation of the Catechism, which she learnt from older clergy.[3]

Keble, too, was brought up in the old High Church tradition.
His latest biographer, Miss Battiscombe, applies to his family tradition, his disciple, Charlotte Yonge's description of her own
parents, 'of the old reticent school, reverent, practical' and refers
to the fact that:

In later years, when Newman and Froude were all enthusiasm
for some item of Catholic faith or practice which had burst
upon them with the force of a new revelation, Keble would
nod approval and remark in tones of the highest commenda-
tion, "Yes, that is exactly what my father taught me."[4]

---

[1] Church, 104.
[2] Church, 104.
[3] H. P. Liddon, *Life of Edward Bouverie Pusey* 1, London 1893[3], 7.
[4] Georgina Battiscombe, *John Keble, a Study in Limitations* London 1963, 11.

Froude himself had been Keble's pupil, and Church says of their relationship that:

> Keble had lifted his pupil's thoughts above mere dry and un-intelligent orthodoxy, and Froude had entered with earnest purpose into Church ways of practical self-discipline and self-correction.[1]

But, however dry and unintelligent, Froude's orthodoxy was of the old Anglican type, derived from his father, the formidable Archdeacon of whom such an unpleasing picture is derived from the recent biography of the other son, James Anthony, 'A fine specimen of a Tory High Churchman of the old school', as Geoffrey Faber describes him:

> He was a landowner, a justice of the peace, a keen rider to hounds. But he was also an artist, an antiquary, a man of wide knowledge – 'very amiable,' said Keble, 'but provokingly intelli-gent, one quite uncomfortable to think of, making one ashamed of going gawking about the world as one is wont to do, with-out understanding anything one sees.' He ran his parish and the bench of magistrates and the whole countryside. Subtleties of doctrine left him uninterested. 'The Church itself he regarded as part of the constitution; and the Prayer Book as an Act of Parliament which only folly or disloyalty could quarrel with.'[2]

So it was, in broad outline, with the others. Newman alone had grown up in Calvinism, even though the Newman family, as Miss Trevor rightly insists, were not Evangelicals.[3] His Calvinism, as he himself says, was derived from Walter Mayers, the young clergyman who was a master at his Ealing school, under whose guidance he experienced an Evangelical conversion in 1816, after a brief period of interest in the scepticism of Paine and Hume.[4] From impressionable adolescence he, alone of the Tractarians, had accepted a closely knit, dogmatic creed which had little in common with seventeenth-century Anglicanism; and yet, para-doxically as we have seen, from Milner's book, put into his hand by Mayers, he had equally derived his first love for the Fathers of the Church.

[1] Church, 41.
[2] Geoffrey Faber, *Oxford Apostles* (2nd. edition) London 1936, 196–7.
[3] Meriol Trevor, *Newman; The Pillar of the Cloud* London 1962, 7.
[4] Tristram, 29; *Apologia*, 4.

To speak of Newman's debt to the Anglican patristic tradition is therefore meaningful only, I would insist, if one realises that this at most added, from about 1834 onwards, to a patristic tradition discovered for himself and already operative. In no way did it create it. Somewhat in the way of M. Jourdain, Newman discovered that, at least from the age of fifteen, he had been speaking patristically, or at least beginning to do so, and that this habit was approved by those he learned to think of as his masters. From whom primarily he learned to turn to the seventeenth century, it is difficult to say, or at least it would need a further investigation. From Keble no doubt he learned something. It is clear from his own statements that his work on the Arians led him inevitably to Bishop Bull. But, to return to the relationship from which I began, I would suspect that it was Martin Joseph Routh who encouraged him to read further in the seventeenth-century divines. In the beginning of February 1834, we are told by J. B. Mozley, in a letter to his sister Maria,

> Newman was closeted the other day two hours with Dr. Routh of Magdalen, receiving his opinions as to his work [*The Arians of the Fourth Century*], which were very complimentary.[1]

What passed in those two hours? Was all the time spent in discussion of the fourth century? Or did Routh, as on a famous occasion, when closeted with Burgon, recommend a course of reading to the man he used thereafter to speak of as 'that clever young gentleman of Oriel, Mr. Newman'? Is it wholly a coincidence that three of the Anglican divines Newman tells us he read in that same year, Laud, Bramhall, and Stillingfleet, appear in the letter of 1837 asking Routh's permission for the dedication to him of the *Prophetical Office*?[2] February is the second month of the year and it is inherently unlikely that Newman could have read many of these authors during January. Did Routh direct him to them? It is an interesting speculation, which further research might confirm or refute. But it is worth consideration. If so, the phrase in the famous dedication – about Routh's being reserved to report to a forgetful generation, 'What was the theology of their fathers' – assumes a fuller significance. Newman already knew much of the Fathers of the Church. Routh was learned in

[1] *Letters of the Rev J. B. Mozley, D.D.* ed. by his sister, London 1885, 39; Middleton, *Routh*, 137; Burgon i, 58.
[2] Middleton, *Routh*, 139.

them before Newman was born; but he had no need to introduce Newman to them in 1834. What he could do, and may have done, was to point out that, besides Bull, many of the great Caroline divines were patristic students and based their theology upon the Fathers.

Whether that be so or not, it is, I suggest, interesting that Newman's reading of the Anglican seventeenth-century authors – barely known, I feel sure, to him earlier – should coincide with what seems to have been his first intimate contact with Routh, the man who, even in his appearance, retaining as he did the old clerical dress, recalled the great figures of the classical Anglican age. Routh was, of course, the great reviver of patristic studies in Oxford, after an interval of relative neglect, with his massive publication of the *Reliquiae Sacrae*; and, no doubt, it was the knowledge of the Fathers displayed in Newman's *Arians of the Fourth Century* which made him anxious to meet a young man who shared his own interests. Nevertheless he was equally, in the view of Oxford, the living representative of a tradition submerged by the metaphysical and apologetic trend of eighteenth-century Anglican theology. If Newman, as I have suggested, was at the beginning of 1834 a man who, from Routh's point of view, had, so to say, entered patristics by the back door, and yet was, by the publication of the *Tracts*, plainly reviving doctrines lost sight of since the Nonjuring Schism, would it not be natural for the great President of Magdalen to point out that the interpretation of Scripture, the Anglican formularies and the Fathers, to which Newman appealed, had been held before and written into a considerable corpus of theological writing?

The theory is plausible, especially since there is no very firm evidence that Newman's Oriel and other Oxford contemporaries – younger when the Oxford Movement began than we are inclined to remember – had had the time or opportunity to study the Laudians closely. In all that Newman says, for example, of the great influence of Keble upon him, he says nothing of his being awakened to the significance of the Carolines. He refers to *The Christian Year* and to Keble's insistence upon the 'living power of faith and love' to produce what Newman could later call the 'illative sense', which converts probability into certainty.[1] To Hurrell Froude's friendship he attributes a weakening of his prejudice against Rome and the communication of a dislike of the

[1] *Apologia*, 18–20.

Reformation. He speaks of Froude as 'a high Tory of the Cavalier stamp.' but never suggests that he held the theology of those who were chaplains to the Cavaliers; indeed he implied that he did not.[1] No doubt Newman, especially after his discovery of Bull's *Defensio* in the course of his work upon the Arian controversy, was quite capable of discovering the theology of which Bull was only one representative for himself. But as one reads all that Newman says of his preparation for his lectures on the *Prophetical Office of the Church*, his enunciation of the *Via Media*, between 1834 and 1836, one has the impression of a man discovering more fully a whole system of theology, that of the Anglican divines, with which, hitherto, he had no more than a nodding acquaintance. The famous passage from the Introduction to the *Prophetical Office*, which he quotes in the *Apologia*, expresses this.

> The present state of our divinity is as follows: the most vigorous, the clearest, the most fertile minds, have through God's mercy been employed in the service of our Church: minds too as reverential and as holy, and as fully imbued with Ancient Truth, and as well versed in the writings of the Fathers, as they were intellectually gifted. This is God's great mercy indeed, for which we must ever be thankful. Primitive doctrine has been explored for us in every direction, and the original principles of the gospel and the Church patiently brought to light. But one thing is still wanting: our champions and teachers have lived in stormy times: political and other influences have acted upon them variously in their day, and have since obstructed a careful consolidation of their judgments. We have a vast inheritance, but no inventory of our treasures. All is given us in profusion; it remains for us to catalogue, sort, distribute, select, harmonize, and complete.[2]

These, I suggest, are the words of one who has only comparatively recently become aware of the full extent of the 'treasures' of which he speaks and who, interestingly enough, is prepared to treat them critically.

> We have more than we know how to use; stores of learning, but little that is precise and serviceable; Catholic truth and individual opinion, first principles and the guesses of genius, all

[1] *Apologia*, 24–5.
[2] *Prophetical Office of the Church* London and Oxford 1837, 29–30. Quoted in *Apologia*, 67.

mingled in the same works, and requiring to be discriminated. We meet with truth overstated or misdirected, matters of detail variously taken, facts incompletely proved or applied, and rules inconsistently urged or discordantly interpreted. Such indeed is the state of every deep philosophy in its first stages, and therefore of theological knowledge.[1]

There is, of course, nothing in this passage referring only to Anglican seventeenth-century divinity, although the reference to 'stormy times' seems to suggest that that is what Newman chiefly had in mind. He seems, too, to think of Anglican theology as a developing system still in 'its first stages'.[2] Once again his historical and dynamic approach to ideas comes out, eventually to find full expression in the *Essay on Development*. He looks to the future as much as to the past. But his attitude is fundamentally that of the man who finds himself a legatee and is considering how best to invest, increase and rationalise his inheritance. Nowhere earlier, as far as I know, in Newman's works is there this feeling. There is nothing corresponding to it in his account of his discovery of the Primitive Church, which seems to have been a gradual process after his initial meeting with it in Milner. It may well be that the need to investigate Anglican theology was a result of the increased sense Newman had of the competition to be faced from Rome. It must not be forgotten that Catholic Emancipation in 1829 may well have sharpened apprehensions of a new attempt by Rome to recover England. Newman indeed speaks of the return of Monsignor Wiseman to England before 1936 and his lectures in London.[3] Hurrell Froude had made him aware that the medieval Church, as well as the early Church, had a theology worth consideration.[4] Newman was also, no doubt, aware of the wealth of post-medieval Roman theology, even if he had not read it, and of its use by Wiseman. With the intricacies of the Calvinist system he had long been fully acquainted. If, as he then felt, the Anglican Church was the true *Via Media*, then it must have a theology of its own, comparable to these systems. This could only come from the specifically Anglican past, which

[1] *Prophetical Office*, 30 (*Apologia*, 67).
[2] See *Apologia*, 66. 'I wished to build up an Anglican theology out of the stores which already lay cut and hewn upon the ground, the past toil of great divines.'
[3] *Apologia*, 64.
[4] *Apologia*, 24.

meant from the seventeenth-century divines, since he was tending to agree with Froude in rejecting the Anglican Reformers. It is not difficult to see why Newman should look in this direction at that particular juncture. And I wonder still, whether, just as Routh earlier in his life had turned the attention of the Americans seeking episcopal consecration, denied them by the Church of England, to the apostolic succession of the Episcopal Church in Scotland, he was not also the finger who pointed the young Mr Newman, already versed in patristics, towards the seventeenth-century exponents of Anglican theology, who drew their inspiration from the same source. Of one thing I am very sure, that, whilst a study of the Laudians did much to consolidate Newman's devotion to the Church of the Fathers, it did not, if chronology means anything at all, create it.

3
The theological vision of the Oxford Movement

A. M. Allchin

In considering the sources of Newman's power, we come inevitably to the years of the Oxford Movement itself, and to his association during that time with the other principal figures involved in its genesis. The fact that Newman's intellectual and spiritual development has received so much more attention than that of any of the other leaders of the Movement, has, I believe, tended to disguise the extent to which during the 1830s a common mind had developed amongst them. After 1845, of course, Newman was separated from Keble and Pusey and their earlier collaboration, practical and intellectual, came to an end. But this fact does nothing to take away from the intimacy of their contact during the years 1833–1840. The shock of the events of 1845, together with the harsh pressures of ecclesiastical controversy within the Church of England, acted as a break upon creative theological reflection among those of Newman's friends who remained in the Church of their baptism. The later writings of the men of the Oxford Movement tend to be erudite and controversial, rather than constructive and systematic. Within this particular strand of Anglican tradition, it was not until the appearance of the Lux Mundi group under the leadership of Charles Gore towards the end of the century that the work of constructive theological thinking was taken up again. In this sense we may say that the strictly theological promise of the Oxford Movement was in its own time unfulfilled. But it remains true, as was pointed out by perceptive contemporaries no less than later commentators, that the years

1833–1840 saw in Oxford, not only an explosion of spiritual energy, but also an explosion of intellectual activity, in which all the leading members of the movement were caught up.[1]

These years were a time of great productivity for Newman, Keble, and Pusey alike. This is perhaps especially true of the year 1836, in which Newman was composing his lectures on the Prophetical Office, in which Keble preached and published his sermon on Apostolical Tradition, and Pusey delivered his lectures on Types and Prophecies, which we shall examine later in this paper.[2] All this of course was in addition to the steady publication of the *Tracts*. In all three at this time one finds a sense of confidence and hope, as together they journey out into new or rediscovered fields of thought and feeling, confirming and supporting one another from their different vantage-points.

For all three had much to contribute. Granted that Newman's was the most powerful and original mind, Pusey nonetheless brought with him a weight of biblical and oriental erudition and a knowledge of current philosophical and theological thought in Germany which no one in Oxford at that time could rival. Almost an exact contemporary of Newman's, he was like him approaching the height of his powers. Keble for his part provided many of the basic insights and convictions out of which the whole movement grew; or rather he embodied that particular combination of insights, moral and aesthetic, spiritual and theological, which was to prove so unexpectedly fruitful. It is true that others were to work out these convictions more fully than Keble himself did, but we should not on that account underestimate either his learning or the acuteness of his mind. There is evidence to show that in private conversation with people he trusted, Keble could surprise those who thought of him primarily as the retiring writer of devotional verse.[3] And at this time he felt a confidence in working out the implications of his position, which he had never known be-

[1] Among contemporaries one may take the judgement of Bishop Connop Thirlwall; among more recent writers, Father Bouyer's verdict, in his life of Newman is striking. See C. Thirlwall, *A Charge to the Clergy of the Diocese of St Davids* London 1842, 36–8; L. Bouyer, *Newman, His Life and Spirituality* London 1953, 223ff.

[2] These lectures, which have never been published, exist in ms. in the library of Pusey House. So far as I know Dr Alf Härdelin was the first to make use of them, in his dissertation on *The Tractarian Understanding of the Eucharist* Uppsala 1965. I am grateful to Dr Härdelin for my own introduction to them.

[3] See the sermon on John Keble in H. P. Liddon, *Clerical Life and Work* London 1895, 339ff.

3*

fore, and was never to know again afterwards. In 1836 he writes to Newman:

> I am extremely obliged to you for looking over my Visitation Sermon. Your and my brother's approbation gave me so much courage that I thundered it out more emphatically than ever I did anything in my life, and to my great surprise they asked me to print it.[1]

The extent to which the three men were living in one another's company during these years, sharing a common enthusiasm, promoting a common cause, makes it difficult to discern exactly the lines of influence and interaction between them. To do so would undoubtedly be valuable, but it would demand more space and much greater knowledge than I have at my disposal. All that will be attempted here, therefore, will be to present some of the central themes of Pusey's unpublished lectures of 1836. To do so will I hope in itself reveal how much there was in common of approach and attitude between himself and Newman at this period. It may also suggest that Pusey deserves more attention as a theologian than he has hitherto received. Under the impulse of events, and doubtless stimulated by the intimacy of his relationship with Newman, his writing has a creative quality at this time which has not been properly recognised. We may suppose that Newman, too, gained much from the constant companionship of a mind very different from but not altogether unequal to his own.[2]

Before we come to an examination of the lectures, however, we must pause for a moment to look at some of the basic convictions, or better perhaps intuitions, which the three men shared at this period: convictions and intuitions which it is not always easy to define, since in them intimate personal feeling was bound up with rapidly developing intellectual views. We cannot do better than to start with a famous passage from Newman's letter to his sister Jemima written shortly after Mary's death in 1828.

> On Thursday I rode over to Cuddesdon with W. and F. and dined with Sanders. It was so great a gain to throw off Oxford

---

[1] Anne Mozley (ed.), *Letters and Correspondence of John Henry Newman During His Life in the English Church with a Brief Autobiography* II, London 1891, 190.

[2] The recent discovery of a list of the names of those who attended these lectures, among the Pusey House Papers, has established the fact that Newman was among them.

for a few hours, so completely as one does in dining out, that it is almost sure to do me good. The country too is beautiful; the fresh leaves, the scents, the varied landscape. Yet I never felt so intensely the transitory nature of this world, as when most delighted with these country scenes. And in riding out to-day I have been impressed more powerfully than before I had an idea was possible with the two Lines: 'Chanting with a *solemn* voice/Minds us of our *better choice*'.

I could hardly believe the lines were not my own, and Keble had not taken them from me. I wish it were possible for words to put down those indefinite, vague and withal subtle feelings which quite pierce the soul and make it sick. Dear Mary seems embodied in every tree and hid behind every hill. What a veil and curtain this world of sense is! beautiful but still a veil.[1]

One may well feel inclined to ask why these two lines from *The Christian Year*, not in themselves particularly memorable, should have made such an impression on Newman's mind. The question is reinforced when one finds Pusey some eight years later using the same stanza to illustrate a crucial point in his lectures on Types and Prophecies. Even when we take the four lines of the stanza together the answer is not immediately evident.

> Every leaf in every nook
> Every wave in every brook
> Chanting with a solemn voice
> Minds us of our better choice.[2]

From the purely literary point of view the lines contain nothing at all striking. What is the clue to their importance for the Tractarians? How did they become the focus of such intense feeling, apparently a sort of tag or motto, charged with hidden associations and allusions?

I believe that the secret lies in the way in which they give expression to two central elements in the Tractarian vision of the world and of God; first that *everything* created shouts the glory of its Maker, whence follows the need to bring all human knowledge, activity, and experience into relation to God's revelation of himself, and secondly, that at the moment of recognising the

[1] Mozley, *Letters and Correspondence* 1, 184.
[2] First Sunday after Epiphany in *The Christian Year*. J. Keble, *The Christian Year, Lyra Innocentium and other Poems*, Oxford 1914, 13.

utter transcendence of God we also experience his agonising nearness, and that this nearness is such that though all the resources
of the human mind and heart must be summoned to its apprehension, in the end no words can express it. It must be known in life.
For a moment they saw the whole world transfigured by uncreated
light, and man in its midst caught up into an awe-ful union with
the divine. And that vision, which certainly owed much to Wordsworth, was understood by them finally in terms which they had
learnt from the Fathers, and above all the Greek Fathers. This
meant that a vision of an aesthetic origin could be integrated into
a larger view of things, which would do justice not only to man's
perception of beauty, but also to his moral and intellectual apprehensions. This was a view which centred upon the mystery of the
Incarnation, seen as providing the key both to the sacramental understanding of the universe, and to an understanding of the
Church wholly centred upon the person and work of Christ, the
redeemer. In the mystery of the Incarnation of the Son of God, in
his death and resurrection, we see the full height and depth of
the miraculous interchange between God and man, and the full
extent and scope of the operation of God's glory, gathering together all things created, making them instruments and vehicles
of the divine presence.[1] This communion of man with God, and
of heaven with earth, is beautifully described in the note which
Keble appended to the poem *Church Rites*, which he set for the
second Sunday after the Epiphany in *Lyra Innocentium*.

The change of water into wine was believed by the ancients to
typify the change which St. Paul in particular so earnestly
dwells on: 'Old things are passed away . . . behold all things are
become new.' And St. John, 'He that sitteth on the Throne
saith, Behold I make all things new.' Accordingly St. Cyprian
applies the first miracle to the admission of the Gentiles into

---

[1] The common theological position of the Tractarians is well expounded by
Dr Eugene Fairweather in the introduction to his selection of texts from the
writings of the Oxford Movement. 'The Tractarians saw the Incarnation, the
Church, and the sacraments as contiguous and inseparable elements in God's
redemptive economy.' For them the twofold truth of the Incarnation implied
'on the one hand, that man's salvation comes from God alone; on the other,
that God's saving action really penetrates and transforms man's world and
man's life. (E. R. Fairweather (ed.), *The Oxford Movement* London 1964, 11.)
It is scarcely necessary to say that 'incarnation' here is thought of as including
death and resurrection, not in opposition to them.

the Church. (Ep. 63, ed. Fell.) And St. Augustine, to the Evangelical interpretation of the Old Testament. (In Joan: Tract 8.) And St. Cyril of Alexandria (in loc.) to the Spirit superseding the letter. This then being the 'beginning of miracles', a kind of pattern of the rest, showed how Christ's glory was to be revealed in the effects of His Sacramental Touch; whether immediately, as when He touched the leper and healed him; or through the hem of His garment; or by Saints, His living members according to His Promise, 'the works that I shall ye do also; and greater works than these shall ye do, because I go unto My Father'. Thus according to the Scriptures, the Sacramental Touch of the Church, is the Touch of Christ; and her system is 'deifica disciplina', a rule which, in some sense, makes men gods, and the human, divine; and all this depends on the verity of the Incarnation, therefore His Mother is especially instrumental in it; besides being, as nearest to Him, the most glorious instance of it. 'The Mother of Jesus is there, and both Jesus and His Disciples are called.' (He as the Bridegroom and Author of the whole mystery, they as ministers, servants and instruments)—to this mysterious, 'marriage', or Communion of Saints.[1]

It is true that these lines were written in 1846, when Keble's understanding of his own position had become more clearly articulate than it was at the outset of the movement. But in substance they express only what Newman tells us in the *Apologia*, that he had learnt from Keble, at the very beginning of their friendship, a belief in the sacramental system and the communion of saints. Indeed they may serve to remind us of the way in which, for the Tractarians, these two articles of faith in some measure expanded so as to cover the whole. 'The sacramental system' taken in this large sense came to include the whole givenness of the Christian religion, and to suggest the Tractarian insistence on revelation, dogma, and liturgical action, while 'the communion of saints' pointed to that strong personal note, the idea of mutual indwelling, which saved the theology of the Oxford Movement from taking the objectivity of divine truths in such a way as to make them "object-like".

When we now turn to the lectures of Pusey on Types and Pro-

---

[1] Keble, *The Christian Year*, 362-3.

phecies given in 1836, we find these same thoughts worked out in relation to the interpretation of the Old and New Testaments. In these lectures we seem to hear a younger and more hopeful Pusey speaking than is familiar to us from his later writings. We see signs of that largeness of mind, if also of a certain indefiniteness of outline, which Newman had noticed as characteristic of his study of the theology of German Protestantism.[1] We can also recognise that sense, common to Tractarian writing at this time, that everything living must be either in growth or in decay, and its immediate application to their own circumstances, beginning to recover great tracts of feeling and understanding which they believed had been for too long abandoned. As Pusey writes:

> Let anyone compare our theology at the present day with that of Bishop Bull and the ancient Church, and he will find that we have altogether lost sight of and forgotten out of mind, much which they dwelt on habitually as part of the Catholic Faith; we have the outline of the truth, but have lost much which gives to it substance and reality, and opens to us a safe and deepening range for our contemplation.[2]

One of the outstanding features of the lectures, both as to style and content, is their romantic quality. The language used, the whole approach with its stress on imagination, is as far removed as possible from the dry lucidity of a William Palmer of Worcester. As Dr Härdelin very justly remarks in relation to them, the leaders of the Oxford Movement were fighting on 'a double front; on the one hand against rationalist anti-dogmatism, and on the other against the intellectualism of older orthodoxy.'[3] Pusey regretted that in his youth he had been made to spend a good deal of time on the eighteenth-century literature of "evidences" of the Christian religion. In these lectures the attack on the old "orthodoxism" of the previous age is so sharp in places that one is

---

[1] Mozley, *Letters and Correspondence* I, 186. 'It is *very* difficult, even for his friends ... to enter into his originality, full-formed accuracy, and unsystematic impartiality'.

[2] Unpublished manuscript volume among the Pusey House manuscripts (p. 9 of the manuscript). In transcribing these lectures I have not altered Pusey's punctuation or spelling, but I have generally expanded his abbreviations, writing 'would' for 'wld' and so on.

[3] Härdelin, 32.

strongly reminded of Coleridge[1], for the very starting point of Pusey's argument, and the theme to which he constantly recurs is the criticism of the old use of individual prophecies as so many predictions or specific evidences of a Christian revelation. It is against this background that he works out his own view of what we should call the image character of biblical thinking.

Speaking of the conventional use of prophecy, Pusey writes:

in becoming clear, it became also shallow. Men wished to grasp the whole evidence of prophecy and to collect it into one focus, and so narrowed their conceptions of it. They were content with nothing but the mid-day Sun and so lost all sympathy for the refreshing hues of its rising or setting light, or those glimpses into a far distant land, which indistinct though they may be, open a wider range of vision.

And here at once comes one of the key conceptions of Tractarian thinking, of which we have already spoken: 'the natural world is an emblem of the spiritual'; and therefore Pusey can confidently go on to make use of his analogy from the natural world:

We see further with diminished light: noon-day beams contract our sphere of vision, although they heighten the intensity of the objects close at hand to us. God and His ways and His Nature we can of course know but in part, and our highest knowledge must be our indistinctest; for that which is most elevated must most surpass our comprehension; it belongs to another sphere, and just touches, as it were, upon that wherein we dwell; its centre is not in this world, and so we cannot survey its compass; its very proportions we can discern only here and there, as we see 'parts of His ways' bearing one upon another; as a whole we see nothing, can judge of nothing; because we are not at the centre whence it can be seen; our most spiritual faculties are just allied to it, and we are in the flesh. Because we are of God, and born of God, we have some sense for beholding the things of God; but because we are in the flesh, and 'no man can see God and live', the light but parts from between the clouds,

[1] It may possibly have been this element in them which made Liddon uneasy about their contents. At any rate he refrains from quoting them in his four volume Life and passes them over with a brief mention. Of course Pusey is very far from accepting the whole of Coleridge's position. In these lectures he speaks of Coleridge's 'flippancy and arrogance' in interpreting the Eden story as an allegory. Unpublished manuscript, 46.

lest we should be struck down to the earth and blinded. Whatever we gain in distinctness and precision we lose in depth; our
furthest point of vision is just where 'light and darkness part' . . .
The soul, thro' that which is divine in it, just putteth forth
itself, and half-seeth things invisible, but cannot declare them
or embody them in words. St. Paul's highest revelations and
visions were unspeakable words which it is not lawful for a
man to utter. This is the case with regard to our whole creed;
by striving over-much at clearness, and practically admitting
only what they could make, as they thought, intelligible to
themselves, men have narrowed it far below that of the ancient
Church, or of our own in former days. So also with prophecy.
Brought within the compass of a system, all those parts were
lost, which lay to the right or to the left beyond the circle which
men had drawn. For prophecy is co-extensive with the whole
system of God's Providence or Dispensations; for every earlier
part of the scheme, in that it is adapted to some later part, pre-
paratory for it, corresponding to it, becomes thereby prophetic
of it.[1]

Here we have already stated some of the major themes of these
lectures. There is the conviction that clarity and immediate intelligibility are qualities dearly purchased in reflection on divine
things; that God reveals himself in images which strike us forcibly
almost in proportion to our inability to capture or define them
fully; that everything in this world can be a type or symbol of
heavenly realities, and that the whole history of God's dealings
with his people foreshadows and is prophetic of his revelation of
himself in Christ. Finally there is the belief that to try to make a
rationally intelligible and complete system of God's ways will inevitably lead to a narrowing and limiting of our apprehension of
them. Clarity and intelligibility are of course in themselves good.
Their danger in theology is that they should give us an external
notion of things, that we should gain a wrong sort of objectivity,
seeking to grasp divine truths from outside, when in fact they are
realities which can only be understood in so far as we are entering
into them and being grasped by them. In a later lecture Pusey
remarks:

It is not in proportion to the clearness of our perception, that
mysteries have their force; how little do we know of the mystery

[1] Unpublished manuscript, 2–3.

of our own sonship to God, yet it is as we put ourselves forth beyond what we know, and endeavour by faith to substantiate what is unseen, and to realise our part in unknown and un-bounded privileges, that its immensity begins to discover itself and to impress us. Not its clearness and distinctness, but its greatness, constitutes its majesty and impressiveness; and that greatness and indistinctness commence together; not the things which we know clearly, but the things which we know un-clearly, are our highest birth-right; for to say this, is only to say, that we see here 'thro' a glass darkly' only the outskirts of God's glory and of his favour towards us, and that it is the very fulness of the light of His countenance, and that His countenance turned to us, which is now hid behind the cloud, and of which only a ray, as it were, breaks thro'.[1]

God speaks to us in images, which can have more than one interpretation, and to understand this is already to escape some of the problems caused by a superficial reading of Old Testament prophecy. Let us now exemplify these points in somewhat greater detail.

What then appears to me of primary importance as a corrective of this narrow view of prophecy is to have well impressed on the mind the significant character of everything, which came from God. The world is full of types and it were probably true to say, everything is a type if we could realise [?] it. The words of a child are constantly typical of the future developed being; they speak greater truth than they themselves (the outward organ of that truth) know: they speak it in reference to some

[1] Unpublished manuscript, 70. With these passages we may compare some words from Wilfrid Ward's summary of the argument of Newman's *University Sermons* '... Clearness of statement, or even of thought, is often not the prin-cipal essential for the recognition of deep truth. Rationalism is ... the clear apprehension of a partial or narrow philosophical system incommensurate with the facts of the world and of human nature. . . . Faith on the other hand, is less clear in its apprehension, but it touches deeper and more numerous grounds of belief. It is the *obscure* apprehension of a profound and comprehen-sive philosophy, while Rationalism is the *clear* apprehension of a narrow and shallow philosophy.' (Wilfrid Ward, *Last Lectures* London 1918, 36.) Para-doxically, it was precisely on grounds such as these, that men like John Keble and R. W. Church based their defence of the Anglican position against the assaults of ultramontane Catholicism. Granted that it was less logically clear and consistent, their system seemed to them to do more justice to the facts of a divided Christendom, and to touch 'deeper and more numerous grounds of belief'.

particular occasion, but indefinitely; they are aware of something kindred to that whole truth, and have some glimmering
of it, but it they grasp not. And yet they who hear it, will
rightly wonder at it, and they who understand it better than
the child itself, will yet confess that they could not have uttered
it so simply and so forcibly. Its very indefiniteness adds to its
reality, comprehensiveness, energy. It comes not from the child
itself, but from a power within it; they are in truth the words
of God, in the mouth of the little one, so lately come from its
Maker's hand. In like manner, the sayings of the Old Testament tho' they often have not the distinct outline of truth,
which belongs to the development, have in then continually a
depth of shade, which impresses the mind in the midst of its
indistinctness, yet more forcibly, and has more religious awe
than would the mere outline, tho' ever so distinct.[1]

This idea of the child as saying more than it knows, is developed
further in relation to the speech of adults, with a curious illustration that suggests vividly the sense of holding a shared
secret which must have characterised the Oxford men at this
time, and also their love of reticence and reserve in speaking of
the things which moved them most. Pusey writes:

Thus everyone has been aware how in mixed society he has
often had pleasure in uttering words, which in his own mind
related to some holier subject, than he thought it expedient
either for himself or others to speak of more plainly; yet one,
who knew him well, would know that the veiled meaning was
his real one, and that it was for the sake of that, that the words
were uttered, altho' he intended also that which lay upon the
surface of the words. And so again, when we are under strong
emotions, words are often uttered which are fuller than we
ourselves are at the time fully aware; we feel only that we have
uttered truths beyond ourselves; and it is upon reflection only
that we find how much the Spirit within us, which gave us
those emotions and the words too, meant by them. One might
even say that no deep saying was ever uttered which was not
capable of many applications and a variety of meanings, which
might very possibly float before our mind together or severally,

[1] Unpublished manuscript, 14.

of which one remains the highest and of that one the rest are fainter and inferior representations.[1]

The fact that God speaks to us in words which contain many levels of meaning, and which are not easily susceptible of precise definition, does not mean that we are left merely with an indistinct impression of the revelation which he intends to convey. One of the most interesting ideas which Pusey develops, both in relation to Old Testament prophecy, and as we shall see later, to the theology of the Fathers, is that the divine mystery is expressed by the conjunction of a number of different images, which for their full apprehension need to be perceived by all the faculties of man working together and in harmony.

In the word, as in the works of God, impression depends, not so much on single objects as on their combination. We single out to ourselves (if we are briefly to give account of our own feelings) the one or the other more striking feature of any scene outspread before us, as that which exercises such power upon us, and yet we are conscious the while, that we are thereby but expressing a part of the truth only, that the whole effect is made up of numerous other parts which we cannot so well analyse but that if they were removed, what remained, altho' in itself the most striking, would lose most of its power. So also in God's word. It is true doubtless that there are prophecies more conspicuous than others, that the hand of the Lord was at times more powerfully upon the Prophets, and they spake of Christ more plainly and more fully, and the types receded from their view and the archetype stands more revealed before us; and yet take these prophecies singly, nakedly as men now are wont to do, apart from the whole system, and the impression will be diminished. Our conviction also is of a compound character and made up of various emotions; in moral subjects it cannot be mainly intellectual; in Divine things, awe, wonder, the absorbing sense of infinity, of purity, or of holiness, infuse conviction more directly than reasoning; nay reasoning in that it appeals to one faculty only, and that for a time is erected into a judge, and so, as it were, sits superior, constantly goes directly counter to the frame of mind wherein belief is received. The chance sight, so to say, of a flower illumined by the sun's rays,

[1] Unpublished manuscript, 19. The resemblance to Wordsworth is particularly remarkable here.

or of the starry heavens, 'the moon and the stars which God has ordained', impress the feeling of God upon the soul more than any artificial reasoning from final causes, however clear it may in itself seem to be, as in Paley.

And then in a sentence which is crossed out, but against which there is a mark which I think indicates 'stet', Pusey draws a parallel which he may well have hesitated to use at this point. 'Like the centurion by the Cross we are awed into belief.'

He goes on to point out how differently the works of the Fathers strikes us in this respect:

> God also has so constructed us, that impression is most strongly made upon us incidentally. Works which like S. Basil or S. Ambrose ... exhibited God's works with a sort of wondering awe, do in fact convince much more than those which, like Paley, make conviction their professed object, and recall our minds from the contemplation of those works to reflect on their own convincingness. We are not formed to seek conviction, but to have it. It is brought to us in the way of duty. In all practical matters we live in belief and through acting on belief, believe in the things of God, and thereby attain a higher kind of belief, and an insight into our belief. ...[1]

From all this there flow interesting consequences, both for our view of the symbolical or typical nature of the whole created order, and for our attitude towards the prophetic character of the Old Testament. Here Pusey seems particularly anxious to set the predictive element in Old Testament prophecy within that larger context, in which alone it can be properly appreciated. He is eager too to stress that it is the history of the Old Testament itself, its events and institutions as a whole, which are prophetic rather than isolated or particular sayings.

> It is remarkable accordingly how in H. Scripture, other feelings are throughout prophecy enlisted, beyond and above contemplation of Divine fore-knowledge. Rather ... that fore-knowledge is presupposed not reflected upon or exhibited. Not time, but the eternal truth contained, is the subject which is alleged. The Old Testament, as cited in the New, might mostly, for the purposes for which it is alleged, have been a contemporary

[1] Unpublished manuscript, 5-6; 6 facing.

document. When time is alluded to, it is not to magnify God's prescience, but to illustrate the harmony and unity of His dispensations Who is 'the same yesterday and today and for ever. . . .' It is the substance which is dwelt upon, not the mode of its delivery.[1]

Holy Scripture does not favour our mechanical views of prophecy, as containing so many items, as it were, as there are striking passages; as though prophecies admitted of being counted up, and the entire evidence of prophecy was to be weighed according to the number and contents and tangibleness of these several predictions. Rather the whole previous dispensation of the O.T., its people, its individual characters, its rites, its sayings, its history was one vast prophetic system, veiling, but full of the N.T.[2]

But perhaps it is in his attitude towards the created order as a whole, and towards the meaning of human history outside the Church, that Pusey's thought is most interesting at this point. I think it would be true to say that in some of Pusey's later writing there is an unhappy lack of concern for the order of creation, so strong is the emphasis on the order of redemption. Here, at least, the balance is more carefully preserved. As Dr Härdelin has pointed out, Pusey is anxious to maintain that the correspondence between heaven and earth, the typical qualities of natural objects, are not simply the product of human imagination. They cannot be perceived without the use of the imagination, but in themselves they are planted in the world by God. They are signs of the continuing goodness and harmony of things, which though marred by sin, is not destroyed by it. Pusey writes that it is not only man who acts as an image of God in the world,

> . . . altho' in him as being the image of God in this lower world, there is most varied development. The other visible creatures of God's Word, and the efflux of his Spirit, do in fact present a continual harmony with an order of things above them; they possess in themselves a relation to things unseen. For as Hooker says (*EP* v, c. 56, 95), 'All things being partakers of God' in that 'God hath his influence into the very essence of all things, without which influence of Deity supporting them, their utter annihilation could not choose but follow', 'they are his offspring',

[1] Unpublished manuscript, 6.
[2] Unpublished manuscript, 8.

and as being such they must (in so far as they have not been marred and deformed by sin) bear a certain impress and image of himself and an analogy, or proportion, or relation to other existences derived from God. For as Hooker again says, 'All things which God in their kind and seasons hath brought forth, were eternally and before all times in God, as a work unbegun is in the artificer, which afterward bringeth it into effect. Therefore whatsoever we do behold now in this present world, it was enwrapped within the bowels of Divine Mercy, written in the book of eternal Wisdom, and held in the hands of omnipotent Power, the first foundations of the world being yet unlaid. So that all things which God hath made are in that respect the off-spring of God; (Acts 17, 28–29) they are *in Him*, as effects in their highest cause, He likewise actually is *in them*, the assist-ance and influence of His Deity being their life.' So that the province of the true poet has been not to invent likenesses, but to trace out the analogies, which are actually impressed upon the creation.[1]

Pusey insists on this point, since it was clearly necessary here to make his position clear both against some tendencies in roman-ticism which gave to the imagination a creative power rather than a capacity for recognition, and also against the eighteenth-century view that creation would simply provide material for a discursive argument by which to approach God.

Nor indeed would external nature convey such direct interests to the soul, and that stronger in proportion to the purity of each, unless it had in it somewhat of God; for it acts upon us not by our own reasoning about the wisdom of contrivances and the like, whereby men now deem (as I said) that they 'ascend from nature up to nature's God,' but by immediate influence; so that nothing exercises so congenial an influence over man's soul, or so harmonised with it, as the visible works of God, ex-cept His words or His works in other human souls. . . . Instances of this expressiveness of nature in conveying moral and re-ligious truth will have been felt by everyone; and they will have felt also, that these religious meanings were not arbitrarily affixed by their own minds, but that they arose out of, and existed in, the things themselves: and if a different meaning is found in the same object, this will be because in fact each

---

[1] Unpublished manuscript, 14–15.

thing contains several such relations, or has several such characters impressed upon it, whereof according to their peculiar
character or susceptibility, different minds have perceived different sides. A proof that this expressiveness really lies in the
objects and is not the work of imagination, (otherwise than as
imagination is employed in tracing out the mutual correspondence of images with their reality, or with each other) is furnished by this, that when religious poets (as Wordsworth or
the author of the Christian Year) have traced out such correspondence, the mind instantly recognises it as *true* not as
beautiful only, and so not belonging to their minds subjectively,
but as actually and really existing (objective). As the Christian
poet just alluded to has well said:

> 'Every leaf in every nook
> Every wave in every brook
> Chanting with a solemn voice
> Minds us of our better choice,'

nor out of Scripture could one learn better to read the book of
God's work than in him.[1]

If we are here touching on one of the deepest common convictions of all the Tractarians, there is another connected with it,
which is less developed in Pusey's thought, but which recurs a
number of times in these lectures, and which is also pointed to in
the verses of the Christian Year. This is the conviction that it is
not only the natural world as God's creation, and the particular
history of the Jewish nation as the story of God's chosen people,
which tell us of God's dealings with men. Obscurely too we are
to trace his hand at work throughout the whole course of human
history, reading by the light of the Gospel something of divine
providence in the history of every nation. In his hymn for the
third Sunday in Lent, Keble had expressed this thought in memorable lines:

> Immortal Greece, dear land of glorious bays
> Lo! here the 'unknown God' of thy unconscious praise!
> The olive wreath, the ivyed wand
> 'The sword in myrtles drest,'
> Each legend of the shadowy strand

[1] Unpublished manuscript, 16–17.

> Now wakes a vision blest:
> As little children lisp and tell of Heaven,
> So thoughts beyond their thoughts to those High Bards
>   were given.[1]

It is interesting to see the image of the child speaking more than it consciously knows, which Pusey had applied to the Old Testament, used here for the poets of ancient Greece. Pusey of course, is careful to distinguish clearly between the history of the Jews, which he believed to have a directly revelatory character, and that of other nations which is only indirectly prophetic. Nonetheless he makes the comparison. In a passage which has been crossed out, possibly because he felt it was carrying him too far beyond his immediate subject, possibly because he found it too daringly speculative, he writes:

> This inherent significance of images receives its full direction and completeness in God's revelation. In heathenism and in the natural world they are significant but not of necessity, prophetic. They express truth, but give no earnest that it shall be realised, unless indeed in so far as we may
>
> > See in heaven and earth
> > In all fair things around
> > Strong yearnings for a blest new birth
> > With sinless glories crowned,
>
> and in some sense the very existence of imperfect good does prophesy of its completion somewhere. Thus the heathen history is instructive, not prophetic, or prophetic in a general way and in broad outlines, of the course of that natural Providence of God whereof it testifies, and whereby it was produced.[2]

Similar thoughts are carried further in a paragraph added to the following page of the lectures.

> And so whereas men have now begun to write sacred history like profane, they ought to have reversed this, and endeavoured to write profane history like sacred, adapting the principles of God's Government which are discovered to them in the one, to the illustration of the other; and tracing out reverentially and with diffidence, but still with what light we have, 'His paths

---

[1] Keble, *The Christian Year*, 54.
[2] Unpublished manuscript, 22.

in the seas, and His footsteps in the dark waters', altho' they be not known until he has cast a light upon the track in the midst of the darkness. 'As language', says a German who has written history on this better principle—'as language and polity are institutions of man's nature, conditions, of his existence, not a spontaneous production, the result of voluntary agreement—so, is there yet another higher Divine institution in the life of mankind, one just as visible, regulating all the phenomena in the life of nations, uniting things of this world with things beyond—which may be called 'the Divine Empire of the World', so far as it is visible and an object of history—'the Kingdom of God' so far as it lives, operates, creates, in the breast of individuals, itself a source of life, invisible as eternal. The history of the Divine empire of the world, is the marrow of the history of all nations on earth, around which everything takes its place, which supports and upholds all history, and it raises history really to a science.[1]

But what is certainly much more central to these lectures than these tentative gestures towards a theology of history, is their sense that the biblical revelation is given through the use of types, symbols and sacramental actions. In the deep understanding that Pusey shows of the characteristic forms of biblical thought, we can see the fruits of his long and intense study of semitic languages. Throughout his life indeed, his theology and spirituality is marked by his knowledge of the Old Testament, and is full of the thought of the transcendence of God, his majesty and glory, so that the absolute priority of the action of the living God in revelation and redemption is never called in question. Yet at the same time there is the sense of the nearness and all-pervading character of the operations of God's glory in the created universe, of the descent of the divine mercy into the depths of man's alienation, which comes not only from the New Testament, but also from the Fathers. Perhaps one of the most important elements in the Tractarian vision of the Christian faith, and one which still has great relevance today, is the way in which it involved a rediscovery of the sense of Scripture and Tradition alike, a new insight into both sacrament and prophecy. For, as we shall see,

---

[1] J. D. von Braunschweig, *Umrisse einer allgemeinen Geschichte der Völker* Leipzig 1833, v–vi. The Bodleian Library copy of this curious work has evidently been used by Pusey.

Pusey is sure that without an understanding of the essential role played by type and sacrament in the process of revelation, we shall be false to revelation itself, losing our awareness of it as a gift from God, into which we are called to enter, and instead transforming it into a mere conceptual scheme of our own devising.

We touch here upon certain of the fundamental issues at stake in the struggle of the early Church against heresy, and its endeavour to maintain the fulness of the biblical revelation, in a hellenic environment. Pusey has very interesting things to say about the meeting of Greek and Hebrew thought forms, even before the Incarnation, in the translation of the Old Testament into Greek. He is commenting on the prophecy concerning the sons of Noah; Ham is Egypt, Shem Israel, Japhet Greece.

> Before the coming of the Lord, as herald of the peace to be renewed, East and West had met in the *language* of Alexandria, (Shem and Japhet in this original dwelling place of Ham); Ham, however gigantic as had been his early civilisation, contributed nothing thereto; Japhet, whose thought as well as dwelling place, "God had enlarged", contributed the precision and clearness and definiteness of the Greek, Shem, whose God the revealed Jehovah was, the mysterious depth and fulness of the language of revelation, [;] and Greek was made the basis, as a sort of earnest that the Spirit which now was, as to its visible form, now [sic] confined to Shem, should penetrate and re-animate and consecrate all the language[s] and thoughts of men. Shem was the soul of the world, since therein God dwelt, and thence was life diffused through all the extremities of the Body. And so a pledge of the future unity was given, in that the thoughts [of] the different nations were thus blended together in one language; and God doubtless illumined in a measure those (the translaters of Alexandria) who gave the first impulse to this union.[1]

But the union was not complete until the Incarnation. On the cross, the wall of partition between Jew and Gentile, between man and God, was thrown down, and at Pentecost the curse of Babel was reversed in the coming of the Spirit. To confess the fullness and reality of the union thus achieved, was the whole

---

[1] Unpublished manuscript, 60.

work of the Fathers in their struggle against heresy, and not least of Athanasius and Cyril of Alexandria for whom Pusey had a special veneration; like the translaters of the Old Testament, though in a still higher way, they were called to bear witness to the unity of all things in God.[1]

The same struggle was, Pusey believed, being worked out in the nineteenth century, in the attempt to reassert the essentially sacramental nature of God's revelation in Scripture and tradition alike.

Since then types are intrinsically significant in themselves, even we who have seen and lived in the reality, still have need of that type to express the reality. It has been well said, that God has appointed, as it were, a sort of sacramental union between the type and the archetype, so that as the type were nothing, except in so far as it represents, and is the medium of conveying the archetype to the mind, so neither can the archetype be conveyed except thro' the type. Tho' the consecrated element be not the sacrament, yet neither can the soul of the sacrament be obtained without it. God has joined them together, and man may not and cannot put them asunder. We think ourselves in no danger of the fleshly system which clung to the type, without looking to the archetype; but in truth, in looking to separate the archetype from the type, by this pseudo-spiritual system we are adding this error to that which is more peculiarly our own. For whereas the type never did exist for itself, but always bearing the character of the archetype impressed upon it, we by separating it therefrom, do as thoroughly empty it of its meaning, as they who saw nothing beyond its outward form. The pseudo-spiritualist and the carnal man alike see in the water, the bread or the wine nothing but the bare element, and thereby each alike deprives himself of the benefits intended for him; the carnal would live on the bread alone, the pseudo-spiritual without it; the carnal mistakes the clouds and darkness for Him who is enshrined within it, the pseudo-spiritualist would behold

[1] I am deeply indebted in these two paragraphs to Fathert Robert Murray, SJ who in the discussion, drew particular attention to the semitic quality in Pusey's thought, suggesting that it was reminiscent of the Syrian Fathers, even more than the Greek. The possibility of a direct influence of St Ephrem the Syrian on Pusey would be worth investigating. It is significant that Father R. M. Benson, after Liddon Pusey's closest disciple, was also a theologian who was first of all a Hebraist, and then a patristic scholar: his whole theology is cast in similar categories; the glory of God revealed in all the dispensations of his mercy.

Him, who 'men cannot see and live', the light inapproachable, 'who no man hath seen or can see': the carnal neglects the revelation, the pseudo-spiritualist would know the unrevealed God. The danger of an age which thinks itself enlightened, is of course this last; only it should be borne in mind that a pseudo-spiritual mind is also unspiritual, that [it is] tho' in a different way equally uncapable of seeing the things of God.

The whole system of religion, contemplative and practical, is one of God's condescension: God cometh down to us, not we mount up to God. Its corner-stone and characteristic is "God manifest in the flesh". And with this, as God has appointed it, all is in keeping. Neither the letter without the Spirit, nor yet the Spirit without the letter—prayers, which God cometh into the midst of us to hear; earthly Sacraments, yet full of Heaven: earthly words, yet full of the Lord, λόγοι proceeding from and setting forth the Λόγος. And we, as we walk still by faith and not by sight must be content to see still the reflected light, "as in a glass darkly", not "face to face".[1]

Thus the images of the Old Testament, no less than the sacraments of the New, are an indispensable element in our apprehension of the Word of God who has become incarnate, who speaks not to our minds alone, but also to our wills, affections, consciences, imaginations. The attempt to reduce the whole economy of God's revelation to conceptual terms is, Pusey argues, radically mistaken.

When moderns then attempt to translate into plain terms the figurative language of Holy Scripture, and to substitute abstract, and as they would fain have it, clearer terms for the types and typical language of the O.T., they uniformly by this transmutation evaporate much of their meaning. We have not, it is true, visible propitiatory sacrifices, a visible theocracy, a visible temple; but it is still thro' the medium of these figures that we understand, (as far as we do understand), the reality: we have

---

[1] Unpublished manuscript, 23. Compare with this Coleridge's words on the nature of symbolism, in the first of his Lay Sermons. '. . . a symbol is characterised by a translucence of the special in the individual, or of the general in the special, or of the universal in the general; above all by the translucence of the eternal through and in the temporal. It always partakes of the reality which it renders intelligible; and while it enunciates the whole, abides itself as a living part in that unity of which it is the representative' (S. T. Coleridge, *Church and State* London 1839, 230).

no better way of understanding the main truths of the Gospel than thro' these very figures, 'the sacrifice of Christ', 'the Kingdom of God', 'the temple of the Holy Ghost'; and he who would lay aside these types and typical language, and understand the mysteries of God without them, would be acting contrary to the teaching of Scr. and so very wrongly and foolishly. Men think that they gain in clearness, but they lose in depth; they would employ definite terms, in order to comprehend that which is infinite![1]

Furthermore actions and events, especially actions in which we ourselves become involved, speak more deeply to us than words.

Thus the mystery of the υἱὸς μονογενής lies veiled in the sacrifice of Isaac, in the brazen serpent, faith in the Crucified, in the passover, vicarious redemption from death and the mystery of the Eucharistic Sacrifice and the Holy Communion. And this perhaps, the rather, because the types being acted, thereby struck [?] more deeply upon the mind, and more deeply affected it, than the word of which men were hearers only. If the sight be more than hearing, how much more oneself acting the truth, and when appealed to, the typical service had this advantage of being, as it were, wound round the conscience and forming a part of the spiritual life, it furnished a mingled argument to the conscience and the understanding.[2]

This whole complex of ideas is worked out most interestingly in later lectures, with reference to the idea of the Eucharistic sacrifice, seen against the background of the sacrificial systems of the Old Testament. Just as Pusey has argued that in the Old Testament, the strength and the impression which is made on the believer comes from the combination of a variety of images which severally reveal different aspects of the central mystery and speak to different faculties in the totality of man, so in the writings of the Fathers, he maintains, different elements of truth are held together in a living synthesis, thereby conveying something of the richness of the divine reality to man's mind and heart. And here the irenic intention in his thought comes very clearly to the surface. Have not the controversies which have divided Christendom on Eucharistic doctrine come from an arbitrary selection of certain

[1] Unpublished manuscript, 24.
[2] Unpublished manuscript, 31.

images, a stressing of certain aspects of the question at the expense of others, a selection which has been followed by a hardening and conceptualising of positions, which ought to have remained more open and full of reverence and awe? He writes:

> In order not to misunderstand the Fathers on this point, one must bear in mind, 1) how deeply impressed they were with the union of the body and blood of Christ with the symbols through which they are conveyed. Not having had to dispute about the Holy Mysteries, they could believe more simply and heartily; they could believe the ὅτι, and not concern themselves with the πῶς. . . . Again, carnal conceptions not having crept into the Church, they could speak the truth without limitation, or restraint. They fearlessly blend the sign and the thing signified, and speak of the reality under the terms under which it was set forth. They might speak the more fully in the one place, trusting to the corrective statements of another; . . . 2) which is in fact the same, the Fathers, from their vivid perception of the relations of the several Chtian. truths (one with another), glide imperceptibly from the mention of the one to the other, or speak of the one under the terms of the other.[1]

In another place he remarks:

> It is very necessary to bear in mind, that they (unlike our dry, hard way of treating things) had the several bearings of the same subject continually in their mind and pass rapidly from the one to the other, so that one unacquainted with their manner, or should [he] take them piecemeal, would easily conclude that they were confounding together different things, or regarded that as the sole object of an institution, which was indeed subordinate, but more to their present point. They use lighter weapons than our massive matter-of-fact age would employ dexterously.[2]

As an instance, St. Augustine passes at once from the mention of the one sacrifice on the cross to our daily refreshment thro' Christ's blood, derived from it. . . . Again with this sacrifice of the Eucharist, the Ancients immediately connected other sacrifices, as the sacrifice of prayer, of thanksgiving, of alms and oblations, of ourselves our souls and bodies, of the whole

[1] Unpublished manuscript, 107.
[2] Unpublished manuscript, 117.

Church, which is the body of Christ, yet it follows not (as some timid Protestants have persuaded themselves) that therefore the Ancients thought of no other sacrifices than these; rather they are parts of the sacrifice, or connected with it, in that all things in Christian faith are connected with Christ; it is not accidental that the Christian Church is called by the same name as the Eucharist—the Body of Christ, for Christ dwelleth in the Church, and it visibly exhibits Him, and He imparteth Himself thro' [the] Eucharist, as the outward and visible sign, and that mystical food, giving life to all the members, and running, as it were, thro' the veins of the whole Church gives it unity in that it keeps it united to Christ, when[ce] St. Paul says (1 Cor. 10) 'For we being many are one bread, one body; for we are all partakers of that one bread'; and the Priest, in presenting the sacred symbols of Christ's Passion, presenteth them as the tokens of God's loving-kindness to the Church which is a part of Christ and in Christ. When Christ is, then, in a measure, in His Church, the Church is to share in the sufferings of Christ, not vicariously, but as part of Him; the Church is offered by Christ, to the Father. In one way there is then a difference between the offering of the symbols of Christ's Body and of His mystical Body the Church; and in another they take place together....

And Pusey clinches his argument by quoting the justly famous passage of St Augustine in the *City of God*, on this subject, underlining the words, 'in that thing which she offers, she herself is offered'.[1]

In these lines Pusey gives eloquent expression to the common Tractarian view of the Church as a sacramental organism centred on the Eucharist and deriving all its life and meaning from Christ himself. He also suggests a way of approach to certain difficult problems in sacramental theology by means of a renewed understanding of the nature of biblical typology. It is one of the places in these lectures where Pusey seems to anticipate more recent theological developments in a remarkable way. One of the interesting features of the vision of the Church stated here is that it stresses the immediate dependence of the Church on God for its whole life and structure. Its unity is to be found in the work of Christ and of the Spirit, and in nothing less than that. This conviction

[1] Unpublished manuscript, 107–8.

about the union of human and divine, visible and invisible, in the Church, which was doubtless one of the reasons which led New-man to leave the Church of England, was also paradoxically enough, one of the principal reasons which made many Catholic-minded Anglicans in the nineteenth century feel bound to remain out of communion with the Roman see. For both the theory and the practice of papal supremacy, as they then saw it, seemed to them to substitute an earthly principle of unity in the Church, for a divine. And though, in the short term, this might seem to make for strength and efficiency, yet they believed it involved a grave distortion of the divine constitution of the Church. God himself is the 'Author and Centre' of the unity of the Church and only when he is recognised as 'the centre of union' may men again 'be safely united, as being drawn in common to that point, where-in alone they can rest'.[1] Only in the Spirit given at Pentecost can there be a union which will not destroy but fulfil the freedom with which God himself has endowed his creatures. To see how the papal primacy may act in the service of, and not in rivalry with the Lordship of Christ and the Spirit in the Church, would seem to be one of the prime theological tasks of our own century, in which all those who, in different ways, acknowledge the primacy of Rome should be able to work together.

In a symposium devoted to the study of the life and work of Newman, there is no need to apologise for a paper devoted to the thought of Newman's friends, Pusey and Keble. It is in no way an accident that intimate and sacred friendships should have played so central a part in the origins of the Oxford Movement. If men are to speak as they did of the indwelling of God in man, really and not notionally, reverently and with awe, how can it be save on the basis of some real knowledge of the way in which men may dwell in, live in, think in one another? It has been my purpose to suggest a little of the intimacy of intellectual contact which existed between these three men at this time. Coleridge re-marked of the first years of his friendship with William and Dorothy Wordsworth, that they were 'three people but one soul', and though in later years that collaboration was to come to an end, its effects have not ceased to be felt in the subsequent history of English letters. The saying might equally well apply to the re-lationship between Pusey, Keble, and Newman in the years be-

[1] Unpublished manuscript, 60.

tween 1833 and 1840. It may be difficult to analyse exactly the separate elements which men bring to such times of intense shared vision and activity, but it seems certain that the power which is released at such privileged moments is something greater than we might have looked for, taking any one of the participants in isolation from the others.

4
Newman and the Empiricist tradition

J. M. Cameron

Bacon aside, it is characteristic of British empiricism that it is preoccupied, almost obsessively, with questions of epistemology. Until these have been got out of the way (it is suggested), no real progress can be made with other philosophical problems. Its fundamental dogma is straight out of Descartes: that the mind is better known than the body, indeed, that the mind (together with what properly belongs to it, thoughts and sensations) is the first object of knowledge and perhaps the only object with which we are acquainted in the strict sense. The acceptance of the dogma has results that are at once overwhelmingly strange and strangely commonplace. We are cast into a world that is a mere hypothesis. We never see physical objects, or touch them, or smell them; we are instead acquainted with mental phenomena that are explained by this or that hypothesis: that of Locke – our perceptions *represent* bodies; that of Berkeley – *esse* is *percipi* or *percipere*, we perceive the ectypes of the Divine archetypes and know ourselves to be agents; that of Hume – we have present 'impressions' whose 'ultimate cause is, in my opinion, perfectly inexplicable by human reason, and 'twill always be impossible to decide with certainty, whether they arise immediately from the object, or are produc'd by the creative power of the mind, or are derived from the author of our being'.[1] The empiricist doctrines of the nineteenth and twentieth centuries, from Mill's 'permanent possibilities of sensation' to the families of sense data, gathered round the for ever

[1] David Hume, *A Treatise of Human Nature* (ed.) L. A. Selby-Bigge, Oxford 1896, 84.

inaccessible physical object, of recent speculation, are no more than rococo developments of the original baroque.

Empiricism thus understood is a syndrome associated with an anxiety state.

> Where am I, or what? From what causes do I derive my existence, and to what condition shall I return? ... What beings surround me?[1]

But an attentive consideration of the syndrome suggests a cure. 'Nature' snatches from us this strange fruit of solitary speculation and will not permit us to reject those beliefs without which we should lose the appetite for life. Or, as Berkeley saw, how we take the world and how we talk about it are not in the slightest degree affected by philosophical theories. No matter how elliptical the penny may seem it is still good and serviceable coin of the realm. A momentary doubt over the causal principle will scarcely disturb our concentration at the billiard table or persuade us to doubt the efficacy of a well-directed cue. Or perhaps empiricism rightly understood is a thesis about meaning.

> The table I write on ... exists, that is, I see and feel it; and if I were out of my study I should say it existed, *meaning* thereby that if I was in my study I might perceive it, or that some other spirit actually does perceive it.[2]

But this allows us to speak with the vulgar and leave it to the learned to use the more faithful but impossibly verbose language of phenomenalism.

Empiricism is thus immensely strange and yet solidly commonsensical. It tells us that most of what we take to be susceptible of categorical statement should strictly be the subject of an indefinitely vast collection of hypotheticals; and yet that this need make no difference to how we talk and how we act. It is terrifying and it is consoling. With one hand it robs us of our familiar world; with the other it restores it to us. From the true proposition that all empirical statements are such that they can be doubted without this entailing any logical absurdity it draws the strange conclusion that all empirical statements are doubtful; but if we ask for a statement that will provide us with the standard that

---

[1] Hume, 269.
[2] George Berkeley, *The Principles of Human Knowledge* in *The Works of George Berkeley, Bishop of Cloyne* II (eds.) A. A. Luce, T. E. Jessop, London 1949, 42. Italics added.

empirical statements fail to come up to, we are offered tautologies and other statements that are true in virtue of the meanings of the terms employed. Whatever is conceivable is possible, Hume tells us; but we have scarcely had the time to savour the thought that for all we know horses may talk to us and lions lay bets on the Derby when irrefragable arguments are proffered to show us that a belief in the miraculous is impossible. In short, the epistemology of empiricism takes us for a wonderful ride, but gets us safely home at last.

Empiricism is not only a doctrine of interest to philosophers and one which provides the layman with the oddest examples of philosophical paradox; its history is also an important part of the history of culture. The doctrine of empiricism, developed so recklessly by philosophers, has in the more general history of intellectual concerns been the handmaid of the experimental method, of the rejection of final causes in the explanation of natural processes and of the expulsion of occult causes from nature. It is this aspect of empiricism Voltaire had in mind when he commended Locke as against the Cartesians.[1] Whatever its epistemological doctrines, empiricism has always been friendly to hardheadedness and sobriety, to caution and self-criticism, in the great inquiries into nature and human society that are the conspicuous achievements of the modern world. It would perhaps be extravagant to claim that Hume is the father of the historical method and of social anthropology; but it seems clear enough that this was the direction in which his thought moved.[2] The logical connections between the theory of knowledge of empiricism and the application of empirical methods in inquiries into matters of fact may be obscure, though they could be elucidated; but the historical connections cannot be doubted. Whether or not we are confronted with modes of thought in philosophy and in positive inquiries that are logically connected is perhaps unimportant for our present purposes. We are at any rate confronted with the kind of elective affinities Max Weber saw between the Protestant ethic and the spirit of capitalism and others have seen between the music, the painting, the architecture, and the politics of, say, the age of baroque. Empiricism has a flavour, a shared style, that is

---

[1] In his *Letters Concerning the English Nation*, English translation, 1733, 97.
[2] See J. A. Passmore, *Hume's Intentions* Cambridge 1952, ch. i; and J. M. Cameron, 'An Incomplete Hume', *Times Literary Supplement*, 22 May 1959, p. 308.

as apparent in Hume's writings on politics and history as in his
writings on perception and the nature of the self, that links Locke
on innate ideas with Butler on conscience; and that stamps un-
mistakably the work of the greatest English theologian of the
nineteenth century: John Henry Newman.

That the empiricist epistemology is centrally important in the
work of Newman I have already shown in my essay on 'Newman
and Empiricism'.[1] In that essay I cite a number of passages from
the sermons, the *Tracts for the Times*, *The Arians*, the *Apologia*,
the unpublished writings kept at the Birmingham Oratory, and
other sources, that, to my mind, place this beyond all possible
doubt. (This point had already been made, effectively but in less
detail, by Mr D. G. James in *The Romantic Comedy*, 1948.) Here
I shall take Newman's rootedness in the tradition of English empiricism for granted. I now go on to ask what use Newman made
of this tradition in his constructive theological work and how far
what we now value in his thought is connected with the cast of
empiricism it always had.

Newman lived at the end of the age of evidences, the age 'when
love was cold',[2] as he tells us; and at the end of the age when
the invincible character of the argument from design, in the form
in which it had been destroyed by Hume, was still commonly
accepted by the devout. The general tendency of his thought,
with few qualifications and few backward glances, is towards the
rejection of the supposedly coercive arguments from 'evidences',
as these were propounded by such theologians as Paley, and of the
demonstrative arguments of eighteenth-century natural theology.
In their place he offers us 'inwardness', faith in the dogmatic
principle, historical inquiry of a cautious kind, far removed from
the jaunty use of historical authorities by the contemporary apologist, and, in his last work, the *Grammar of Assent*, an account
of belief and judgement that is marked by that hostility to formal
logic (or what he took formal logic to be) that is a perpetually
recurring note in his writings. It is in the *Grammar of Assent* that
he cites, with approval, a passage from his brilliant pamphlet,
The Tamworth Reading Room. It is as good an account as any
of his general attitude to rationalism. The thought is aphoristic,

---

[1] *Victorian Studies*, Indiana IV, 2 (1960), 99–117 reprinted in J. M. Cameron,
The Night Battle London 1962, 219–43.
[2] John Henry Newman, *Sermons Chiefly on the Theory of Religious Belief*
London 1843, 189 (*University Sermons*).

rather than continuous, and we do no serious violence to the passage if we pick out from it the following remarks:

> The heart is commonly reached, not through reason, but through the imagination, by means of direct impressions, by the testimony of facts and events, by history, by description. Persons influence us, voices melt us, looks subdue us, deeds inflame us. Many a man will live and die upon a dogma; no man will be a martyr for a conclusion. ... Logic makes but a sorry rhetoric with the multitude; first shoot round corners, and you may not despair of converting by a syllogism. ... I would rather be bound to defend the reasonableness of assuming that Christianity is true, than to demonstrate a moral government from the physical world. Life is for action. If we insist on proofs for everything, we shall never come to action: to act you must assume, and that assumption is faith ... no religion yet has been a religion of physics or of philosophy. It has ever been synonymous with revelation. It has never been a deduction from what we know; it has ever been an assertion of what we are to believe. It has never lived in a conclusion; it has ever been a message, a history, or a vision. ... Moses was instructed not to reason from the creation, but to work miracles. Christianity is a history supernatural, and almost scenic: it tells us what its Author is, by telling us what He has done. ...[1]

Here is a religion conceived as having no foundations external to itself. This or that consideration, historical or moral, derived from common knowledge or from reading, may indeed for individuals and upon particular occasions be persuasive; but this will be something that speaks to the condition of a single man in a unique situation. But there are no demonstrative arguments of a historical or philosophical kind – such arguments would in principle speak to the generality of men – which, existing prior to the act of faith, serve as necessary conditions for this act. The use of the expression 'direct impressions' in the first of the passages quoted above is not accidental. I do not suggest that Newman's use of the term 'impression' is precisely that of Hume. It is looser and less technical. But it stands all the same for something that is an original existence from which everything else is derived, and is thus analogous in its role to 'impression' in Hume's system. Con-

[1] John Henry Newman, *An Essay in Aid of a Grammar of Assent* 1906, pp. 92–6.

sider, for example, the following passage from the last of the *University Sermons*:

> Theological dogmas are propositions expressive of the judgments which the mind forms, or the impressions which it receives, of Revealed Truth. Revelation sets before it certain supernatural facts and actions, beings and principles; these make a certain impression or image upon it; and this impression spontaneously, or even necessarily, becomes the subject of reflection on the part of the mind itself, which proceeds to investigate it, and to draw it forth in successive and distinct sentences.[1]

Later in the same sermon he remarks of a 'body of dogmatic statements' that 'what was an impression on the Imagination has become a system or creed in the Reason'.[2] Again, he makes an explicit comparison between the impression made by Divine revelation and sense perception:

> This may be fitly compared with the impressions made on us by the senses. Material objects are real, whole, and individual; and the impressions which they make on the mind by means of the senses, are of a corresponding nature, complex and manifold in their relations and bearings, but considered in themselves integral and one. And in like manner the ideas which we are granted of Divine Objects under the Gospel, from the nature of the case and because they are ideas, answer to the Originals so far as this, that they are whole, indivisible, substantial, and may be called real, as being images of what is real. Objects which are conveyed to us through the senses, stand out in our minds ... with dimensions and aspects and influences various, and all of these consistent with one another ... while we contemplate the objects themselves; thus forcing on us a persuasion of their reality from the spontaneous congruity and coincidence of these accompaniments, as if they could not be creations of our minds, but were the images of external and independent beings. This of course will take place in the case of the sacred ideas which are the objects of our faith.[3]

Revelation, then, is of an object that is given, known in us by an impression which is self-authenticating in the way the impres-

---

[1] *University Sermons*, 320–21.
[2] *University Sermons*, 331.
[3] *University Sermons*, 331–2.

sions of normal sense perception authenticate the reality of the objects to which they correspond. Such impressions prompt us to analyse and describe their objects, and the validity of such analysis and description rests upon the authenticity of the original perception. Analysis and description are always inadequate to represent the richness and immediacy of what is first bestowed upon us.

The model of perception, taken from Locke and Hume, presupposed by Newman is, of course, open to devastating criticism; but its use as a model to bring out what is peculiar to the relation between the datum of revelation – event, vision, personal encounter, whatever it may be – and theological discourse does not rest upon its adequacy as an account of what it is to perceive physical objects. At bottom Newman may be concerned to advance a theory of the connection between language and the subject matter of religious discourse. He says, in the fourth of the *University Sermons*, that 'moral Truth'

> cannot be adequately explained and defended in words at all. Its views and human language are incommensurable. For, after all, what *is* language but an artificial system adapted for particular purposes, which have been determined by our wants?[1]

This is why religious communication is frequently, of necessity, indirect.

> When the mind is occupied by some vast and awful subject of contemplation, it is prompted to give utterance to its feelings in a figurative style; for ordinary words will not convey the admiration, nor literal words the reverence which possesses it; and when, dazzled at length with the great sight, it turns away for relief, it still catches in every new object which it encounters, glimpses of its former vision, and colours its whole range of thought with this one abiding association.[2]

This, too, is why the mind is seized with a certain giddiness and even nausea before dogmatic statements and why 'freedom from symbols and articles is abstractedly the highest state of Christian communion, and the peculiar privilege of the primitive church'.[3]

A consequence of Newman's use of the empiricist model is that we begin from what is within: the impression. This is not the

---

[1] *University Sermons*, 70.
[2] John Henry Newman, *The Arians of the Fourth Century* London 1883, 57–8.
[3] *The Arians of the Fourth Century*, 36.

object of faith, but this is how the object of faith is apprehended; it is from the content of the impression that religious utterances are drawn and by which their fidelity to the object of faith is tested. The terminology of within and without generates a great many difficulties, but it seemed to him unavoidable. Once we set up the mechanism by which we derive from the impression, that which is logically private, authentic discourse about what is logically public, the object, we are bound to push the distinction between what is logically private, the inward impression, and what is logically public, the correlative object, to the limit at which the two split apart; we are then left with a scepticism about the object for which there is no remedy short of deciding that the very way the problem has been set up must be defective.

Newman, certainly, had no suspicion that the model he takes for granted, so far as sense perception is concerned, has something fundamentally wrong with it, and this leads him to an excessive reliance upon the model in all its details. If, however, we take him to be saying no more than that the object of faith necessarily transcends our capacity to say what it is, and that religious discourse is necessarily bound by the subjectivity of the believer, even in the case of that believer who is a commissioned teacher and steward of the mysteries, then what he says has point, since it enables us to make the necessary distinction between what is given in revelation and the historically limited forms of thought and language in which we speak about it.

What is communicated with a certain awkwardness, the empiricist model being, as it were, so obtrusive, in the analytic works is expressed with more grace in the *Parochial Sermons*. There is a remarkable passage in which Newman speaks of soul and body:

... we are made up of soul and body. Now, if we did not know this, so that we cannot deny it, what notion could our minds ever form of such a mixture of natures, and how should we ever succeed in making those who go only by abstract reason take in what we mean? The body is made up of matter; this we see; it has a certain extension, make, form, and solidity: by the soul, we mean that invisible principle which thinks. We are conscious we are alive, and are rational; each man has his own thoughts, feelings, and desires; each man is one to himself, and knows himself to be one and indivisible; – one in such sense, that while he exists, it were an absurdity to suppose he can be

4*

other than himself; one in a sense in which no material body which consists of parts can be one. He is sure that he is distinct from the body, though joined to it, because he is one, and the body is not one, but a collection of many things. He feels moreover that he is distinct from it, because he uses it; for what a man can use, he is superior to. No one can by any possibility mistake his body for himself. It is *his*; it is not he. This principle, then, which thinks and acts in the body, and which each person feels to be himself, we call the soul. We do not know what it is; it cannot be reached by any of the senses . . . to ask what shape the soul is, would be as absurd as to ask what is the shape of a thought, or a wish, or a regret, or a hope.[1]

So far Newman has been treading a familiar path and one that, so most of us would now think, ends in an intellectual morass. (For example, if the soul lacks extension, what is the force of saying it is *in* the body? Again, is it really the case that it would be correct – I am not making a point about mere usage – to say: I went to church and took my body with me? or: I used my tongue to say my prayers? or: You pricked my body and caused me to have a pain? The vein of the passage is Cartesian rather than Humeian, except perhaps for the 'we do not know what it is' said of the soul; and the reference to a 'thought, or a wish, or a regret, or a hope' as having no extension perhaps echoes Hume's 'a moral reflection cannot be plac'd on the right or on the left hand of a passion'.[2]) And yet, under the pressure of the logical violence the mode of discourse he has chosen engenders, he finally comes to the following conclusion, after admitting that 'it is as incomprehensible as any thing can be, how soul and body can make up one man' – an admission strictly incompatible with what he has already said.

No part of a man's body is like a mere instrument, as a knife, or a crutch might be, which he takes up and may lay down. Every part of it is part of himself; it is connected into one by his soul, which is one. Supposing we take stones and raise a house, the building is not *really* one; it is composed of a number of separate parts, which viewed as collected together, we

<hr>

[1] John Henry Newman, *Parochial Sermons* IV, 1839, 323–24.
[2] David Hume, *Treatise* I.iv.5.

call one. . . . But the hands and the feet, the head and trunk, form one body under the presence of the soul within them.[1]

Now this is (as he himself goes on to state) to contradict what he has earlier laid down as the right way of talking about soul and body. My body is, *qua* living body, myself; my body is not related to me as tool to user. The question that arises is why, if in the end Newman is compelled to assert what is fundamentally a non-dualistic view of human nature, he feels he has to engage in a Cartesian or Humeian excursion first. In part, we are inclined to say, this is because it is the merest philosophical orthodoxy of the day. That another view is possible had been forgotten, despite the availability of Holy Scripture and the writings of Aristotle. But this procedure by which he first, as it were, drives us to the edge of sanity by recounting the empiricist fable, and then casts the fable aside and utters another doctrine, is so characteristic of his work on a number of topics that it may better be viewed as a hermeneutic or rhetorical device.

For Hume there are only two kinds of connection between phenomena: psychological and logical. Habit establishes connections between impressions and ideas and the associations thus established are to the world of the mind what the forces of Newtonian physics are in the world-picture of physical science. In logic and mathematics we deal with connections, the nature of which is guaranteed because we are concerned with relations of ideas. Here the mind is free to determine the necessary features of its own discourse. But matters of fact are entirely loose and unconnected in themselves. How they are is simply given and there can therefore be no demonstrative reasoning concerning them, for there is no reason why they should have the order they have. To the picture of a perceiving subject the prisoner of his own impressions is added the picture of a world of fact in which perceptible order is a property of our habits and expectations, and of these only. Just as Newman uses the empiricist account of perception as a device to weaken the comfortable assumptions of common sense, so he uses this latter picture to contrast the

[1] *Parochial Sermons* IV, 325. But with this should be compared the much more wonderful sermon, 'The Resurrection of the Body', in *Parochial Sermons* I, in which he advances the entirely biblical doctrine of man, as in, *e.g.*, the following passage: 'God graciously called Himself *the God of Abraham*. He did not say the God of Abraham's *soul*, but simply of *Abraham*. He blest Abraham, and He gave him eternal life; not to his soul only without his body, but to Abraham as one man.'

unintelligibility of the world of nature and of its processes, and of the world of history, too, with the same worlds as they are partially illuminated by faith.

> ... faith, without asking for one ray of light more than is given, muses over the wonderful system of Providence, as seen in this world, which is ever connecting events, *between which man sees no necessary bond*. The whole system of what is called cause and effect is one of mystery. ...[1]

What is true of the world of nature is also true of the human world of history, the very world within which we should expect to find evidence of purpose and design since it is in this world that men seek to bring states of affairs into existence in accordance with their desires and purposes. But when the religious man looks out upon the world of history he finds something quite different.

> Starting then with the being of a God ... I look out of myself into the world of men, and there I see a sight which fills me with unspeakable distress. The world seems simply to give the lie to that great truth, of which my whole being is so full; and the effect upon me is, in consequence, as a matter of necessity, as confusing as if I denied I am in existence myself. If I looked into a mirror, and did not see my face, I should have the sort of feeling which actually comes upon me, when I look into this living busy world, and see no reflection of its Creator. ... Were it not for this voice, speaking so clearly in my conscience and my heart, I should be an atheist, or a pantheist, or a polytheist when I looked into the world.[2]

To look into the mirror of the world and to see in it no trace of that which is so vivid an inward reality for the believer, this is for Newman the nightmare experience liable to cast a man into a state of unbelief. But – and the movement of argument is precisely the same as when Newman uses the empiricist account of what it is to perceive to press us into a total reliance upon faith – it is this apparent absence of God from the world of men that compels the conclusion that the absence is a sign of God's having absented himself, not a sign of his non-existence; for

> either there is no Creator, or this living society of men is in a true sense discarded from His presence ... *if* there be a God,

---

[1] *Parochial Sermons* 11, London 143, 237. Italics added.
[2] John Henry Newman, *Apologia pro Vita Sua*, 1955 (Everyman), 217.

since there is a God, the human race is implicated in some terrible aboriginal calamity.[1]

Once again, what is inward is the primary reality and saves what is without from absolute unintelligibility; but in this mode of argument – better, perhaps, persuasion – the absolute unintelligibility of what lies beyond inwardness has first to be experienced before what is inward can show its power to rescue the world from its deficiency of perceptible order. At his weakest, Newman is capable of appealing simply to the voice of Nature and of making the same appeal as Hume to a kind of easy pragmatism. We trust our senses 'from a secret instinct, so it need not be weakness or rashness, if upon a certain presentiment of mind we trust to the fidelity of testimony offered for a revelation'.[2] Again, in *Tract 85*, as a persuasive to convince us that it is a blessed thing to believe, he tells us, echoing Hume, 'that Nature certainly does give sentence against scepticism'.[3] But at his most serious he does not give us this easy advice, but rather asks the believer to look into the mirror of the world and find in it no answering image of man; and, since human inwardness is the only secure testimony of the divine image in man, no trace of God's presence and work.

If the structure of argument comes from the empiricists in general and from Hume in particular, the spirit of the argument is rather that of Pascal. How far Newman was directly influenced by Pascal is, as is almost always the case when we try to estimate his intellectual debts, uncertain. In a great crisis of his life it was a fragment of Pascal, 'Je mourrai seul', that came to his lips.[4] We know that in 1840 he recommended the reading of the *Pensées* to a correspondent[5] and it seems tolerably certain that he had read Pascal in Taylor's translation with some attention. It is interesting, too, that, as Dean Church remarked, there was something of Pascal in the character of Hurrell Froude. 'Both had that peculiarly bright, brilliant, sharp-cutting intellect which passes with ease through the coverings and disguises which veil realities from men.'[6]

[1] *Apologia*, 218.
[2] *University Sermons*, 206.
[3] *Tracts for the Times* v, London 1840, No. 85, 72.
[4] *Apologia*, 200.
[5] Anne Mozley (ed.), *Letters and Correspondence of John Henry Newman* ii, London 1891, 307.
[6] R. W. Church, *The Oxford Movement* London 1922, 56.

But spiritual affinity rather than literary influence is what is in question. Here we note, first, the remarkable correspondence between what Pascal has to say about the order of thought with what was, for Newman, not so much an order of thought chosen from among alternatives, as the native inclination of the mind. Pascal writes: 'Or l'ordre de la pensée est de commencer par soy, et par son auteur et sa fin.'[1] This is Newman's method, as we have seen, to begin with what is inward and from this inward consciousness to go straight to God. This Newman traces back to his 'childish imaginations'; and the effect of his 'inward conversion' at the age of fifteen on his later opinions consisted 'in isolating me from the objects that surrounded me, in confirming my mistrust of the reality of material phenomena, and making me rest in the thought of two and two only supreme and luminously self-evident beings, myself and my Creator'.[2]

There are other parallels with the thought of Pascal. Both stress the inefficacy of demonstrative reason in matters of faith.[3] Both think it an error in apologetics to attempt with infidels 'prouver la Divinité par les ouvrages de la nature'.[4] Both have the same view of the role of the imagination, 'that the world overcomes us, not merely by appealing to our reason, or exciting our passions, but by imposing on our imagination'.[5] Most important of all, each is driven by the force of his dialectic to say, of the great choice between belief and unbelief: *il faut parier.*

> . . . let us suppose two persons of strong mind, not easily excitable, sound judging and cautious; and let them be equally endowed in these respects. Now there is an additional reason why, of these two, he who is religious will believe more and reason less than the irreligious; that is, if a man's acting upon a message is the measure of his believing it, as the common sense of the world will determine. For in any matter so momentous and practical as the welfare of the soul, a wise man will not wait for the fullest evidence, before he acts; and will show his caution, not in remaining uninfluenced by the existing report of a divine message, but by obeying it though it might be more

---

[1] Blaise Pascal, *Pensées*, translated by H. F. Stewart, 1950, p. 82 (bilingual edition).

[2] *Apologia*, 31.

[3] *Pensées*, 132; *University Sermons*, 55.

[4] *Pensées*, 132; *University Sermons*, 55.

[5] *University Sermons*, 110. See '. . . cette partie dominante dans l'homme, cette maîtresse d'erreur et de fausseté', *Pensées*, 38.

clearly attested. If it is but slightly probable that rejection of the Gospel will involve his eternal ruin, it is safest and wisest to act as if it were certain.[1]

Thus Newman in an early sermon. In a later sermon he says of the true Christian that

when Christ comes at last, blessed indeed will be his lot. He has joined himself from the first to the conquering side; he has risked the present against the future, preferring the chance of eternity to the certainty of time. . . .[2]

There is a difficulty here for Newman, if not for Pascal. Here *il faut parier* is given as a *reason* for believing; and this line of thought is in plain conflict with his more usual view that religion begins with what is given inwardly and is not a matter of calculation. We may conjecture that it is not an easy matter to rid oneself of the view that there must be intellectual foundations for faith, that faith cannot be self-authenticating. It is true, *il faut parier* seems sophistical and it would be hard to think well of a man for whom it was the sole persuasive to the obedience of faith. That it is the only *reason* Newman can give is evidence of the extent to which he has repudiated the apologetic style of his contemporaries and immediate predecessors.

It has already been remarked that the strangeness of empiricist epistemology is linked with extreme sobriety in dealing with matters of fact in such fields as natural science and history. Since in these matters we cannot go beyond experience, scepticism about large speculations is joined to a strict attention to evidence, to experiment, and to the coherent testimony of the senses. In so far as the natural scientist or the student of society is concerned with causes, these will be causal sequences established and checked by observation; and the passage from one state or event to another will not exhibit a necessary connection the existence of which can be inferred as we infer a conclusion from given premises. The contrast here is with human action where the connection between, say, belief and the action which exhibits it is not causal but conceptual; and explanation by final causes is the application to natural processes of an explanatory model derived from human action. It is this which gave final causes their immense plausibility

---

[1] *Parochial Sermons* II, 23.
[2] *Parochial Sermons* IV, 271, 33.

as explanations of natural processes. That the connections are here merely conceptual explains their inability to give us any information we do not already have. If we explain the soporific powers of opium by stating that it has a *virtus dormitiva* we have uttered no more than a barren tautology.

Here Newman is as much a child of the empiricist tradition as in his theory of knowledge, and it is this aspect of Newman's thought that in part accounts for the impression of an astonishing modernity we sometimes derive from his writings. He was, in relation to natural science, a modern man, whereas many of his friends and contemporaries were in such matters men of a pre-scientific mentality. The proof text is a comment on Darwin's evolutionary hypothesis written in a notebok at the end of 1863, four years after the appearance of *The Origin of Species*. He wrote:

> There is as much want of simplicity in the idea of the creation of distinct species as in those of the creation [of] trees in full growth (whose seed [is] in themselves) or of rocks with fossils in them. I mean that it is as strange that monkeys should be so like men, with no historical connexion between them, as that there should be, or the notion that there was, no history or course of facts by which fossil bones got into rocks. . . . I will either go the whole hog with Darwin, or, dispensing with time and history altogether, hold, not only the theory of distinct species, but that also of the creation of the fossil-bearing rocks.[1]

As we know, many divines of this period did hold this last theory, Keble among them. We may wonder why Newman kept his being prepared to 'go the whole hog with Darwin' to himself. It seems likely that he felt he had in any case a strong tendency to get into scrapes and saw no particular duty to get into this one. Had he done so, it would certainly have gratified all those who believed that the deepest tendency in Newman's thought worked towards infidelity. In any case, Newman had the strongest objection to forcing theology and natural science into a close partnership. In his lecture on 'Christianity and Scientific Investigation' he speaks of

> religious men, who, from a nervous impatience lest Scripture should for one moment seem inconsistent with the results of

---

[1] Unpublished papers at the Birmingham Oratory, note of 9 December 1863.

some speculation of the hour, are for ever proposing geological or ethnological comments upon it, which they have to alter or obliterate before the ink is well dry, from changes in the progressive science, which they have so officiously brought to its aid.[1]

When we recall the rapacity with which some theologians have fastened upon the Uncertainty Principle of Heisenberg or the 'big bang' theory of the origin of the universe, we may think that Newman's remarks have not lost their point.

Perhaps the most remarkable instance of Newman's acuteness in a matter which belongs to the philosophy of both the natural and the social sciences is contained in a letter to T. W. Allies who had asked him a question about the philosophy of history, whether it was not 'the results of history viewed by the light of final causes'. In his reply Newman wrote:

> For myself, I cannot help thinking that laws are a sort of facts *in* the subject matter which is in question. In chemistry latent heat involves certain laws. These the religious mind rightly considers to have been determined by the Creator for a good end; but the end is not part of the law, as in the corresponding case of morals, 'finis praecepti non cadit sub praeceptum'. Bacon seems to me to state correctly, that the doctrine of final causes (when actively introduced) *spoils* physics. First let us ascertain the fact – then theologize upon it. Depend upon it, when once the laws of human affairs are drawn out, and the philosophy into which they combine, it will be a movement worthy of the Lawgiver, but if we begin speaking of Him first of all, we shall never get at His laws. I can quite understand a Professor drawing religious conclusions from historical laws or ordinances, as from physical, but he must first find his laws.[2]

This letter was written in 1854 and we may suspect that it echoes, in what he has to say about 'the laws of human affairs', a theme in Mill's *Logic*.[3] We know that he was a student of Mill. There is no doubt a certain amount of confusion in this passage, notably in the almost unanalysable 'laws are a sort of facts *in* the subject matter'; but he is clear as to the main point, the useless-

---

[1] John Henry Newman, *On the Scope and Nature of University Education* London 1915 (Everyman), 252; *Idea of a University* London 1925, 472.
[2] Cited in A. Dwight Culler, *The Imperial Intellect* New Haven 1955, 269.
[3] See John Stuart Mill, *A System of Logic*, Book VI, *passim*.

ness for scientific purposes of final causes in physical science. There is a remark in a notebook of 1861 which suggests that so far as the logic of the science is concerned on one occasion at least he advanced beyond Mill: 'The logical evolutions of science (induction &c.) are a rule of the game, not in the nature of things.'[1]

The three volumes of *Historical Sketches* remind us that Newman was always an amateur of history. The *Essay on Development*, his most influential if not his greatest work – this is surely the *Lectures on Justification* – is not a historical work as such, but it deals with a historical problem. The *Apologia* itself is an important historical work and a primary source for the ecclesiastical history of the period. His inopportunist opposition to the project of an Infallibility Decree and his resentment against the 'insolent and aggressive' faction that dominated English Catholicism down to the end of the pontificate of Pius IX both rested upon a lively appreciation of historical considerations. In what sense is Newman here, too, a child of the empiricist tradition?

It would not be an exaggeration to say that Newman's theory of Anglicanism as the *Via Media* rested upon historical interpretation; and his abandonment of the attempt to offer a rationale of the *Via Media* and his decision to submit to the Roman Church were consequences of his perception that this interpretation had broken down. It would be excessive to say that his conversion – he might well have objected to this term, but it is convenient – rested upon a changed view of history; but it is certain that it was in part motivated by a strong sense of what he took to be historical reality. A starting point of the *Essay on Development* is that Protestantism, in so far as it claims to be primitive Christianity, is untenable on purely historical grounds; for 'whatever history teaches, whatever it omits, whatever it exaggerates or extenuates, whatever it says or unsays, at least the Christianity of history is not Protestantism. If ever there were a safe truth, it is this'[2] And whatever the weight we give to the apparatus for distinguishing between true and false developments constructed in the course of the *Essay*, and no one would seriously defend it as it stands, it is clear from the *Essay* itself that what in the end conquered the heart and mind of Newman was what he took to be historically

[1] Oratory manuscripts, note of 16 November 1861.
[2] John Henry Newman, *An Essay on the Development of Christian Doctrine* London 1890, 7.

given, the inescapable conclusion before a particular constellation of facts.

> No one doubts ... that the Roman Catholic communion of this day is the successor and representative of the Medieval Church, or that the Medieval Church is the legitimate heir of the Nicene; even allowing that it is a question whether a line cannot be drawn between the Nicene Church and the Church which preceded it. On the whole, all parties will agree that, of all existing systems, the present communion of Rome is the nearest approximation in fact to the Church of the Fathers, possible though some may think it, to be nearer still to that Church on paper. Did St. Athanasius or St. Ambrose come suddenly to life, it cannot be doubted what communion he would take to be his own.[1]

It is important to notice, however, that for Newman attention to this constellation of facts in itself is not enough to convince one of the conclusion he draws from it. In the great sermon on 'Faith and Reason contrasted as Habits of Mind' he shows that neither history nor Scripture, viewed from a scientific standpoint, compels the assent of faith.

> It is difficult to say where the evidence, whether for Scripture or the Creed, would be found, if it were deprived of those adventitious illustrations which it extracts and absorbs from the mind of the inquirer, and which a merciful Providence places there for that very purpose. Texts have their illuminating power, from the atmosphere of habit, opinion, usage, tradition, through which we see them.[2]

What holds of Scripture holds *a fortiori* of secular history. Apart from that inwardness possessed by the believer which, since it is the witness of the Spirit, is able to make Scripture come alive and history to show, fitfully and here and there, the Divine action, men's conclusions are merely probable, even after long and earnest study, and do not in themselves compel the practical judgement. Newman is so far an empiricist that he is infinitely removed both from the pious chroniclers, such as Bossuet, and from those philosophical historians – Vico, Hegel, Marx, and

---

[1] *An Essay on the Development of Christian Doctrine*, 97–8.
[2] *University Sermons*, 183.

Engels – who have seen in the pattern of secular history the march of God in the world.

Newman does, in the *Essay on Development*, make one astonishing remark which strikes one as being of a highly metaphysical character. He asks a question that must at times trouble every believer, namely, why the burden of evil is not removed by a Divine decree that the end should now come. His answer is: 'Let the Church be removed, and the world will soon come to its end.'[1] This is to assert the final dependence of secular history upon sacred history. That any history should be known to be sacred history is, for Newman, a gift of the Spirit and not the fruit of study; it is known inwardly, by the believer, and does not rest upon observation and the testing of evidence by scholars, though there is an implicit assumption that it should not come into direct and permanent conflict with what the scholars establish. We look into the world of men and see no trace of God's presence; we look upon historical existence and see no sufficient reason for such existence. That, nevertheless, there is sacred history and that, more wonderfully, the existence of secular history should be preserved through its dependence upon sacred history, these are not conclusions to which we are driven as we are driven by what is evidence for historians. These positions, therefore, do not conflict with the scepticism of the empiricist tradition: they transcend it. Newman never denied that to the natural man, and to the believer in that first, decisive vision of a world without God, the world, its religious phenomena included, was 'a riddle, an aenigma, an inexplicable mystery'.[2] If in the end he rejected Hume's verdict, it was not that he thought the verdict unjustified: it was also his own, when he set aside his antecedent presumption in favour of Christian belief. It was rather that he found more in his inwardness than Hume found in his. Hume never got farther than *l'esprit de géometrie*. Newman was a master of *l'esprit de finesse*.

My conclusion, then, is that Newman's philosophical deficiencies provide, accidentally, as it were, and through a trick of the history of ideas, the ground for his theological virtues. The epistemology of empiricism is as dead as argument can make it; but it still offers a wild poetry which creates in us a strange view of

---

[1] *An Essay on the Development of Christian Doctrine*, 204.
[2] David Hume, 'The Natural History of Religion', in *Essays and Treatises on Several Subjects* II, London 1822, 449.

the commonplace, much as an unusual light will give a familiar scene a look of enchantment. Its genuine intellectual content is quite other than the empiricists themselves, Newman included, supposed: roughly, that informative statements are not analytic and are thus in principle always doubtable and always corrigible; and that analytic statements are not informative, except in the trivial sense that a man may stand in need of having their analysis exhibited to him. But the whole sub-structure of 'impressions', sense data, the belief in the uniquely informative character of introspection, 'the egocentric predicament', the agonising questions about what colour and shape bodies *really* are, and the rest, this has vanished into a limbo where the whole brood may live happily for ever with phlogiston, animal spirits, the round square, the present King of France and the unheard music of the spheres. It is all the same true that empiricism is an experience that has to be lived through if one is to grasp the mentality of the modern educated man. Newman had had this experience, and this is one of the reasons why what he writes strikes so sympathetically upon the ear, and why so much Catholic writing of that time, and later, grates.

A further advantage that Newman derived from his empiricist background is that he was never tempted to amalgamate philosophy with theology or to fidget because his theology lacked a philosophical 'foundation'. Perhaps his knowledge of the history of Gnosticism would always have saved him from the first error; but the second error is subtler and more pervasive. Two things should be distinguished. First, it is true and inescapable that there should be a close relation between philosophy and theology; for in so far as the theologian asks questions about the meaning of first-order theological statements either in Scripture or in doctrinal formularies he is engaged in what is as much a philosophical enterprise as an inquiry into the conceptual structure of scientific or moral statements. Again, if we look at the history of doctrine we are bound to notice that doctrinal formularies draw heavily upon the philosophical word-books of their periods, so that familiarity with philosophical terminology and the problems which dictated the terminology is an exegetical requirement. But the picture of dogmatic theology as a superstructure resting upon a foundation of natural theology, that is, of assured philosophical conclusions, is an absurdity if we take the idea of revelation seriously; for this would be to say that the work of God, revelation, is helpless except it be brought into a certain relation with a work of man, philosophy. It is true that the *conclusions* of natural theology are presupposed by any kind of theological discourse[1]; but not as conclusions of chains of argument prior to theological discourse but as, so to speak, the underlying grammar of such discourse. Men may fail to grasp this grammar and, through this failure, take religious language to be without sense. For this there are no philosophical remedies, except by chance and for this or that individual man.

We may be grateful, therefore, that Newman lacked architectonic power in philosophy; for such power would have been a standing temptation to shift his attention from the ineffable acts and events in which he found the data of revelation. And we may also be grateful that he was never touched by idealist metaphysics. This was what stupefied Coleridge and corrupted so much Scottish Presbyterian theology in the later nineteenth century. The experience of empiricism is able to confer upon those who undergo it something of the Socratic irony. Only this irony can check the insatiable appetite of philosophy to make a meal of all things, the sacred science of theology included.

[1] This is how I understand the first chapter of the Letter to the Romans.

A note on Newman's historical method

J. D. Holmes

Newman's philosophical scepticism extended to his interpretation of history and, in particular, to his method of dealing with the problem that, although Christianity is a historical religion, history can only give probability, whereas faith demands certainty. Is a relation possible, therefore, between the Christian demand for certainty and the apparent failure of historical inquiry to produce results that are more than probable? Newman's solution is to posit, in his theory of development, antecedent considerations independent of demonstration.

'It is undoubtedly an hypothesis to account for a difficulty'[1], which was 'the want of accord between the early and the late aspects of Christianity'; and its purpose was to show how an argument could be grounded upon the history of 'the doctrine and worship of Christianity'. The effect of the theory in the Catholic Church was to undermine that position referred to by Bishop Butler as 'non-historical orthodoxy'[2]; and Newman did more than anyone to oppose the obscurantism of some of the Ultramontanes, when they threatened to play down or reject historical inquiry. Father Ryder of the Birmingham Oratory pointed out that W. G. Ward, for example, had an 'aversion for Ecclesiastical history as hampering, or defining Ecclesiastical authority'.[3]

Far from permitting his theory of development to be used to dismiss inconvenient facts, Newman was prepared for the *logical* possibility of its empirical refutation. Thus no theory of doctrinal development could explain away the fact, if it was a fact, that

[1] *Essay on the Development of Christian Doctrine* London 1906, 30.
[2] Bishop Butler, 'Newman and the Second Vatican Council', p. 240.
[3] H. I. D. Ryder, *Idealism in Theology, a Review of Dr Ward's Scheme of Dogmatic Authority* London 1867, p. 8.

Honorius formally taught heresy[1]; whilst the hypothesis of development itself could be destroyed if there were distinct or positive evidence that the Church had actually contradicted herself.[2] Newman vigorously rejected the dishonest distortion of history for the sake of some gratuitous theory.[3] On one occasion before 1845, he had condemned Catholic editions of the works of Ambrose and Augustine which omitted what was considered questionable. When he republished his book as a Catholic, he simply commented that those who cared to do so, could defend Medina's language or the conduct of the editors of St Augustine.[4]

As Professor Cameron has pointed out[5], the theory of evolution is a crucial example of Newman's willingness to accept scientific or historical evidence against the apparent testimony of Scripture; but Newman was equally emphatic about the bearing of historical investigation upon the Bible generally:

> Why do you take for granted that I admit no historical errors in the Bible? This is a question of fact – fact is fact, and can be proved. Perhaps what I might think short of a proof, another might think a demonstration – Perhaps what another would think sufficient for moral conviction, I, from reverence and tenderness towards a sacred writer, might pick holes in – but certainly I will not shut my eyes to historical proof, nor am I inconsistent, as a Catholic in saying so. When indeed you come to the 'Moral Authority' of the written word the case is different; because, as I think, we have not the same natural ability to resolve moral questions as to ascertain facts.[6]

At the same time, history could not simply be discussed as a technical science:

> Physical facts are present; they are submitted to the senses, and the senses may be satisfactorily tested, corrected, and verified. . . . But it is otherwise with history, the facts of which are not present.[7]

---

[1] See the letter reprinted in the *Dublin Review* 229, 1955, 450–52.
[2] *Essay on the Development of Christian Doctrine*, 121.
[3] J. H. Newman, *Historical Sketches* II, 342.
[4] J. H. Newman, *The Via Media of the Anglican Church* London 1877, 82. Conclusion referring to 73–5.
[5] Cameron, 'Newman and the Empiricist Tradition', 23–4.
[6] Newman to Hutton, 3 June 1865, Oratory P.C. copy.
[7] *Essay on the Development of Christian Doctrine*, III.

There was also a personal element in history. Historians differed from each other in estimating testimonies or facts, because

> that estimate is simply their own, coming of their own judgement; and that judgement coming of assumptions of their own, explicit or implicit; and those assumptions spontaneously issuing out of the state of thought respectively belonging to each of them; and all these successive processes of minute reasoning superintended and directed by an intellectual instrument far too subtle and spiritual to be scientific.[1]

To have read the original sources diligently and reported them accurately was a great achievement, but it was far more difficult to combine and adjust the materials, to bring out the course of events so that the reader had a definite impression on his mind of what had passed through it.[2]

While admitting the intrinsic value of evidence, therefore, Newman insisted that it could only be appreciated in the light of antecedent moral or political considerations. This may seem ambivalent, or even paradoxical; but it is not contradictory: evidence can overcome antecedent probabilities, and antecedent considerations can supersede contrary evidence. Both positions are true, and both must be maintained.

This is what brings Newman so close in spirit to modern historians – his scepticism of an over-riding and systematic philosophy, as distinct from a theology, of history.

---

[1] J. H. Newman, *An Essay in Aid of a Grammar of Assent* London 1870, 364.
[2] J. H. Newman, *Essays, Critical and Historical* II, London 1871, 254.

5
The biblical basis of Newman's ecumenical theology

C. S. Dessain

Newman's teaching on the Divine Indwelling – its origins

Dr Owen Chadwick, in his book *The Mind of the Oxford Movement*, speaks of the Parochial Sermons of Newman as embodying 'the "typical" doctrine of the Movement at its highest', and adds, 'It is of the essence of the Movement that its best writing should be enshrined in parochial sermons.'[1] It can hardly be sufficiently emphasised that Newman was first and foremost a pastor. His pastoral work at St Clement's, and then at St Mary's and Littlemore, begun long before the movement, continued during it. The Parochial Sermons, while they benefited, as the third decade of the century opened, from Newman's maturity and deeper hold on the content of revealed truth, remained always plain and pastoral. Thus as late as 1841 Peter le Page Renouf could write, after hearing the University sermon, 'Wisdom as contrasted with Faith and Bigotry,' that 'it was very different from his Parochial Sermons, when he never says anything which the most illiterate person cannot understand.'[2]

Newman's deepest influence was exercised through these Parochial Sermons, and that even more when they were published than when they were preached. As the first volumes came out several thousand copies were sold, and there are many testimonies to their effect, to how they set people living a more Christian,

[1] Owen Chadwick, *The Mind of the Oxford Movement* London 1960, 42.
[2] *The Life Work of Sir Peter le Page Renouf* First Series, iv, *The Book of the Dead* Paris 1907, xv.

prayerful life. Newman himself was convinced that his written was more effective than his spoken word. Looking back in 1849, he wrote, 'I do think that my influence among persons who have *not* seen me, has been indefinitely greater than among those who have.'[1] The influence of the sermons was due to their content, their matter, the saving truth they put forward, and not merely to their manner, or their delivery.

There has been printed recently by Mr David Newsome, part of a correspondence in which Newman was led to explain his aim and purpose in publishing them. Samuel Wilberforce received from the author a presentation copy of the first volume of the *Parochial Sermons*. He was still very much an Evangelical and felt that in it Newman limited the power of God's Spirit in a most unscriptural way. He seemed to put on one side the possibility of the Holy Spirit effecting sudden or rapid conversions. Newman's defence, in a letter of 4 February 1835, was that

> My Sermons are on subjects connected with sanctification. My reason for dwelling on the latter subject was my conviction *that we required the Law* not the Gospel in this age – we want rousing – we want the claims of duty and the details of obedience set before us strongly. And this is what has led me to enlarge on our part of the work not on the Spirit's.

And he concludes:

> In truth men *do* think that a saving state is one, where the mind merely looks to Christ – a virtual antinomianism.

A few lines further on Newman added that it was necessary to bring out the details of the Christian life as matters of fact. The Evangelicals were ready to confess that they were sinful in the abstract, but there was nothing definite or tangible in their teaching. To this he makes Wilberforce reply, 'I do not quarrel with you, for speaking in detail, but for not making mention of the Holy Spirit.' Newman answers, 'I will never be so irreverent as to (if I may so say) lug in any doctrine, much less so sacred a one'.[2] He appeals then to the immediate pastoral aim of his sermons, to justify his reticence. Yet, in fact, he held at this time not merely

---

[1] C. S. Dessain (ed.) *The Letters and Diaries of John Henry Newman* XIII, London 1962, 99.

[2] David Newsome, 'Justification and Sanctification: Newman and the Evangelicals', *Journal of Theological Studies*, April 1964, 43. See also David Newsome, 'The Evangelical sources of Newman's Power', p. 25 above.

that the Holy Spirit could influence men, but much more – the doctrine of his indwelling presence in their souls. In a letter to Wilberforce, a few days earlier than the one just quoted, he defined it as

> the great gift of grace, marvellous beyond words, exceeding in bounty, and freely given to those whom God has chosen in Christ and brings to baptism. It is the indwelling of the Holy Spirit in the soul as in a Temple – the Spirit of adoption. In the first place it has (so to say) a physical, or (as we term it) a mystical influence on the soul, uniting it to Christ – it distinguishes the Christian from all unregenerate men.

Wilberforce had mentioned the text, 'Grieve not the Holy Spirit'. This, Newman says, does not refer 'to the case of *a sinner* who is to be roused. It is exhortation to Christians not to profane their peculiar privilege.'[1] This privilege in spite of his unwillingness to 'lug in' the doctrine of the Holy Spirit, was to become more and more prominent in the Parochial Sermons, because of the important place it occupied in the Christian revelation, and because it had such practical religious value.

It is surprising that this should have been the case when we consider how this central doctrine of God's indwelling was, and was to remain, neglected in Western Christendom. It suggests how complete and balanced was the hold Newman had managed to acquire on revealed religion by the early 1830s. It had been the New Testament teaching that he who accepted Christ possessed within him, in the friendship and intimacy of a personal relationship, the presence of the Father, his Father, the Son, and the Holy Spirit. This 'partly realised eschatology', this gift, was meant to lead him to the love and service of his neighbour, of other persons. Indeed, the promise of the indwelling of the Holy Spirit in the soul, and through him, of the Father and the Son, was the culminating point of the Christian revelation, whether we consider it historically as it is to be found in the middle chapters of Romans and in the Last Discourse, or whether we arrange it in systematic form. Grace, in Scripture, is the favour, the generous kindness of God. This is primarily and essentially *personal*. God takes possession of man and is present in him. This is what may be called the revealed foundation of the Christian life, so sacred that reverence

---

[1] Newsome, 'Justification and Sanctification', 41.

has undoubtedly been one cause of reticence concerning it. Biblical scholars will not deny its primary importance, and contemporary Catholic theologians are admitting more and more that this truth is the real basis of the treatise on Grace.[1]

How did Newman discover it? In spite of his child's delight in reading the Bible, he tells us that as a boy of fifteen he did not see the *meaning* of loving God. He wanted to be virtuous, not religious. All this was changed by his Evangelical conversion. He gave himself to God, and, with the help of the works of Thomas Scott, accepted with his whole heart and mind the doctrine of the Blessed Trinity.[2] It was no mere abstract speculation he had discovered, but a saving relationship with Father, Son, and Holy Spirit. His was now a religion of persons. He understood the meaning of loving God, and it is clear that when he went up to Oxford he was trying to live in his presence. He grasped a fact which he reiterated in old age, in *A Grammar of Assent*, that the Holy Trinity is never spoken of in Scripture or in the Creeds as a mystery, but as a saving truth and as the basis of a Christian life.[3]

That was Newman's religious attitude from 1816 onwards. With it he accepted the Evangelical, the Protestant theology. He continued to hold a doctrine of imputed righteousness for the next ten years. He thought the *experience* of conversion was what made the true Christian. Only gradually did he come to believe in baptismal regeneration, but his own personal underlying religious attitude was not so far removed from the doctrine he would later make his own. Life is larger than logic, whose 'chain of conclusions', as Newman tells us, 'hangs loose at both ends'.[4] The special Evangelical tenets did not hinder him from leading a religious life that was Trinitarian. His first conversion was the

---

[1] Thus Joachim Jeremias, in his lecture on 'Justification by Faith', in *The Central Message of the New Testament* London 1965, 61–6 brings out strongly how the new Christian life begins with 'the gift of God's Spirit'. He speaks of the antedonation, the firm present possession of God, of life with Christ already here, as the teaching of the Gospel. For the theologians, see Karl Rahner, SJ, *Theological Investigations* 1, London 1961, 319–46.

[2] J. H. Newman, *Apologia pro Vita sua* London 1913, 1; H. Tristram, *John Henry Newman, Autobiographical Writings* London 1956, 169.

[3] J. H. Newman, *An Essay in Aid of a Grammar of Assent*, 132–41. See also *Parochial and Plain Sermons* 1, London 1910, 210.

[4] J. H. Newman, *An Essay in Aid of a Grammar of Assent*, 284. Newman's theological development until the early thirties has been excellently described from the unpublished manuscripts by Thomas L. Sheridan, SJ, in *Newman and Justification, a Study in the Development of a Theology*, a thesis submitted to the Faculty of Theology of the Institut Catholique de Paris, 1965.

turning-point of his life, when he gave himself to Father, Son, and Holy Spirit, and when, thanks to his familiarity with Scripture, he began to understand the meaning of God's grace. The implications were not worked out until he was a man of thirty.

About the year 1834 he wrote for Pusey a paper on baptismal regeneration, and the consequent special Divine Presence. By way of replying to the objection that no one who had experienced conversion in the Evangelical sense, could hold the doctrine of baptismal regeneration, Newman was led to become autobiographical. He spoke of those who

> were taught that at a certain time of religious emotion and anxiety, which they had experienced, they were regenerated and believed it; yet that, in spite of their love for their instructors and their memory of their own inward struggles, they deliberately changed their minds, that they were led year by year more and more to understand and to approve a system of doctrine which they once identified with the religion of the world, that year by year they saw more of the reasons for it, its scripturalness, its consistency with itself, its uses; lastly, that having thus wrought out their view for themselves, they have had an opportunity, which before was not afforded them, of knowing the proofs and explanations of the doctrine given by the great teachers of the Primitive and the modern Anglican Church, and to their surprise and great thankfulness they have found almost their own words in their writings, so as to have a full sanction for maintaining openly as the sense of Scripture what they had privately attained.[1]

Others will discuss the contribution of Evangelicals and of the Caroline divines to Newman's thought, but the above quotation seems to be the nearest we can get in Newman's own words, to what the evidence suggests – namely that the source of his teaching on the indwelling of the Blessed Trinity was primarily Holy

[1] MS 'Holy Baptism', 3–5. Newman's paper was never published, although the substance of it was turned into sermons, because Pusey wrote instead his long tract, *Scriptural Views of Holy Baptism*, Tracts 67, 68, and 69, Oxford 1835. There he spoke indeed of the indwelling, but did not develop the subject until his sermons published fifteen years and more later. The Caroline divines, when they wrote on grace, were preoccupied with the controversies of their day, whether against Rome or Protestantism, and hardly did more than mention the doctrine of God's presence in the soul.

Scripture. It has been by returning to the same source that others have rediscovered it in more recent times.[1]

Religious application in the Parochial Sermons

We must now see what part the divine indwelling and the relationship of the Christian with the Father, the Son, and the Holy Spirit, played in the Parochial Sermons, which, as Dr Chadwick says, contain the 'doctrine of the Movement at its highest', and show us Newman in possession of the body of revealed truth, to which he would later make only minor additions or alterations. The first three volumes were published as the Oxford Movement was beginning, in 1834–1835 and the beginning of 1836 respectively. There was an interval of three years before the appearance of the second batch, and by then the Movement had passed its zenith. We will consider for the moment only the first three volumes.

In the first volume, as Newman explained to Samuel Wilberforce, he was rousing people to the claims of holiness and the need for detailed obedience. He was saying comparatively little about

---

[1] How far was Newman helped in his discovery by the Fathers, whose writings he began to read consecutively in 1828? He always speaks of finding the doctrine in Scripture, and he was never satisfied with the way he studied the Fathers at this period. In 1842 he wrote to T. W. Allies: 'When I began to read the "Fathers" many years ago, I began at the Apostolical, and took a great deal of pains with them and Justin Martyr—all of which I count now almost wasted— and that for this reason, that I did not understand *what* was in them, what I was to look for, what were the strong and important points, etc. I measured and systematised them by Protestant doctrines and views, and by this sort of cross division I managed to spend a good deal of time on them and got nothing from them. The result was something like that described in the case of the unobservant boy in the story of "Eyes and No Eyes".' (*Correspondence of John Henry Newman with John Keble and Others, 1839–1845*, edited at the Birmingham Oratory, London 1917, p. 196.) Newman did, however, make notes of his patristic studies in a large vellum-bound manuscript book. He wrote down two references in the Epistles of St Ignatius to our being the temple of God. Under the word 'indwelling' he listed authorities for the fact that soul *and* body were sanctified. Perhaps entered later was a remark about possible differences between Greek and Latin theology. For the former 'justification consists in a gift dwelling within the soul', for the latter 'in a change of the soul'. On the Divine Presence he made a reference to the works of the Caroline scholar John Gregory, who speaks of the Shekinah dwelling with individuals. (*The Works of John Gregory* London 1665, pp. 132–41.) This does not amount to very much. It should be added that Newman, when he was preparing to write his *Arians of the Fourth Century*, studied Petavius. From the eighth book, he could have learned much as to the teaching of the Fathers on the indwelling, but everything seems to suggest that his real source was simply the New Testament.

the Holy Spirit. The very first sermon of all, 'Holiness necessary for Future Blessedness' is typical in this respect, yet it concludes:

> While we labour to mould our hearts after the pattern of the holiness of our Heavenly Father, it is our comfort to know, what I have already implied, that we are not left to ourselves, but that the Holy Ghost is graciously present with us, and enables us to triumph over, and to change our minds.[1]

Similarly, at the end of the second sermon, 'On the Immortality of the Soul', Newman says:

> What a blessed discovery it is to those who make it ... that really they are ever in their Saviour's presence. This is a thought which it is scarcely right to enlarge upon in a mixed congregation ... for why should the privileges of the true Christian be disclosed to mankind at large.[2]

Elsewhere in the volume it is explained how the Christian is a temple of the Holy Spirit, and how he is like St Ignatius, who called himself Theophorus, because he carried Christ in his breast.[3]

The second volume is more explicit, and Newman insists strongly how scriptural the doctrine of God's indwelling is:

> The Gospel teaches us another mode in which man may be said to be united with Almighty God. It is the peculiar blessedness of the Christian, as St. Peter tells us, to be 'partaker of the Divine Nature'. . . . And further we are assured of some real though mystical fellowship with the Father, Son, and Holy Spirit, in order to this: so that both by a real presence in the soul, and by the fruits of grace, God is one with every believer, as in a consecrated temple.[4]

There are a number of such quotations. It must suffice to turn to the sermon for Whit Sunday on 'The Indwelling Spirit', which begins:

> God the Son has graciously vouchsafed to reveal the Father to His creatures from without; God the Holy Ghost by inward

[1] *Parochial and Plain Sermons* I, 13–14.
[2] *Parochial and Plain Sermons* I, 26.
[3] *Parochial and Plain Sermons* I, 293.
[4] *Parochial and Plain Sermons* II, 34–5.

communications. [Newman then says], On this Festival I propose, as is suitable, to describe as scripturally as I can the merci-
ful offices of God the Holy Ghost towards us Christians. [We
have] that great privilege of receiving into our hearts, not the
mere gifts of the Spirit, but His very presence Himself, by a
real not a figurative indwelling. [He is] the seal and earnest of
an Unseen Saviour, ...

Newman proceeds to weave together and develop the relevant
texts in Romans and the two Epistles to the Corinthians.[1] He tries
to make us realise the Scripture teaching:

The Holy Ghost, I have said, dwells in body and soul as in a
temple. Evil spirits indeed have power to possess sinners, but
His Indwelling is far more perfect; for He is all-knowing and
omnipresent, He is able to search into all our thoughts, and
penetrate into every motive of the heart. Therefore, He pervades us (if it may be said) as light pervades a building, or as a
sweet perfume the folds of some honourable robe; so that, in
Scripture language, we are said to be in Him, and He in us.
It is plain that such an inhabitation brings the Christian into a
state altogether new and marvellous, far above the possession
of mere gifts, exalts him inconceivably in the scale of beings,
and gives him a place and an office which he had not before. . . .
Such is the great doctrine, which we hold as a matter of faith,
and without actual experience to verify it to us.[2]

The presence of the Spirit enables us to cry 'Abba, Father', and
gives us the fellowship and presence of the Incarnate Son.

There is not time to do more than call attention to one sermon
in the third volume, that entitled 'The Gift of the Spirit'. Again
there is a long Scripture proof of the gift, which is received by
the Christian at baptism.

By this new birth the Divine Shechinah is set up within him,
pervading soul and body, separating him really, not only in
name, from those who are not Christians, raising him in the
scale of being. . . .[3]

[1] *Parochial and Plain Sermons* II, 217–21.
[2] *Parochial and Plain Sermons* II, 222, 224.
[3] *Parochial and Plain Sermons* III, 261–6.

5+

And the practical conclusion follows:

> It were well if the views I have been setting before you, which in
> the main are, I trust, those of the Church Catholic from the be-
> ginning, were most understood and received among us.

This would put a stop to the two extremes of enthusiasm and cold
religion. The gift of Grace is unseen and unless this is understood,
people who read in Scripture of its greatness, will either think it
must be a kind of religious ecstasy, an emotion and a feeling
which they must exhibit in their conversation; or else sober religious men will react in the opposite direction and look on the
Scripture privilege almost as something that did not outlast the
Apostles' day. 'For ourselves, in proportion as we realise that
higher view of the subject, which we may humbly trust is the
true one, let us be careful to act upon it. Let us adore the Sacred
Presence within us with all fear.'[1]

It might be thought that such teaching, instead of rousing
people and causing them to obey God in detail, would lead to
some kind of quietism. Among its benefits in Newman's eyes was
that it provided an answer to the preoccupation of the Evangelicals with feelings and emotion, which he regarded as the prevailing religious ill. The indwelling was an exacting privilege. The
business of the Christian was to 'walk in all the ordinances of the
Lord blameless . . . all along looking reverently towards the Great
Object of faith, the Father, the Son, and the Holy Ghost'. . . .[2]

> Do we not try to persuade ourselves [he asks] that to *feel* re-
> ligiously, to confess our love of religion, and to be able to talk
> of religion, will stand in the place of careful obedience, of that
> *self-denial* which is the very substance of true practical re-
> ligion?[3] Yet how many there are who sit still with folded hands,
> dreaming, doing nothing at all, thinking they have done every-
> thing or need do nothing, when they have merely had these good
> *thoughts*, which will save no one.[4] [He condemns the system]
> which makes Christian faith consist, not in the honest and
> plain practice of what is right, but in the luxury of excited re-
> ligious feeling, in a mere meditating on our Blessed Lord, and
> dwelling as in a reverie on what He has done for us; – for such

[1] *Parochial and Plain Sermons* III, 267–9.
[2] *Parochial and Plain Sermons* II, 159.
[3] *Parochial and Plain Sermons* I, 30.
[4] *Parochial and Plain Sermons* III, 172.

indolent contemplation will no more sanctify a man *in fact*, than reading a poem or listening to a chant or psalm-tune.[1]

Possession of the three Persons depends on love for the persons around us, and this not in any mere general way. 'Schemes of an expansive benevolence' can be an obstacle to 'the charities of private life', and 'the best preparation for loving the world at large, and loving it duly and wisely, is to cultivate an intimate friendship and affection towards those who are immediately about us'.[2]

Newman, then, was preaching what may be called the mysticism of the New Testament. In his day the word "mysticism" was generally used in a pejorative sense. He reminds us, some years later, that God is everywhere.

> And He who lives in all creatures on earth in order to their mortal life, lives in all Christians in a more divine way in order to their life immortal, [and then insists that] if this notion of the literal indwelling of God within us, whether by way of nature or of grace, be decried as a sort of mysticism, I ask in reply whether it is not a necessary truth that He is with us and in us if He is everywhere? And if He is everywhere and dwells in all, there is no antecedent objection against taking Scripture literally, no difficulty in supposing that the truth is as Scripture says, – that as He dwells in us in one mode in the way of nature, so He is in us in another in the way of Grace.[3]

Newman brought out strongly, too, the ecclesial nature of the divine gift, which is not a private grace, but establishes a common fellowship. There is only time to notice this in passing, fundamental though it is. Grace comes to us through Christ's body, and baptism and the Eucharist are social by their very nature. Newman emphasises this, and tells us, for instance, that

> The Church of Christ, as Scripture teaches, is a visible body, invested with, or (I may say) existing in invisible privileges. Take the analogy of the human body.... When the soul leaves the body it ceases to be a body, it becomes a corpse. So the Church

---

[1] *Parochial and Plain Sermons* II, 373.
[2] *Parochial and Plain Sermons* II, 52–3.
[3] J. H. Newman, *Lectures on the Doctrine of Justification* London 1908, 144–5.

would cease to be the Church, did the Holy Spirit leave it; and it does not exist at all except in the Spirit.[1]

The Holy Spirit is given to individuals through the Church's sacrament of baptism, and through the Church too, the Eucharist strengthens in them the presence of the indwelling Christ, and binds them to each other.

This was the teaching which Newman as a pastor thought it so necessary to put before his flock in order to promote a genuine Christian life among them. It was teaching that had been revealed for that very purpose, and yet it was to a great extent overlooked in a religious world divided between Protestants, who mostly believed in imputed righteousness and Catholics who mostly regarded grace as a quality infused into the soul. Newman, at any rate, during the years which followed, continued to preach the doctrine of the indwelling with more earnestness than ever. The second batch of *Parochial Sermons*, the three volumes published in 1839, 1840, and 1842 contain expositions of it even finer and more developed than those already quoted.[2]

Ecumenical application in the Lectures on Justification

Besides seeing the religious value of the doctrine of the indwelling, the revealed foundation of the Christian life, Newman came to realise that it provided the true solution of the divisive controversies over justification. It had what would now be called an ecumenical value. It was over the doctrine of Grace that the Western Christian world had split at the Reformation, but the two sides could be reconciled by a return to the real teaching on the subject to be found in the New Testament. Newman lectured on it in Adam de Brome's Chapel in St Mary's, and in the summer of 1837 decided to publish these *Lectures on the Doctrine of Justification*. He wrote on 6 June to J. W. Bowden:

> I almost incline to publish a volume of Lectures on Justification at Christmas – Pusey wishes it and I see advantages.

What these were Newman explained at the beginning of his preface:

---

[1] *Parochial and Plain Sermons* III, 224; *Parochial and Plain Sermons* II, 223–4, 144, 148.
[2] e.g. *Parochial and Plain Sermons* IV, 145–6, 168–71, 227–9, 247–9, 253–6; V, 57, 138–40, 157–8, 235–6, 315–26; VI, 120–5, 174–89.

The present Volume originated in the following way. It was
brought home to the writer from various quarters, that a
suspicion existed in many serious minds against certain essential
Christian truths, such as Baptismal Regeneration and the Apostolical Ministry, under the impression that they fostered notions
of human merit, were prejudicial to the inward life of religion,
and incompatible with the doctrine of justifying faith, nay with
express statements on the subject in our Formularies.

Newman wished to trace out the true doctrine from Scripture and
to consolidate the theological system of Anglicanism.[1] In a pen-
cilled note on his own copy of *Lectures on the Doctrine of Justification*, which he made use of when describing that work in the
Apologia, Newman wrote:

The object of my book is this – to show that Lutheranism is
either a truism or a paradox; a truism if with Melancthon it is
made rational, a paradox if with Luther it is made substantive;
Melancthon differs scarcely more than in terms from the Catholic; Luther scarcely in sense from the Antinomian. My book
then is of the nature of an Irenicon in the doctrine of which it
treats.

In the *Apologia* he explained that it

was aimed at the Lutheran dictum that justification by faith
only was the cardinal doctrine of Christianity.... I thought
that the Anglican Church followed Melancthon, and that in
consequence between Rome and Anglicanism, between high
Church and low Church, there was no real intellectual difference on the point. I wished to fill up a ditch, the work of man.[2]

How then do the lectures effect this reconciliation? What is considered to be Luther's view, the doctrine of imputed righteousness, is rejected because it means that Christ's obedience long ago
is imputed to us. 'But that applying or imputing is the act of
God; and the question before us is, not what is God's act in justifying, but what is the state of the justified soul.'[3] There remained
the two views, roughly the Protestant and the Catholic, that our
state of justification in God's sight consists either in faith, or in a
renovating quality in the soul.

[1] *Lectures on the Doctrine of Justification*, v.
[2] *Apologia*, 72.
[3] *Lectures on the Doctrine of Justification*, 134.

Now, however intelligible each of these answers may be. [New-man proceeds] neither will be found sufficient and final.... When Faith is said to be the inward principle of acceptance, the question rises, what gives to faith its acceptableness?... faith is acceptable as having something in it, which unbelief has not; that something, what is it? It must be God's grace, if God's grace act *in* the soul, and not merely externally, as in the way of Providence. If it acts in us, and has a presence in us, when we have faith, then the having that grace or that presence, and not faith, which is its result, must be the real token, the real state of a justified man. [On the other hand,] if we say that justification consists in a supernatural quality imparted to the soul by God's grace, as the Romanists say, then in like manner, the question arises, is this quality all that is in us of heaven? does not the grace itself, as an immediate divine power or presence, dwell in the hearts which are gifted with this renovating principle?... if it does, then surely the possession of that grace is really our justification, and not renewal.... And thus, [Newman concludes] by tracing farther back the lines of thought on which these apparently discordant views are placed, they are made to converge; they converge, that is, supposing there to be vouchsafed to us, an inward divine presence, of which both faith and spiritual renovation are fruits. [He then proceeds to show at length] that justification actually *is* ascribed in Scripture to the presence of the Holy Spirit, and that immediately, neither faith nor renewal intervening.[1]

In eloquent pages he draws out the Scripture proof that 'This is to be justified, to receive the Divine Presence within us, and be made a Temple of the Holy Ghost', and also that Christ 'is our Righteousness by dwelling in us by the Spirit; He justifies us by entering into us, He continues to justify us by remaining in us. *This* is really and truly our justification, not faith, not holiness, not (much less) a mere imputation; but through God's mercy, the very Presence of Christ.'[2]

Newman thought that both Evangelical and Roman divines, not to mention the high and dry anti-Evangelicals took a low and impersonal view of Grace, which had serious practical con-sequences, to which as a pastor he frequently adverted.

---

[1] *Lectures on the Doctrine of Justification*, 136–7.
[2] *Lectures on the Doctrine of Justification*, 144, 150.

I say, the view of justification taken by Romanists and by a school of divines among ourselves, tends to fix the mind on self, not on Christ, whereas that which I have advocated as Scriptural and Catholic, buries itself in the absorbing vision of a present, an indwelling God.

Instead of merely telling us our duties, or urging us to seek a mere title of righteousness or else a holiness of our own, the Scripture doctrine points to 'the glorious Shekinah of the Word Incarnate'. Newman asks:

When are we the more likely to dread sinning, when we know merely we ought to dread it, or when we see the exceeding peril of it? When are we the more likely to keep awake and be sober, when we have a present treasure now to lose, or a distant reward to gain? [And again] Has not this thought [of God within us] more of persuasiveness in it to do and to suffer for Him than the views of doctrine which have spread among us? is it not more constraining than that which considers that the Gospel comes to us in name, not in power; deeper and more sacred than a second, which makes its heavenly grace a matter of purchase and trade; more glowing than a third, which depresses it almost to the chill temperature of natural religion?[1]

As we have seen, Newman claims to derive from Holy Scripture his teaching on justification as being the indwelling of God, and as he elaborates it further, that continues to be his court of appeal. In fact it is the source of a difficulty, for his teaching seems to mean that justification was effected differently under the Old Testament and under the New.

If under the Gospel it consists in the inward Presence of the Incarnate Word, therefore, this gift being peculiar to the Gospel, Abraham (for instance) who was justified, was justified in some other way; whereas St Paul certainly does liken the one justification to the other. [However, Newman maintains that] There is nothing contrary to St Paul's argument in supposing that that same blessing which was conveyed before Christ came in one way, should under the Gospel come to us in another and more precious way.[2]

[1] *Lectures on the Doctrine of Justification*, 190–1. In a note to the 1874 edition Newman described his judgement on Roman divines as 'unreal and arbitrary'.
[2] *Lectures on the Doctrine of Justification*, 192–3.

This corresponds to St Paul's teaching on the old dispensation as the 'shadow', and on the new creation, and with the text in St John, 'As yet the Spirit had not been given, because Jesus was not yet glorified'.[1] Newman insisted in his sermons and elsewhere, that there was an essential distinction between Grace under the Old Law and under the New. In 1837, when Pusey was attacked by the Evangelical *Christian Observer* for maintaining this, and for saying that Noah and Moses and Abraham were not regenerate, Newman replied to it in *Tract 82*. He claimed to show that Pusey's view was scriptural and added:

> In truth his view is simply *beyond*, not *against* the opinion of your Magazine. It is a view which the present age cannot be said to deny, because it does not see it. The Catholic Church has ever given to Noah, Abraham and Moses, all that the present age gives to Christians. You cannot mention the grace, in kind or degree, which you ascribe to the Christian, which Dr Pusey will not ascribe to Abraham, except, perhaps, the intimate knowledge of the details of Christian doctrine. But he considers that Christians have something beyond this, even a portion of that heaven brought down to earth, which will be for ever in heaven the portion of Abraham and all saints in its fulness.[2]

Rediscovery in modern theology

Yet for centuries the doctrine of the indwelling of the Blessed Trinity in the soul was quite astonishingly neglected. The historians of dogma trace this neglect to the emphasis placed by the Scholastics of the idea of grace as a quality in the soul. Grace in this sense, for which there is a certain warrant in Scripture, was first mentioned explicitly by Alexander of Hales, and explained by St Bonaventure as a proof of man's fundamental impotence. It was described by St Thomas as a habit or disposition enabling the Holy Spirit to act in the Christian. Soon, however, this lesser grace, this quality in the soul began to be treated independently of the Holy Spirit. Ever since, as Peter Fransen says, it 'had been cut off from its one and only source, that is, from the interior operation of the indwelling Holy Ghost, it had come to look increasingly like a personal possession, some sort of capital that

---

[1] In 7 : 39 (Revised Standard Version).
[2] *Tract 82*, John Henry Newman, *The Via Media* JJ, 167–8.

could be treasured up or put to use at will'.[1] It was against this idea of grace as something separate from God that Luther reacted. We were justified *sola gratia* exclusively by God's love for us. Luther wished to re-emphasise the personal relations between God and man. Unfortunately the doctrine of justification by faith only, at least when imputed righteousness was its corollary, could leave the way open to even greater forgetfulness of the divine indwelling than decadent scholastic teaching about grace.

For reasons that history makes clear the Council of Trent contented itself with reasserting that grace inheres in us, and that the one formal cause of justification is the justice of God, by which he makes us just. Until quite recent times the Catholic theologians were for the most part content merely to explain the existence of grace as defined at Trent. As Fransen says:

> By and large they failed to give serious thought to what is in fact the ultimate root of man's ulterior sanctification: the living indwelling of the Blessed Trinity. And so created grace was understood by the ordinary faithful to be a thing by itself.[2]

Nor was it the ordinary faithful only who suffered. As the Benedictine Father Vandenbroucke has pointed out, the earlier monastic Middle Ages still lived out the New Testament mysticism of St Paul and St John. This was not forgotten, but from the period of the Scholastics onwards, the mystical experience was described '*dans le cadre, avec la garantie* de ces données, bien plus que comme l'expérience de ces données'.[3] Even St Thomas, who began by admitting a contemplation of the three divine Persons, later passed, no doubt under the influence of the Pseudo-Denis, from a theological notion of the object of contemplation to a more psychological one. He was thus considered to be a link in the tradition which was for long preponderant in Catholic spirituality.[4] Fortunately Ruusbroec and others preserved the older tradition, and this was kept alive after the Council of Trent by a small but distinguished group of theologians. They protested against the preoccupation with grace as a quality in the

[1] Peter Fransen, SJ, *Divine Grace and Man*, revised edition, New York 1965, 124.
[2] Fransen, 130.
[3] F. Vandenbroucke, OSB, 'Le divorce entre théologie et mystique', *Nouvelle Revue Théologique*, April 1950, 389.
[4] F. Vandenbroucke, OSB, 'Notes sur la théologie mystique de saint Thomas d'Aquin', *Ephemerides Theologicae Lovanienses*, July–December 1951, 489–90.

5*

soul, and deliberately based their teaching on Scripture and the Fathers. Lessius and Petavius were the greatest names among them.

In the Protestant world also the doctrine of the divine indwelling was forgotten. Fortunately the devout reading of the New Testament must have kept it alive in many hearts, but as has been said, the widely held doctrine of imputed righteousness was inimical to it. Then also the emphasis on religious experience had led the England of the first half of the nineteenth century to a preoccupation with feelings, to 'self-contemplation', the antithesis to the contemplation of an indwelling God. As Newman says:

> Luther found in the Church great corruptions countenanced by its highest authorities; he felt them; but instead of meeting them with divine weapons, he used one of his own. . . . He found Christians in bondage to their works and observances; he released them by his doctrine of faith; and he left them in bondage to their feelings.[1]

Clement Webb made a fair comment:

> As Bacon saw in Aristotle chiefly the idol of a degenerate scholasticism, so Newman sees in Luther the patriarch of the tendency which, in much of the Methodist and Evangelical preaching of his day, seemed to him to identify justifying faith with an emotional crisis, compared with which both obedience to the moral law and aspiration after the holiness of life to which the Christian is called fell, as it were, into the background.[2]

In preaching grace as the indwelling of the Blessed Trinity, Newman was helping to reconcile Protestants and Catholics. Since his day there has been a full recovery of this revealed truth, which both sides had neglected. But that is not the only part of the subject in which Newman was a preacher of forgotten truths. The place of Easter in the Christian scheme had fallen into the background for centuries, in the consciousness of Western Christendom. Here also there has been a recovery recently, and the work of modern exegetes and theologians has born fruit in the decrees of the Second Vatican Council, with their emphasis on the paschal mystery. The same emphasis, frequent and

[1] *Lectures on the Doctrine of Justification*, 339–40.
[2] C. C. J. Webb, *Religious Thought in the Oxford Movement* London 1928, 88.

eloquent, on the saving value of the Resurrection, is to be found in Newman's *Parochial Sermons*, while in his book on *Justification*, he devoted a whole lecture to showing from Scripture that Christ's Resurrection was the source of the Christian's possession of the Holy Spirit. He appealed to the text that

> [He] 'who was delivered for our offences was raised again for our justification' [and commented] in saying that Christ *rose again* for our justification, it is implied that justification is through that second Comforter who after that Resurrection came down from heaven.

The relevant texts had already been quoted and the argument now was rather that of 'the harmony of sacred doctrine and the light which the view in question throws on particular texts'.

> [The Son] 'came first in the flesh, and secondly in the Spirit. As in God's counsels it was necessary for the Atonement that there should be a material, local, Sacrifice of the Son once for all; so for our individual justification, there must be a spiritual, ubiquitous communication of that Sacrifice continually. There was but one Atonement; there are ten thousand justifications. ... He said that unless He went, His Spirit would not come to us ... Thus He died to purchase what he rose to apply.'[1]

This soteriological aspect of Easter was something almost forgotten both in the ordinary Roman teaching, and among the Evangelicals. It was a return to the doctrine of Scripture and the early Church, not to mention that of Eastern Christendom. Once more a ditch was being filled, an obstacle to unity cleared away. Clement Webb noted how

> the opponents of the Oxford Movement have often tended to see in it chiefly a reaction to medievalism. ... But more characteristic is its return to a primitive consciousness of organic participation in the risen life of Christ, with which the concentration of Western medieval piety on the Passion has less in common than it has with Evangelical devotion to the Precious Blood.[2]

A further point where Newman approximates to the East, is in the way he maintains the separate action and relation of the three

[1] *Lectures on the Doctrine of Justification*, 203–6.
[2] Webb, 91.

Persons of the Holy Trinity in the work of salvation. He keeps too close to Scripture to follow the timid minimising teaching of so much Western theology in this matter. He does not play down the supernatural privilege of the Christian, the 'half-realised eschatology'. In the course of his explanation of the soteriological value of the Resurrection he says:

> Here I would observe of this part of the wonderful Economy of Redemption, that it has been the gracious will of God the Son and God the Holy Ghost so to act together in their separate Persons, as to make it difficult for us creatures always to discriminate what belongs to each respectively. Christ rises by his own power, yet the Holy Ghost is said to raise Him; hence, the expression of St Paul, 'according to the Spirit of Holiness,' as applied to His resurrection, may be taken to stand either for His Divine nature or for the Third Person in the Blessed Trinity. The case is the same as regards the mystery of the Incarnation itself. The Word of God descended into the Virgin's womb, and framed for Himself a human tabernacle, yet the man so born was 'conceived of the Holy Ghost. . . .' I notice this merely by way of explaining myself, if in speaking upon this most sacred subject I have said, or may say, anything which would seem to 'confound the Persons' of the Son and the Spirit, which are eternally distinct and complete in Themselves, though in nature and operation One.[1]

In the smallest as in the greatest matters, Newman's approach was always personal. There is not to be found in him that 'attenuation of the "Trinity in the economy of salvation" into a kind of pre-Christian monotheism' which Karl Rahner discerns 'in the history of Western piety', and which he maintains, has so sadly 'diminished the significance of the Holy Trinity in concrete religious life'.[2]

Again the question arises, how was Newman able to rediscover so many truths that were half forgotten in the West for centuries? By 1837 he was deeply learned in the Fathers. Much was to be found in St Athanasius, also in the Cappadocians and others. But Newman wished to convince people who would not be impressed by the appeal to Antiquity. As he said in the original preface to the *Lectures*, 'nothing would meet the evil but plain statements

[1] *Lectures on the Doctrine of Justification*, 208–9.
[2] Karl Rahner, SJ, *Theological Investigations* I, London 1960, 346.

on the subject argued out from Scripture'.[1] In his *Lectures* he quoted Protestant and Catholic theologians in an attempt to reconcile them, but they afforded him little guidance in the work of composition. On 16 July 1937 he wrote to Pusey:

> I am at my Lectures on Justification – but have hopes they will not take me very long. It is curious, all parties confess it was a new subject at the Reformation – and the Schoolmen scarcely touch upon it. I do not find it form even one head in the four books of the Master of the Sentences – yet respectably sized volumes have been written on it since. It is a very curious phenomenon in the history of the Church. I have long looked in vain for the peculiar or ἦθος in antiquity – and this fact just fits in with its absence.

'The peculiar or ἦθος' was, of course, that of the Evangelicals.

Newman found his task more complicated than he had expected. In the new year he was telling his sisters how he was obliged continually to correct and rewrite. When the work was finished, he told them:

> My book is rather longer than I expected – it has taken me more pains and thought than any book I have done – at least, I think so. The great difficulty was to avoid *being* difficult – which on the subject of Justification is not a slight one. It is so entangled and mystified by irrelevant and refined questions.[2]

People sometimes think that Newman kept all his papers; he burnt six hundred pages of drafts of his *Lectures* when the book was published. It is possible that they would have revealed how he was able to elaborate the doctrine of Grace in such fullness. He himself seems, however, to confirm that his only real source was Holy Scripture. On 17 January 1838 he wrote to J. W. Bowden:

> Then about my own work *Lectures on Justification* I am a good deal fussed. It is the first voyage I have made proprio marte, with sun, stars, compass and a sounding line, but with very insufficient charts. It is a terra incognita in our Church,

---

[1] *Lectures on the Doctrine of Justification*, v.
[2] Anne Mozley (ed.), *The Letters and Correspondence of John Henry Newman* II, London 1891, 250.

and I am so afraid, not of saying things wrong so much as queer and crotchetty – and of misunderstanding other writers. For really the Lutherans etc. as divines are so shallow and inconsequent, that I can hardly believe my own impressions about them.[1]

There were no charts, no theological writings to guide him. He was later to praise Bishop Bull for defending 'in a measure' 'the true doctrine of justification', but this was only on the level of controversy with Protestantism, and he criticised him at the same time for 'his homeliness and want of the supernatural element'.[2] In the long and very learned appendix to the *Lectures*, 'On the formal cause of Justification', which had an irenical purpose, that of showing there was little or no difference of view between the disputants, he interpreted Hooker and also the Calvinist writers benignly.

Great divines [he also noted] have approximated to an agreement, thus Lombard and St Thomas, and, in modern times, Petavius, declare that grace, or the Holy Spirit Himself indwelling, is the formal cause of justification, and thus appear to have avoided an intellectual difficulty [that of making our righteousness external], without falling into what is worse a moral one [that of making our righteousness something of our own].[3]

Newman's conclusion as to the proper formal cause of justification was that

with the Romanists he would consider it as an inward gift, yet with the Protestants as not a mere quality of the mind, [and he added] numerous passages might be cited from the Fathers in point, but it would be scarcely to the purpose to do so, for Scripture itself, to go no further, is as clear, as far as words go, on the doctrine of a Divine Indwelling, as the Fathers can be; and the question is as to its *interpretation*, whether literal or not.[4]

The sun and the stars had shown Newman the way clearly enough.

[1] Mozley, 249.
[2] John Henry Newman, *Certain Difficulties felt by Anglicans in Catholic Teaching* I, London 1908, 2, 139.
[3] *Lectures on the Doctrine of Justification*, 377–8.
[4] *Lectures on the Doctrine of Justification*, 389.

The central truth of revelation which Newman first began to grasp at the age of sixteen, and which he developed so persuasively in his *Parochial Sermons* and in *Lectures on Justification*, continued to be the nourishment of his religious life as his posthumously published *Meditations on Christian Doctrine* bear witness.[1] Also, in the preface to the third edition of the *Lectures* he wrote:

Unless the Author held in substance in 1874 what he published in 1838, he would not at this time be reprinting what he wrote as an Anglican; certainly not with so little added by way of safeguard.

And he reiterated the irenical purpose of the *Lectures*:

Their drift is to show that there is little difference but what is verbal in the various views on justification whether found among Catholic or Protestant divines; by Protestant being meant Lutheran, Calvinistic, and thirdly that dry anti-evangelical doctrine, which was dominant in the Church of England during the last century, and is best designated by the name of Arminianism.[2]

Speaking recently of the answer given to Luther by the Council of Trent, Father Fransen says:

If the Church intended to take into account this 'reformed adjustment,' she had to show how all human relations with God, without exception, can be reduced to *one living contact*, the contact we have in the indwelling of the Blessed Trinity. It was the tragedy of the times that such an attempt could not be made then because the theology of those days was powerless to elaborate a truly satisfying answer. Several centuries later, Cardinal Newman would guess the ecumenical significance of an adequate answer when he wrote the Catholic foreword to the new edition of his formerly Anglican *Lectures on Justification*, but by that time it was too late. Christendom lay riven apart for ages.[3]

[1] J. H. Newman, *Meditations and Devotions* London 1893, 548-9, 554-6.
[2] *Lectures on the Doctrine of Justification*, ix.
[3] Fransen, 127. Hans Küng, too, who, in his *Justification: The Doctrine of Karl Barth and a Catholic Reflection*, New York 1964, has performed a task similar to Newman's, relies on the latter's work, which he describes as 'one of the best treatments of the Catholic theology of justification', 212 (London 1965, 202-3). Both of them emphasise that Grace is essentially *personal*, the generous favour of the living God.

Newman, then, demonstrated in the *Lectures*, the ecumenical significance of the doctrine of the indwelling, just as he showed its religious importance in his sermons. This side of his achievement, so close to the best theological insights of the present revival, has tended to be overlooked. The principle lesson to be learned from him is surely that the effectiveness of a revealed religion depends on its fidelity to the revelation it has received, and that if people are to lead truly Christian lives, no other foundation can any one lay than that which is laid, namely the revealed mysticism of St John and St Paul, which Newman expounds in a way that is both inspiring and exacting.

6
Newman on the church— his final view, its origins and influence

John Coulson

Newman's response to the First Vatican Council was strong and definite: he referred to it as thunder in a clear sky and to its exploitation by an aggressive and insolent faction.[1] Not only did it provoke him to write about liberty within the Church in his *Letter to the Duke of Norfolk* (1875), but it compelled him to return to a fundamental problem and its corollary – how ought we to describe the presence of Christ to his Church, and what is the principle by which the Church, as transmitting that presence, is duly ordered or 'regulated'?

To his opponents – the victorious Ultramontane party – no such problem arose; for them the Church was an authoritarian regime whose regulating principle was the absolute rule of the Pope; by such means, and by such means alone could the presence of Christ be transmitted. Newman could not accept this account because it substituted a part of the Church system for that antecedent unity from which its life-giving character as the Body of Christ derived[2]; and he developed this argument in a preface written in 1877 for the third edition of the *Via Media*.[3]

In the years immediately following Vatican 1 Newman's attempt to put such a question, where it was not openly resented, was merely ignored; yet here in the preface to the *Via Media* is a

[1] W. Ward, *The Life of John Henry Newman* II, London 1912, 288.
[2] *University Sermons*, 330.
[3] Composed when he republished his *Lectures on the Prophetical Office of the Church*, 1837 as volume I of *The Via Media of the Anglican Church*, 1877.

tradition of the Church more ecumenical and more in keeping
with the needs of his time and ours than the incomplete definitions produced by Vatican I. It was not entirely without fruit,
since it directly influenced von Hügel, whose celebrated analysis
of religion into three elements in *The Mystical Element* is derived from Newman's preface; and it anticipates much that is to
be found in later European writing on the Church, particularly
in Blondel. Newman shares our presuppositions and asks our
kind of questions: no wonder, therefore, that his findings should
so closely anticipate the more ecumenical teaching of *De Ecclesia*
– that we must first understand our response to the Church *as a
whole* before we can effectively define how we should understand its component parts.

In the manuscript of his preface, then, Newman writes that
he wishes to speak 'concretely of the Church as the body of
Christ'. His purpose is to show how the different and apparently
contradictory faces of the Church may be reconciled: if the mission of the Church is to restore all men to Christ by serving them,
how can this be reconciled with the needs of internal Church
discipline; and how are those needs to be reconciled with the
rights of the individual conscience to seek truths and to follow
them? His problem is how to define the parts of the Church
without compromising its antecedent unity; and he succeeds by
deriving his definitions from the three offices of Christ:

> He is Prophet, Priest, and King; and after His pattern, and in
> human measure, Holy Church has a triple office too; not the
> Prophetical alone and in isolation, as these Lectures virtually
> teach, but three offices, which are indivisible, though diverse,
> viz. teaching, rule and sacred ministry. This then is the point
> on which I shall now insist, the very title of the Lectures I am
> to criticize suggesting to me how best to criticize them.
>
> Christianity, then, is at once a philosophy, a political power,
> and a religious rite: as a religion, it is Holy; as a philosophy, it
> is Apostolic; as a political power, it is imperial, that is One and
> Catholic. As a religion, its special centre of action is pastor and
> flock; as a philosophy, the Schools; as a rule, the Papacy and its
> Curia. [*Via Media*, xl.]

Although the words 'imperial', 'political', and 'curia' strike
sharply on modern ears, Newman had his reasons for using them,
as I hope to show; but his is still a very different way of describ-

ing the Church from anything we find until very recent times. And I wish to suggest that why it comes in the form of a preface to a book written when he was still an Anglican is because Newman's method of description derives initially from the Anglican tradition. In the *Apologia* Newman speaks of gaining his understanding of 'a visible Church' and of 'the historical nature of revelation' from Butler[1], of 'the doctrine of Tradition' from Hawkins[2], and of 'the idea of the Church' as independent of the state from Whateley.[3] Newman also speaks of the Romantic movement as preparing the imagination of the nation for the reception of Catholic truth, and of the contribution of Coleridge in particular.[4] For reasons which I hope will become apparent during the course of this paper, it is with Coleridge that I intend to begin.

As far back as 1802 Coleridge in his notebooks had written: 'every season Nature converts me from some unloving heresy and will make a Catholic of me at last'. In his history of the Oxford Movement, R. W. Church emphasises the influence of Coleridge upon the climate of opinion in which the Movement arose; and he instances Coleridge's contribution to a better understanding of the 'idea, history and relations, to society of the Church', and to his having lifted the subject to a very high level. Newman read Coleridge for the first time in the spring of 1835[5], and although he was 'surprised how much I thought mine is to be found there', there is no evidence that Coleridge had a direct influence on the formation of Newman's ideas.[6] What he and Newman have in common is that they were both old enough to belong to a tradition not yet extinguished which could still point to its truths as if to self-evident facts. F. D. Maurice noticed this tendency in 1838[7], as did Hort, and spoke of it as a kind of Platonism. But it was a Platonism derived ultimately from the Fathers and mediated by the seventeenth-century Anglican divines, to whom

---

[1] *Apologia* Oxford ed., 1913, 113.   [2] *Apologia*, 112.
[3] H. Tristram, *John Henry Newman Autobiographical Writings* London 1956, 69; *Apologia*, 115.   [4] *Apologia*, 195.
[5] At the instigation of T. D. Acland (1809–1898), members of whose family had known Coleridge when he lived in Somerset.
[6] The Library of the Birmingham Oratory, however, possesses copies of most of Coleridge's chief works which appear to be annotated by Ambrose St John and Joseph Bacchus; and this is at least evidence for a continuing tradition at the Oratory that Coleridge has relevance.
[7] Frederick Maurice, *Life of Frederick Denison Maurice*, 1 London 1884, 251.

Coleridge (so Hort considered) owed his understanding of the nature of the Church.

This tradition emphasises the distinction between distinguishable parts, and the antecedent unity in which those parts actually co-exist.[1] It is of this distinction that Coleridge and Newman are speaking when they use the terms 'concepts' and 'ideas'. To Coleridge an *idea* was

> an educt of the imagination, a Form presenting or presupposing an ultimate end appropriately, an intuition not sensuous... suggested by two contradictory positions. Of all realities it is the most real and of all operative powers the most actual.[2]

To speak, for example, of the democratic spirit or of the life of the Church would be to use words in this sense as terms for *ideas*. They characterise our grasp of something as a whole, and they are therefore to be distinguished from a reductive analysis into clear and distinct parts or strictly definable concepts. Nowadays we might call *ideas*, as Coleridge defines them, terms for what we can experience, but cannot precisely define; or, in Coleridge's own words

> which the mind can know but which it cannot understand, of which understanding can be no more than the symbol and is only excellent as being the symbol.[3]

The successful application in our own day of this type of explanation to literary criticism is, for theological purposes, highly significant, especially as Coleridge specifically applies it to the Church which, he says, 'is in the Christian sense an idea'.[4] Newman, independently of Coleridge, adopts this kind of 'ideological' explanation, and it is the root of his method in the *Development of Christian Doctrine* (1845). He speaks of ideas as having the power

[1] *Biographia Literaria*, ch. xiv, 149.

[2] S. T. Coleridge, *Church and State*, 1839, 18.

[3] *Philosophical Lectures*, 168–9. He goes on to speak of such symbols as constituting a medium between literal and metaphorical, and as partaking of the reality which they have rendered intelligible. Coleridge, *Church and State*, 230.

[4] *Literary Remains* iii, 270. In seeking to account for the power of works of the imagination 'to bring the whole soul of man into activity', Coleridge ascribes it to our response, concretely, to the poem as a whole. This, he adds, is distinct from, but uniquely compatible with our response to a poem's component parts. [*Biographia Literaria*, cf. xiv; and see L. C. Knights, 'Idea and Symbol: some Hints from Coleridge', in the symposium *Metaphor and Symbol*, subsequently republished in *Further Explorations* London 1965, 155–68.]

to live in the mind; and it is this which is the process of development:

> the germination of and maturation of some truth or apparent truth on a large mental field ... [which] is carried on through and by means of communities of men ... ; and it employs their minds as its instruments, and depends upon them, while it uses them.

Newman, too, speaks of the distinguishing mark of an *idea* as being its ability to bring contrary and opposite aspects into harmony, so that 'no one term or proposition will serve to define it', since 'whole objects do not create in the intellect whole ideas, but are to use a mathematical phrase, thrown into series, into a number of statements ... approximating, as they accumulate, to a perfect image'.[1]

To Coleridge as to Newman it was in this sense that the Church was an idea, and our acquaintance with it was not with a simple series of concepts or propositions, but with an object[2] as indefinable, complex, and concrete as a living thing, and thus easily misrepresented by impatient demands for clear definition and simple recognition. Since, therefore, our response is both to a whole and to its component parts, the Church cannot be confined to one mode of presence: it will be both as diverse as the human personality, and as unified. To expect such a diversity of modes and functions will encourage us to make distinctions. Thus Coleridge distinguished between the ecclesia and the enclesia, between the Church universal in application and existing eternally, and the Church as a social force and a recognisable political entity.[3]

As an Anglican Newman makes a similar simple two-fold distinction between what gives the Church life – the prophetical tradition – and what gives the Church form – the episcopal tradition. At this stage he still regards the Church as a "generalised idea", and the episcopal tradition possesses no greater authority than what is handed down from bishop to bishop or what can be recognised in Scripture as 'an outline of sound words'. The prophetical tradition, on the other hand, is rather what St Paul calls 'the mind of the spirit', the thought and principle which breathed

---

[1] *Essay on the Development of Christian Doctrine* ed. C. F. Harrold, 1959, 36, 32, 33, 51.
[2] *University Sermons*, 330–31.
[3] Coleridge, *Church and State*, 48.

in the Church, her accustomed and unconscious mode of viewing things, and the body of her received opinions, than any definite and systematic collection of dogmas elaborated by the intellect.[1]

It was in this sense that the Church was 'that new language which Christ has brought us'[2]; and although Newman was subsequently to speak of these lectures on the Prophetical Office as coming to pieces – it is possible that he found their distinction between form and life too simple – he repudiated neither their insights nor their terminology. Instead, he assimilates them to what from the very outset enriched his response to the Church – his strong and abiding sense of the presence of Christ. It is this which most sharply distinguishes him from Coleridge, deriving as it does from Newman's Evangelical background, and it is to be seen most clearly in their differing views of conscience. For Coleridge conscience is a principle – it is Kant's practical reason. For Newman such a view is but natural religion: it is inadequate to the fact of revelation. It is in the very university sermon in which Newman acknowledges a similarity between his views and Coleridge's that the difference is most clearly given between a philosophical and theological view of conscience: 'The philosopher aspires towards a divine *principle*; The Christian towards a divine *Agent*'. And in the next paragraph Newman defines this as a 'method of personation' which is 'carried throughout the revealed system'.[3] In 1836, Newman himself spoke of Coleridge as 'looking at the Church, sacraments, doctrines etc rather as symbols of a philosophy than as *truths* – as the mere accidental types of principles'.[4]

Nowadays, of course, if we attempted to begin by defining an institution like the Church or Parliament in terms of their leading *ideas*, as if they were self-evident facts, we should be asked to justify the logic of our description; and if we spoke of contradictory aspects as being unified by their *idea*, we should be accused of using an umbrella term to evade logical difficulties. In the early nineteenth century it was still possible for Coleridge to rest his case upon an appeal to self-evidence. Newman's approach, however, is more contemporary. He starts the other way round: not

[1] J. H. Newman, *The Via Media of the Anglican Church* I, 260, 249, 251.
[2] J. H. Newman, *Parochial and Plain Sermons* v, 44.
[3] *University Sermons*, 28.
[4] Anne Mozley (ed.), *Letters and Correspondence of John Henry Newman* London 1891, 156.

with the idea, but with what the idea is of – the institution or polity which is the Church existing here and now – warts and all. Coleridge, on the other hand, far from making such a distinction seems to deny it, speaking as if the *idea* were the reality.[1] But, as Newman could see, this was to forget that religious propositions have a double function, being held as theological definitions and as statements of religious fact: the 'notion and the reality assented to are represented by one and the same proposition, but serve as distinct interpretations of it'.[2] Otherwise we fail to distinguish theology from religion, explanation from what seeks explanation in order to survive and adapt itself to changing human needs. The facts of religion, because of their living and developing nature, require for their expression this essentially ambiguous language of metaphor and symbol: otherwise 'the intellect runs wild; but with the aid of symbols, as in algebra, it advances with precision and effect'.[3]

To equate the Church, as Coleridge seems to do, with an idea or symbol gives us no means of verification and no way of distinguishing between one organisation and another, between the Church before Christ and after, or, between 'the dry bones of the prophet's vision' and 'the organs of one invisible governing soul'.[4] Although Newman accepts Coleridge's assumption that 'the mind embraces more than it can grasp'[5], and that what it thus embraces can be identified in terms of ideas, an *idea* is not reality at its most real but an image of what acts upon us in the manner of objects of sense-perception.[6] Thus to speak of the Church as an *idea* and to leave it at that is to have nothing more substantial than

[1] Ideas are spoken of as 'partaking of the reality which they have rendered intelligible', and 'of all realities the most real'. See also footnote 3 on page 126 above.

[2] *An Essay in Aid of a Grammar of Assent* ed. C. F. Harrold, 1947, 91. Language performs a similar function in poetry. In speaking of the period which came to an end with Donne, T. S. Eliot says, 'the intellect was immediately at the tips of the senses. Sensation became word and word was sensation' (*Selected Essays*, 210). And Dylan Thomas remarked: 'When I experience anything, I experience it as a thing and a word at the same time.'

[3] *Grammar of Assent*, 200.

[4] *Parochial and Plain Sermons* IV, 169–70.

[5] Mozley II, 311.

[6] *University Sermons*, 330. 'The ideas which we are granted of Divine Objects under the Gospel . . . answer to the Originals so far as this, that they are whole, indivisible, substantial, and may be called real, as being images of what is real.'

a paper Church; since to start from an *idea* is—as it were—to start in mid-air: we must begin with what the *idea* or symbol is *of*:

> As God is one, so the impression which He gives us of Himself is one; it is not a thing of parts; it is not a system ... it is the vision of an object.[1]

For Newman the starting-point must be the objectified presence or 'Body' of Christ existing in the world. It is to be identified by what Newman calls his 'method of personation', a method which would itself be even more arbitrary than Coleridge's if it were grounded solely on introspective self-evidence; but where, even as an Anglican, Newman appears to differ from the Evangelicals, is that Christ is not encountered directly and introspectively as an *alter ego*, but always through the Church and its sacraments, or, in other words, through the Church concretely as the Body of Christ. Christ is uniquely present to each Christian when the Church is gathered to form the Eucharistic community, since this is that special mode of approaching Him which he has bequeathed.[2]

> He has shown us, that to come to Him for life is a literal bodily action; not a mere figure, not a mere movement of the heart towards Him, but an action of the visible limbs; not a mere secret faith, but a coming to church, a passing on along the aisle to His holy table ... If then a man does not seek Him where He is, there is no profit in seeking Him where He is not. What is the good sitting at home seeking Him, when his presence in the Holy Eucharist[3]?

If the precondition for Christ's indwelling is neither successful ideological analysis nor introspection, but the bodily act of placing ourselves within the people of God as they offer the Eucharist, then worship becomes as fundamental a note of the Church as its prophetical and episcopal traditions; and the Church's establishment as a visible polity becomes essential for its effective acts of worship. Thus it is the Church which is visible, not Christ, 'whose more perfect powerful presence which we now enjoy, being in-

---

[1] *University Sermons*, 330, also 340. Newman seems to be specifically refuting Coleridge's doctrine of symbolism in his *University Sermon* xv, para. 31, p. 338.

[2] *Parochial and Plain Sermons* II, 144. See Dessain, 'The biblical basis of Newman's ecumenical theology', p. 109 above.

[3] *Parochial and Plain Sermons* VII, 149.

visible, can be discerned and used by faith only'; but 'what is seen is not the whole Church but the visible part of it'.

The Anglican tradition prevented Newman from accepting the legal fiction, current among Roman Catholics, of the Church and Tradition as 'a list of articles that could be numbered'[1]; instead, by encouraging his patristic scholarship it prepared him to expect a living and antecedent unity, complex of definition, perpetually in growth, and seemingly contradictory in its behaviour. His identification of the Church with the presence of Christ which came from his Evangelical background led him to see that the problem – then as now – was how to account for the 'double aspect' of the Church: how to square its superstitions and tyrannies with its function as the 'visible part' of the Body of Christ.

This preoccupation is to be seen especially – as we should expect – in those sermons preached as he was moving towards his conversion. First published in 1843 as *Sermons on the Subjects of the Day* they are chiefly concerned to study the nature of the Church and its effect upon the world. The distinction between life and form can be seen to give way to a more complex discrimination, as the outlines emerge of what Professor Nédoncelle has called 'une théologie des abus ecclésiastiques'.[2] It was Kingsley's error that he confused such analysis with advocacy.

The sermon for Christmas Day 1840 contains the first reference by Newman to the triple offices of Christ as prophet, priest, and King, and he notes that they relate to thought, endurance, and active life; but he does not yet relate them in any detail to the Church, except for noticing that knowledge, endurance, and power are the three privileges of the Church. In a footnote to these sermons occurs Newman's remark about his being 'impelled' towards the Roman Church by 'a present living and energetic heterodoxy', and this together with his publication of *Tract 90* would seem to indicate a growing determination to put the Anglican Church to the test as a living Catholic polity.[3] By now Newman had come to hold that the Church's free exercise of its kingly function was the precondition for the effective exercise of its

---

[1] Letter to Flanagan 1868, *Journal of Theological Studies*, October 1958, 324–35.
[2] Maurice Nédoncelle, *L'Apologia de Newman dans l'histoire de l'autobiographie et de la théologie* (p. 583 of a volume of studies presented to Romano Guardini on his eightieth birthday, and published by Echter Verlag, Wurzburg).
[3] J. H. Newman, *Sermons Bearing Upon Subjects of the Day* London 1873, 54, 56, 341.

priestly function, since Christ could only be 'uniquely present' when the people of God were effectively embodied as a worshipping community.

After his conversion his target changes, but his concern remains the same—with the ills that befall Christianity when the antecedent unity of prophetical, priestly and kingly functions is threatened by disproportionate emphasis. Now he had to concern himself with the over emphasis of the kingly function; and in each of his main works between 1859 and 1875 he is trying to show how within the Catholic polity there can be life and liberty.[1] By 1877, when he prepared to republish the *Via Media*, he was ready to encounter the formidable and final adversary referred to in the MS as 'the writer whom I am undertaking to answer'[2] – the Newman of his Anglican past.

The problem he faces is clearly defined: it is 'the recurring contrast between the theological side of Roman teaching and its political and popular side'[3], and the question to which this contrast gives rise – is the Church's claim to function as the visible part of the body of Christ invalidated by what, as an Anglican, Newman had criticised as 'Romanism', viz, the superstitions of peasants and the tyranny of men in power? In republishing the *Via Media* he retained these criticisms, but added an ironical footnote:

> There is a certain truth in this remark but a man must have a large knowledge of Catholics and of the effect of their system upon them, to assert with confidence what is here imagined of them.[4]

That Newman was not merely being ironical at his own expense, can be seen from a letter written to von Hügel at the same time, 30 June 1877, in which Newman said:

[1] At first he is concerned to temper the Church to those converts who have accepted its discipline; but each successive study takes his theology of the Church a stage deeper. *On Consulting the faithful in matters of Doctrine* (1859); *The Apologia* (1865): each is a response to a particular challenge since, as a Roman Catholic, Newman became solely an 'occasional' writer. After the Vatican Council he was silent until Gladstone gave him his opportunity – and the *Letter to the Duke of Norfolk* (1875) is the result.
[2] Unpublished manuscript at Birmingham Oratory, 38.
[3] *Via Media*, xxix.
[4] *Via Media*, 102 *n*. 6. Almost the same words are used with reference to 'Romanism' and to the view that obedience justifies in a footnote added to page 186 of the *Lectures on Justification* in the revised edition of 1874.

but to argue, 'the existence of evil in the *Church* is a proof that
the Church is not from God', is not going to the root of the
matter, but trifling with a mere instance of a great and fearful
fact instead of going straight to that fact itself. . . . The disasters
and defeats of the Church are pre-supposed in scripture.

This does not mean that Newman was advocating a form of
quietism. He was profoundly disturbed by the state of the Church
in the 1870s which he attributed to the Ultramontane belief that
the Church's survival depended upon imposing its power upon
its members and, defensively, upon the rest of the world. This
policy split Catholics into two camps. The disapproval of the
dominant Ultramontane element towards all that was being done
to extend political and social freedom at the expense of traditional
authority sprang as much from despair as from reflection. So
radical was their disjunction of nature from grace that they believed natural man to be so feeble that he was unable to move
towards God unless constrained by an external authority – for
them, as Blondel observed, 'nothing in man echoes or calls to the
gift'.[1] Instead they sought security in an imposed and life-destroy-
ing uniformity, whose results Newman anticipated as an Anglican:

> when religion is reduced in all its parts to a system there is a
> danger of something earthly being the chief object of our con-
> templation instead of our maker.[2]

It was this judgement which he did not withdraw and to which
the ironical footnote was appended. Newman never turned his
back upon the principle that 'Revelation . . . does but complete
what nature has begun'.[3]

By the 1870s Newman had come to believe that in a Church
which, under the influence of the Ultramontanes, had become too
highly systematised, centralised, and clericalised, the first task
was to emphasise the right of individual conscience; since however pure the Church's power might be at the summit, it suffered
from 'a great deal of Roman malaria at the foot'. Not only had it
to be reminded of the supremacy of conscience, but of the func-
tional autonomy of the spiritual and temporal in Church and

---

[1] A. Dru in *Downside Review*, vol. 81, 1963, p. 244.
[2] *Via Media* I, 102.
[3] *Via Media*, lxxi.

State which the rise of Christianity required and made inevitable. Above all, the Ultramontanes had to be told that however the Pope's infallibility might be interpreted it could never supersede conscience – hence Newman's challenge that he 'would drink to the Pope, if you please, – still, to Conscience first, and to the Pope afterwards'. Such sentiments allied Newman with the liberal Catholics and with Acton in particular: what was then not understood, and sometimes not even now, is that Newman never ceased to preserve a sound theological balance. He qualifies his account of conscience by speaking of it as 'at once the highest of teachers, yet the least luminous'; and as requiring for its fulfilment 'The Church, the Pope, the Hierarchy (who) are in the Divine purpose, the supply of an urgent demand'. Although to deny conscience was to deny the presence and power of the indwelling presence of Christ, that voice of God within us is incomplete, and requires the Church and its sacraments for its true identification, location, and fulfilment.

Newman, therefore, could not rest on the unaided power of conscience as the sole alternative to the abuses of authority, and here is the source of his divergence from liberal Catholicism as represented by Acton – a divergence completely consistent with his position theologically. Both Newman and Acton were for the separation, in the sense of the autonomous functioning, of Church and State, spiritual and secular; and Newman would not have cavilled at Acton's statement of the central problem of Catholicism as 'How private virtue and public crime could issue from the same root'.[1] They both opposed, therefore, the Ultramontane integrisme that saw the Church as confined to one mode – the political ultra-devotional.

But since 1870 the papacy for Acton was 'the fiend skulking behind the crucifix'[2], and his religion had become his flag, while his politics had become his faith.[3] For him there was no alternative to papal autocracy other than an autonomous conscience. Yet this was to obliterate that very distinction between conscience as a divine agent and as divine principle which separates Newman from Coleridge or Catholic from Protestant. Conscience is as much the effect or sign of a healthy spiritual sensibility as its

[1] Acton, *Historical Essays* 1908, 301.
[2] *Acton Correspondence* 1, 56.
[3] *Letters of Acton to Mary Gladstone*, 199.

cause, depending as it does upon the Church for its fulfilment.[1]

The proper question to ask then is what ensures that the Church functions as a living whole instead of an abstraction of discordant and self-conceived parts? Newman's answer is that it is the prophetical office, not the unaided power of conscience, which has to be opposed to the institutional excesses of the Church. 'Theology', he says, 'is the regulating principle. Its absence has been the cause of our late and present internal troubles', since never is religion in greater danger than when 'the Schools of theology have been broken up and ceased to be'.[2]

And here is the nerve of Newman's argument in his preface to the third edition of the *Via Media*:

I say, then, Theology is the fundamental and regulating principle of the whole Church system. It is commensurate with Revelation, and Revelation is the initial and essential idea of Christianity. It is the subject-matter, the formal cause, the expression, of the Prophetical Office, and, as being such, has created both the Regal Office and the Sacerdotal. And it has in a certain sense a power of jurisdiction over those offices, as being its own creations, theologians being ever in request and in employment in keeping within bounds both the political and popular elements in the Church's constitution, – elements which are far more congenial than itself to the human mind, are far more liable to excess and corruption, and are ever struggling to liberate themselves from those restraints which are in truth necessary for their well-being. [xlvii–xlviii.]

In failing to recognise the prophetical function as the regulating principle, both Acton and the Ultramontanes were making the same mistake. Both saw the Church in political terms: Acton opposed conscience to papal tyranny, but conscience without theology is at best sensibility, at worst emotion. For all Ultramontanes, power without theology was exercised in unreflecting imitation of secular power – the Pope must have the status of a Prince, the bishop of a lord mayor, and so forth – and it produced that monstrous contradiction between Scripture and practice known today as "triumphalism". It is theology's function to recall the systems and abstractions of Churchmen to the fullness of their origins in Scripture and in the traditions of the people of God.

[1] The discussion in the *Grammar of Assent*, v, i, 81–3.
[2] W. Ward, *The Life of John Henry Newman* II, 288.

Theology is the perpetual critic of abuses and abstractions: it shows that the descriptions of the Church in Scripture, since they are 'educts of the imagination', are in terms of metaphors and symbols, since we are dealing not with static concepts but with developing functions. By these means Newman had come to regard the Church as 'a divine indwelling'; whose 'instruments are not even so much as instruments, but only the outward lineaments of Him'.[1] It was a complex unity of many offices – of the Pope, the bishops and of the consensus fidelium – whose union was not political but 'musical'. In an unpublished letter to Dr Jenkins of 6 April 1877, he puts it thus:

> the Pope as the key note, the Bishops the 3rd, the priests the 5th, the people the octave, and the Protestants the flat 7th which needs resolving.

By the introduction of theology as the regulating principle, Newman abandons his former distinction between life and form, returning to Scripture for a three-fold description of the Church as a community for teaching, worship, and ministry. It is a description in terms of offices or functions, presupposing an antecedent unity, and aiming at an harmonious resolution of institutional, liturgical and theological claims in which no one element must preponderate at the expense of the others. This is the ideal: the fact tends to be otherwise:

> Truth is the guiding principle of theology and theological enquiries; devotion and edification, of worship; and of government, expedience. The instrument of theology is reasoning; of worship, our emotional nature; of rule, command and coercion. Further, in man as he is, reasoning tends to rationalism; devotion to superstition and enthusiasm; and power to ambition and tyranny.

This is what accounts for "Romanism" or the practices tolerated in Catholic countries which are at odds with Catholic theology. They are yet another example of that notorious 'double aspect' of the Church which, rather than a remediable defect, is part of its enduring condition.

> Men talk of our double aspect now; has not the first age a double aspect? Do not such incidents in the Gospel as this, and

---

[1] *Lectures on Justification*, 196.

the miracle on the swine, the pool of Bethseda, the restoration of the servant's ear, the changing water into wine, the coin in the fish's mouth, and the like, form an aspect of Apostolic Christianity very different from that presented by St. Paul's Pastoral Epistles and the Epistle General of St. John? Need men wait for the Medieval Church in order to make their complaint that the theology of Christianity does not accord with its religious manifestations? [lxvii.] [The motives for accepting this apparent contradiction are pastoral.] They illustrate at once both these elements of her divinely ordered constitution; for the fear, as already mentioned, of 'quenching the smoking flax', which is the attribute of a guide of souls, operated in the same direction as zeal for the extension of Christ's kingdom, in resisting that rigorousness of a logical theology which is more suited for the Schools than for the World. In these cases then the two offices, political and pastoral, have a common interest as against the theological; but this is not always so. [lxxix.]

It is at this point, and only after making these reservations, that Newman is prepared to accept the Ultramontane emphasis upon the institutional character of the Church; and Newman agrees that her survival depends upon the Church maintaining, through the exercise of her kingly or institutional power, 'a strict unity of polity'.[1]

As I have said Newman's language falls sharply on modern ears, but it is chosen deliberately to conciliate the Ultramontane party, and its subsequent restatement by von Hügel may be more to our taste. What Newman is saying is that religious sensibility and the language of theology, like all language, arise not from

---

[1] 'The Catholic Church is by its very structure and mission a political power, by which I mean a visible, substantive body of men, united together by common engagements and laws and thereby necessarily having relations both towards its members and towards outsiders. Such a polity exists simply for the sake of the Catholic Religion, and as a means to an end; but since politics in their nature are a subject of absorbing interest, it is not wonderful that grave scandals from time to time occur among those who constitute its executive, or legislative, from their being led off from spiritual aims by secular. These scandals hide from the world for a while, and from large classes and various ranks of society, for long intervals, the real sanctity, beauty, and persuasiveness of the Church and her children.' (page 107 *n.*)

'It is not a mere question of succession. The Catholic Church is not a mere (spiritual) family or race, the essential idea of which is propagation, but a polity, of which the essential idea is union and subordination, and of which propagation is but the condition and necessity.' (page 345 *n.* 5.)

self-evident ideas, but from the life of a community, and that they are meaningful only in so far as they continue to reflect a continuing community life. Hence the community as such must be safeguarded if the rights of conscience and the language of theology are to continue to function. This is the sense which Newman gives to the term 'tradition' which like 'Scripture' is the expression of this continuing community.[1]

How far he was prepared to go can be seen in the MS to his preface to the *Via Media*, where he expands paragraph 26, p. lxxxiii to read:

> I say then, that a conclusion of the executive in the Catholic Church may become a dogmatic conclusion in her theology on the principle that what is absolutely essential to her well-being must be intended by her Divine Founder to take its place among her doctrines.

But this executive power depends upon what might be called a dialectic of functions within the Church: it must not be exercised in a vacuum. Instead it must expect challenges and clashes. These however are to be regarded not as the sources of error and weakness, but as evidence of a power to adapt and to survive, since 'whatever is great refuses to be reduced to human rule and to be made consistent in its many aspects with itself' (xciv).

Such a conception of the Church and its tradition as living and developing was diametrically opposed to the official and dominant view of the nineteenth-century papacy: hence Newman's description of its action in 1870 as 'thunder in a clear sky'. But the line Newman was adopting – and it is the line of *De Ecclesia* – did not lack propounders. In the Church of England the writings of F. D. Maurice on the kingdom of Christ show most interesting similarities, which now have great consequences for ecumenism. And Maurice, of course, derives from Coleridge.

For our immediate purposes, however, the most important development of Newman's teaching is to be found in von Hügel,

---

[1] 'The early Christians, when teaching and proving Christianity, had nothing tangible to appeal to but the Scriptures. As time went on, and a theological literature grew up, the appeal exclusively to Scripture ceased. Intermitted it never could be. Scripture had the prerogative of inspiration, and thereby a sacredness and power, sui generis; but, from the nature of the case, it was inferior as an instrument of proof, in directness and breadth, to Councils, to the Schola, and to the Fathers, doctors, theologians, and devotional writers of the Church' (*Via Media*, 321).

whose analysis of the three-fold elements of religion, which he published in part one of the *Mystical Element of Religion* in 1908, has had great influence upon Anglican theologians. These have to some extent been tempted to regard von Hügel as something of a rogue-elephant, theologically, and not at all representative of his Church in his descriptions of its nature. For von Hügel the Church was the 'greatest possible multiplicity in the deepest possible unity', because 'every truly living unity is constituted in multiplicity' – hence his celebrated remark that monism was the enemy of religion. The three offices of Christ – the kingly, prophetical, and priestly – are by von Hügel taken to correspond to the external, intellectual and mystical elements of the human soul.[1] Each of these three elements of religion seeks to suppress the other and to exercise a totalitarian domination. Thus when the external or historical and institutional element predominates religion is conceived as a thing fixed in itself and given one for all, and to be defended against all change and interpretation. This is that view which nowadays we have learned to condemn as 'essentialism' – a view which in von Hügel's words conceives the Church as a paste from which 'all yeast must be kept out'. The proof that von Hügel derived this interpretation of the three-fold nature of the Church directly from Newman is reasonably conclusive.

Newman may have met von Hügel in 1869, but there are full records of a week's conversation in June 1876; and it is clear that Newman's influence upon von Hügel was at its height during the seventies – the period of the composition of the *Letter to the Duke of Norfolk* and of the Preface to the *Via Media*. Of the books which most influenced him von Hügel mentions (13 December 1874) *Loss and Gain*, *The Apologia*, *Anglican Difficulties* and the *Grammar of Assent*. What is not generally known is that in 1878 he was writing to Newman and suggesting that some of his works should be translated into German:

> I have long been hoping that I might some day be the means of getting your minor writings better known among the many Germans who do not read English. And now a friend of mine, a Baron Stockhausen, is desirous of translating some of your shorter pieces. . . . We propose to translate . . . the preface to the Via Media and the 5 lectures on the notes of the Church, which

---

[1] *Mystical Element of Religion* London 1927, I, XVI, 66–7.

6+

make up part II of Anglican Difficulties – I had also thought of the nine discourses on university teaching. [9 November 1878.]

A good deal of work must have been done, since Newman is writing on 26 January 1879 'of a passage or sentence in my Preface to the *Via Media* which ought to be made clearer', and he sends it in a letter of 4 February 1879.[1]

But Newman gives von Hügel even more than a way of looking at the Church under three modalities, as von Hügel himself admitted when on Newman's death in 1890 he wrote of his influences as 'too general and far-reaching, too secret and deep to be thus tangible and self-evident to a generation bathed in and penetrated by them'. To both men the enemies of religious insight were shallowness and its ally over-simplification. 'This clarifying business', von Hügel wrote, 'misleads and impoverishes us.' Although T. S. Eliot was right in saying that we value von Hügel chiefly for his religious sensibility, nevertheless in telling us what a mature religion is like 'from the inside', he also succeeds in expressing the institutional or kingly office of the Church in terms which are, perhaps, ecumenically more acceptable than Newman's. Both men hold this office or element of the Church to be neither an accident nor an unrealisable ideal, but a mysterious precondition of effective religion. This is what von Hügel means when he uses that favourite term 'appurtenance'; and he explicitly acknowledges that it was Newman who 'first taught me to glory in my appurtenance to the Catholic and Roman Church'.[2]

> Cease to worship God in particular places [he writes] and your worship will become less vivid, less concentrated ... the history of religion teaches us that it ... requires to be developed *socially*. ... And this social worship ... will not be fully normal and complete unless it contains a central element of action as well as of saying and teaching. A simple mental cultus is too brainy for mere man.[3]

We need to be trained, therefore, 'in the creaturely mind, so richly furnished by Church appurtenance', and to reject this institutional element is to upset the balance within the Church. Thus von Hügel deplored the excesses of the Reformation, be-

---

[1] von Hügel directly acknowledges Newman's Preface to the *Via Media* in a footnote to *Mystical Element of Religion* I, 53.

[2] *Mystical Element of Religion* I, xxxi.

[3] *Essays and Addresses*, II, 67.

cause they eradicated 'a difficult and delicate discrimination' which had until then been operative within the Christian consciousness.[1]

Both Newman and von Hügel insist upon our taking the Church as it is – warts and all – since entry into it is both privilege and danger. Von Hügel often speaks of the Church as his hair shirt or his purgatory, because conflict is inevitable in what cannot be confined to one modality since it is in perpetual growth. 'What is a religion worth,' he asks, 'which costs you nothing?'

There is, however, a difference of approach. Von Hügel was interested in religion generally, Newman in the Christian Church specifically – a difference which is attributable partly to the diminished status of Christian belief at the end of the nineteenth century, and partly to Newman's 'Evangelical' preoccupation with the presence of Christ. This preoccupation may well have accounted for the 'rigorous' tone in his sermons which von Hügel found 'depressing'. What Newman gave von Hügel was a logical model for the analysis of religion into its elements; but whereas von Hügel starts with a general theory, with which the three offices of Christ are subsequently shown to be compatible, Newman is entirely concerned with these offices as they elucidate the structures of the Church. This enabled him to anticipate our contemporary emphasis upon the priestly function of the Church as being, through its liturgy, to embody the people of God. Von Hügel, however, equates the priestly with the mystical, and seems to speak of the Church as if it were but the institutional *element*, instead of that 'Divine Object' to which we must respond as a whole before we can understand or identify its parts.

Conclusion

I have tried to show that Newman's final view of the Church is not idiosyncratic, but part of an old and potentially ecumenical tradition which persists even into the nineteenth century and in spite of the unfinished business of the First Vatican Council. This tradition holds the Church to be an organism given once for all and yet capable of infinite growth. And the Christian must first respond to it as a whole before he can effectively respond to its component parts, which are its acts of policy, its liturgical function of making us one with Christ in the people of God, and its

[1] *Essays and Addresses* 1, 265, 282.

descriptions of itself in the metaphors and symbols of Scripture. It is theology which alone can teach us how to interpret this, the Church's language, and how best to perform the actions which this language demands, since in these matters we must first act in order to see.

When one aspect of the Church seeks and gains totalitarian predominance then there arises that tyranny of the spirit which is so disquieting a feature of recent Roman Catholicism. It was what provoked most of the upheavals within the Church after 1870. Newman in his criticisms of the policies of Pius IX and in his writings on the Temporal Power, the modernists in their attempts to distinguish the Jesus of history from the Jesus of the Church, or Blondel in his opposition to L'Action Française, when an atheist, Charles Maurras, came to be accepted by Catholics as the defender of spiritual order – all revolve around the same question: is the life of the Church coterminous with its external and institutional rule? Each in his own way came to the same answer: the Church is the multi-dimensional Body of Christ. If its action is confined to one of its dimensions then it will fail to fulfil its mission, which is to show Christ so that he may draw all men to him.

The relevance of my starting-point in Coleridge is now I hope apparent. When he speaks of our response to the Church as to an *idea* presupposing a living unity, or as to a symbol which is a living educt of the imagination, what he is emphasising is a tradition which was in danger of being overlooked by Roman Catholics until Möhler, Newman, von Hügel, and Blondel re-affirmed it: that the essence of the Catholic response is never to a sterilised deposit or to an imposed uniformity, but to a unity which is complex of definition and discernment because it lives, and has the power 'to bring the whole soul of man into activity'. But where for Coleridge this assent could rest upon self-evident truths or *ideas*; for the others it was an assent to a social unity, to a personal relationship with the Body of Christ. And this is what links Newman's 'method of personation' with the personal-ism of von Hügel and Blondel, since for Blondel 'tradition' in the technical sense came to mean the continuing and developing experience of Christ, collectively, by the Church. Where he, von Hügel and Newman are at one is that for this tradition, or Christ's presence, to be effectively perceived, it must be permitted to live generously and through all its dimensions or, as we should now say, functions of liturgical embodiment, social action, and theological realisation. And to this trio of functions theology must be restored to its rightful place as 'the fundamental and regulating principle of the whole Church system'.[1]

The error of the Church in the nineteenth century was to confine itself to one modality, or at the most, two. Blondel denounces this as 'monophorisme'; in our own time Schillebeeckx has called it 'essentialism'. Von Hügel spoke of the emotional elements of religion uniting with the institutional and imposing themselves upon the analytic and speculative elements. We might, however, prefer Newman's racier but no less exact remark that the Church had fallen into the hands of the political ultra-devotional party.

To neglect theology is to defer an inevitable reckoning with what von Hügel described as 'the arrears of some twelve generations'. But the consequences of theological procrastination are more than intellectual; they involve that separation of intellect from feeling which is the dissociation of sensibility. Claudel characterises this crisis in the nineteenth-century Church as 'the tragedy of the starved imagination'[2]; and there is indeed a dramatic irony in Newman's forecast while still an Anglican that 'When the Church displays her proper gifts, she prospers: when she uses them, she declines'.[3]

It has needed two World Wars and a Second Vatican Council to recall Roman Catholics to a proper understanding of such an observation and of what it implies for all who remain separated in Christ.

[1] *Via Media*, xlvii.
[2] Quoted in Maurice Blondel, *Letter on Apologetics* and *History and Dogma*, texts presented and translated by Alexander Dru and Illtyd Trethowan (London 1964), p. 21.
[3] J. H. Newman, *Sermons on the Subjects of the Day*, 243.

Part III

The development of Newman's influence

1
Newman's influence in France

B. D. Dupuy, OP

A paragraph of the decree on ecumenism promulgated by the Second Vatican Council states a rule for the theological investigation to be carried out in the Catholic Church; it is a rule which ought to have considerable consequences in the future.

> In ecumenical dialogue [it is stated in paragraph 11] Catholic theologians standing fast by the teaching of the Church and investigating the divine mysteries with the separated brethren must proceed with love for the truth, with charity and humility. When comparing doctrines with one another, they should remember that in Catholic doctrine there exists a 'hierarchy' of truths, since they vary in their relation to the fundamental Christian faith. Thus the way will be opened by which through fraternal rivalry all will be stirred to a deeper understanding and a clearer presentation of the unfathomable riches of Christ.

The Second Vatican Council was only enabled to make this call upon its theologians – viz, to proceed to a new evaluation of the truths of Catholic doctrine in their relationship with sacred Scripture and the data of tradition – because of work already done in this field within the Catholic Church. I want to show that Newman's work was not unconnected with this quest for new ways and indeed contributed to it in large measure.

For it was Newman's writings much more than his personal destiny in Anglicanism and in the Oxford Movement which have interested French Catholics. His unblemished life, his readiness to respond to the calls of grace, his faithfulness to each day's guidance – these were, of course, recognised from the start. They were

6*

loved and reverenced by Catholics who encountered in what he wrote truths which they did not find expressed with such simplicity or fervour in the classical masters of spirituality. In France, especially, Newman was first accepted as a devotional writer; it was not until the beginning of the twentieth century that P. Thureau-Dangin's great work, *La Rennaissance catholique en Angleterre*, and Henri Bremond's biography were published, and a beginning was made to assigning a historical place to Newman's thought and examining the significance of his approach. But the *Essay on the Development of Christian Doctrine* and the *Apologia* were both translated immediately on publication, and the great works of the middle years were studied as they appeared. Thus, unlike English writers of the time who were interested particularly in Newman's life and situation in the Church, French writers made a particular study of his works in order to compare them with contemporary Catholic positions.

Newman's influence in French-speaking countries has passed roughly through three successive periods. Throughout the nineteenth century the *Essay on the Development of Christian Doctrine* was his best known work and was studied more than any other. Then his philosophy of belief came to the forefront; attention was paid to his *University Sermons*, to certain of the *Parochial and Plain Sermons* and to the *Grammar of Assent* which until then had not been translated, but was at this period. After the First World War, in the general reaction against modernism, Newman's work was under something of a cloud in France and Belgium, but since 1935 we have been witnessing a general revival of Newman studies. Without any doubt the stimulus of Vatican II will enable this revival to develop further; and a number of recent publications already give promise of this development.

I

The idea of dogmatic development, although it was new to a number of theologians between 1845 and 1850, was at once accepted and provoked unconcealed interest.[1] Only a few considered it somewhat suspect. There was never any radical criticism in France like that, for example, in America of

[1] See also my article 'L'influence de Newman sur la théologie catholique du développement dogmatique' in *Newman Studien* VI, Nuremberg 1964, 143–65.

O. Brownson. The favour shown to a convert, even when he is not very well understood, no doubt played its part in this general approval. But theologians are not always so kind as the general public to new adherents to the Catholic faith, and if they gave such a favourable welcome to the idea of dogmatic development it was because in reality it answered a need. The hypothesis put forward by Newman had been in men's minds for a long time and was becoming increasingly urgent with the advance of historical knowledge, and increasingly plausible.

The idea of dogma prevailing until then in ecclesiastical teaching had been fashioned in a world that was solely conceptual and strictly theological in outlook. Since the last of the great Gallican historians and after the destruction caused by the French Revolution very little was known about the history of doctrine. This ignorance, as Newman noted in a letter of the period to Lord Adare[1], did not make for an understanding of the *Essay on the Development of Christian Doctrine*. Nevertheless, theologians perceived in it the work of a master imbued with the sense of tradition, of one possessing a decided gift for philosophy, of a master who was profoundly Catholic.

Even in Rome it was admitted that Newman's argument was substantially correct. But as Professor Owen Chadwick has shown, it was reinterpreted in the terms of scholastic theology which seemed to be clearer and safer.[2] Newman proposed criteria of the *homogeneity* of dogma which could be recognised *a posteriori*. The Roman theologians desired to establish criteria of *definability*, which could be determined *a priori*. Perrone, who was always very friendly to Newman, for the whole of his life held an interpretation of the canon of Vincent of Lérins different from Newman's.[3] Fundamentally, the two views were rather far from each other.

It must be acknowledged that even nowadays different interpretations of the *Essay on the Development of Christian Doctrine* can be given. Directly after its publication the French philosopher, Emile Saisset, hailed the book as a work of rationalist inspiration.

---

[1] 31 August 1846. See C. S. Dessain (ed.), *Letters and Diaries* xi, London 1962 238–41.
[2] Owen Chadwick, *From Bossuet to Newman* Cambridge 1957, 164–84.
[3] F. M. William, 'J. H. Newman und P. Perrone' in *Newman Studien* ii, Nuremberg 1955, 120–45.

He thus shared the opinion of James Mozley and of several English writers. He wrote:

> We see in Christianity a perfectly new and original idea, one which has been able to assimilate other ideas which had appeared previously or which it found beside it, but which it incorporated into itself by mastering them. We believe that this idea was at first only a seed, that this seed developed only gradually under the influence of a great number of causes and minds.... We should be very sorry to cloud the joy of those who are now hailing the conversion of Mr Newman, but we advise them not to be too triumphant. That Rome should receive with honour a theologian of such worth and virtue is worthy of her policy and her maternal indulgence, but whether she knows it or not, in absolving Pusey's disciple she is granting an amnesty to rationalism.[1]

This unfounded and mistaken interpretation, entirely contrary to Newman's mind, was refuted by Abbé Darboy, the future Archbishop of Paris.[2] For the latter the *Essay* was, on the contrary, a work of faith, 'a fine fragment of what can be called a philosophy of Church history', and it brought new light to the understanding of Catholic dogma.

New light is what it was for many; and several theologians were only brought round to accepting certain definitions of the Church by calling on Newman's help. Thus Mgr Sibour, Archbishop of Paris, who had been an opponent of the definition of the Immaculate Conception, in his pastoral letter of 29 November 1854 declared that it could and must be understood by means of the idea of development.[3] On several occasions in 1871 a similar view was expressed. Thus the American, Archbishop Kenrick, a member of the minority at Vatican I and an opponent of the definition of papal infallibility, explained it and determined its mean-

---

[1] Emile Saisset, 'De l'origine et de la formation du Christianisme, à l'occasion du livre de M. Newman' in *La Liberté de penser* 15 March 1848, 337–57.

[2] G. Darboy, 'Comment y a-t-il progrès doctrinal dans le catholicisme?' in the *Correspondant*, 23 1848, 281–93. G. Darboy devoted another article to Newman in the *Correspondant* (1851), 385–407.

[3] Mgr Sibour, 'Lettre pastorale sur l'Immaculée Conception de la Sainte' (23 November 1854) in *Mandements, lettres et instructions pastorales* II, 213–33, es. 219–20.

ing and precise implication by relying on the work of Newman.[1] Mgr Mignot also acknowledged the debt that he owed to the *Essay* in the discussions of this period.[2]

All the same the *Essay* did not at once gain acceptance among the theologians of the Catholic universities. The First Vatican Council did not deal with development.[3] After 1871 the theory of development worked out by Franzelin was taught in the schools, and this theory was appreciably different from Newman's.

An incident shows this to be true. In 1880, Abbé Duchesne, the youthful and brilliant professor of history at the Institut Catholique was taken to task by Abbé Rambouillet, an unknown curate in Paris. According to the latter, Duchesne, in his course on Christian origins, was making use of an idea of development which depended on the theories of Gunther, Rosmini, and Ubaghs rather than on those of Franzelin. For greater safety in this matter, Mgr d'Hulst, rector of the Institut Catholique, wrote to Franzelin, explaining to him that the idea of development followed by Duchesne could be linked with those of Newman and Petau, and that he thought it compatible with what was taught in Rome. Franzelin answered that Newman's and Petau's position was 'beyond reproach', but that it was not opportune for it to become the object of teaching which might well soon spread to the Roman schools. Nor did he desire his 'own ideas to be interpreted in this sense so that they might appear to be only slightly dis-similar'.[4]

Franzelin's answer proves that the eminent Roman professor allowed a plurality of ideas on the subject among Catholics. On the other hand, he was not anxious to see Newman's theory taught in the schools, especially in Rome. Yet this is what happened fairly soon, as can be seen from the book on theological criteria by

[1] Mgr P. R. Kenrick, letter to Lord Acton (29 March 1871) published in J. von Schulte, *Der Altkatholizismus* Gissen 1887, 267–70. During the Vatican Council Mgr Kenrick made two speeches on these lines (J. Friedrich, *Documenta* I, 187–246; II, 281–9). See also Dom Cuthbert Butler, *The Vatican Council, 1869–70*, London, Collins 1962, 424.

[2] Mgr E. I. Mignot, Preface to the French translation of the *Essay*, published by H. Brémond, Paris 1906.

[3] M. G. McGrath, *The Vatican Council's Teaching on the Evolution of Dogma*, Santiago, Chile, Catholic University 1961, has shown that the few lines in Vatican I aimed at the idea of development (Denz.-Schönm. 3020) concerned only the work of Günther.

[4] See A. Baudrillart, *Vie de Mgr d'Hulst* I, Paris 1912. 458–65.

a follower of Cardinal de Angelis, Canon Salvatore di Bartolo.[1] This well-informed and careful author prepared a treatise on the *loci theologici* in which one of the principal sources was the *Letter to the Duke of Norfolk*. It is true that the book was placed on the Index, but for its over-generous view of scriptural inspiration, not for its idea of development which was not called in question.

Thus, at the end of the nineteenth century the idea of dogmatic development was, it can be said, established in Catholicism. But its significance and scope remained to be determined. As we know, the Catholic theological schools have for long wavered between two positions which, in their most extreme form, are in opposition.[2] According to the first, development occurs only in the formulas; there is a phychological reason for it, and this accounts for it (Thomas Aquinas). According to the second, it affects the very substance of revelation; development explains how doctrines that are only latently to be found in Scripture can become *de fide*; there is then the emergence of what hitherto was only there implicitly, it is made explicit (Suarez and the theologians of the University of Salamanca in the sixteenth century). It is possible to hold that each of these theories contains a part of the truth, but a proper presentation of the development of doctrine ought to put forward the two aspects inclusively and not exclusively.

The theory proposed by Newman in 1845 approached development in a totally different way. For Newman considered the *idea* of development and not only the *concept* of dogma. But the old dispute, forgotten for a time, was necessarily to break out anew. It was in France in 1904 that this occurred at the time of the publication of Abbé Loisy's 'little red book', *L'Évangile et l'Église*. Loisy, guided towards Newman by Friedrich von Hügel, had read the *Essay on the Development of Christian Doctrine* and de-

---

[1] Salvatore Di Bartolo, *Les Critères théologiques* Paris 1889. The author had received several approbations of his work, and one in particular from Cardinal Manning. The later, revised edition *Giudici sovra i criteri teologici Rome* 1891, was not translated into French.

[2] See Chadwick, 21–48. C. Pozo, *La teoría del progreso dogmático en los teólogos de la Escuela de Salamanca* Madrid 1959; F. C. Martinez, 'La Solución de Suarez al problema de la evolución e progreso dogmático' in *Estudios Ecclesiásticos* 31 (1957), 17–41.

voted a discerning article to it in 1898.[1] A few years later he had occasion to explain, in an answer to Harnack's *Das Wesen des Christenthums*, his own idea of development. Of Newman's argument Loisy retained the vitalistic, biological elements and deliberately interpreted the idea of development in an evolutionary sense. For Loisy, the symbols of revelation led immediately to the formulations of the Church. But was not the distance between them greater than had at first been thought? Loisy did not raise the question directly, but that is the impression remaining from his book. The centuries-old controversy on doctrinal development was at once reopened. Loisy deliberately rejected the idea that the formulations of the Church were merely the explanation of the revealed deposit. Revelation is for him rather like a germ, the Church like a living being, and dogmas are the expression of its life. To account for the transition from primitive symbol to dogma new elements must be made to intervene, as happens when a seed grows into a tree or a child develops morally into an adult. Thus it was much more than a question about development that was raised by Loisy; it was a question about the nature of revelation and dogma. This French context of the early 1900s must be considered if the role of Newman's work in the theological discussions of this period is to be understood. Loisy's work itself is difficult to understand apart from this climate of idealist and evolutionistic philosophy, which he often referred to and with which he was thoroughly imbued.

For these reasons theological interest, which hitherto had been almost exclusively concentrated on the *Essay on the Development of Christian Doctrine*, now turned towards other works – to the *University Sermons* and to the *Grammar of Assent*.

II

In an article appearing in 1901 Wilfrid Ward investigated the revived popularity at that time of Newman's thought in France, and especially the interest aroused by his philosophy of religious

---

[1] A. Firmin (A. Loisy) 'Le développement chrétien d'après de cardinal Newman' in *Revue du clergé français*, 1 December 1898, 5–20. In *Revue d'histoire et de littérature religieuse*, 1913, 570, Loisy explained that during this period Newman had taken the place of Renan among his favourite authors. It is odd that in reprinting this article in his *Mémoires* (vol. iii, Paris 1931, 268) Loisy omitted this passage.

knowledge.[1] This revival of interest was surprising. No work of Newman's had appeared in the previous years; the *Grammar of Assent* was still not translated, and the *Essay on the Development of Christian Doctrine*, which had gained a considerable public, owed its fame more to its leading idea than to its details or to its philosophical formulations. This unexpected revival seemed therefore to have specifically French causes, and Wilfrid Ward felt that Sabatier's *Esquisse d'une philosophie de la religion* to a great extent accounted for it.

Wilfrid Ward was well informed. His judgement deserves to be remembered. Before being invoked by Blondel's disciples Newman's name had in fact been mentioned on several occasions by the Catholic critics of Auguste Sabatier. The first of these was doubtless Mgr E. I. Mignot, at that time Bishop of Fréjus, a former disciple of J. B. Hogan's, that excellent follower of Newman, as Mignot himself had been for a long time past. He was in touch with French and Roman circles concerned with biblical criticism and religious philosophy. When Sabier's book came out he devoted some discerning pages to it.[2] This study, published in one of the most widely read reviews in Paris, cannot have been unknown to Loisy who, in the following year, dealt with the same subject in the *Revue du clergé français* in a whole series of articles. They follow each other in logical sequence: 'Christian Development according to Newman (on dogma and development); 'The Individualist Theory of Religion' (on Sabatier's philosophy of religion); 'The Definition of Religion' (on the nature of revelation); 'The Religion of Israel' (on the origin of revelation). Before comparing Harnack and Newman Loisy had made a long comparison between Newman and Sabatier.

Both Newman and Sabatier, as Wilfrid Ward noted, could be compared in several ways. Their points of similarity were the more striking and interesting in that their investigations issued from very different viewpoints and almost opposite considerations. Sabatier, seeking a way to account for dogma in terms of religious symbolism had found in the idea of evolution an argument against Catholic doctrine, whereas by the same means he could also have drawn closer to it. Newman, criticising the doctrinal principle of

[1] Wilfrid Ward, 'Newman and Sabatier' in *Fortnightly Review* 69, London 1901, 808–22.
[2] E. I. Mignot, 'L'évolutionnisme religieux' in the *Correspondant* 187, 1897, 3–42. Reprinted in *L'Eglise et la critique* Paris 1910, 3–87.

the Council of Trent, had discovered in the development of doctrines the proof of the truth of Catholicism against which he had
for long held out.

Sabatier and Newman both had a keen perception of the different standpoints and aspects of a single truth; they shared a
mutual concern for psychology and history; they agreed on the
impossibility of intellectual solutions adequate to the deepest problems, on the need to clarify the intellectual element of a truth
subsequently to its other aspects and as a part of them, and on
the need to affirm the primacy of religious conscience over dogmatic formulations.

The similarities as well as the contrasts compelled recognition.
Thus the best theologians considered that, without denying the
doctrinal divergences between the two trends, it was possible to
initiate a comparison between them which had not been possible
in the more intellectualised and scholastic setting of previous
generations.

The prevailing tendency of recent studies in religious philosophy [wrote F. Dubois in the *Revue du Clergé français*[1]] is
to relegate the intellectual element of religion, belief and dogma
to the background, and to regard religion principally as a feeling, an emotion or rather, according to the most popular
formula, as a higher life, that is, an immanent activity in which
spontaneity and the unconscious have a part to play equal at
least to that of reflection. This tendency certainly appears to be
a 'Protestant infiltration':[2] it is derived from Schleiermacher,
Benjamin Constant, Vinet and Edmond Scherer, but it should
not be condemned out of hand as defective in origin, for, after
all, the soundness of an idea is more important than its origin,
and it recurs, with appreciable variations, among Catholics like
Cardinal Newman and Fr Tyrrell, S.J.,[3] in England, in France,
in M. Ioisy, and in general among the apologists of the school
of M. Maurice Blondel.

[1] Florimond Dubois, 'Dogme et piété' in *Revue du clergé français* 41, 1905,
480.
[2] Allusion to a work by the publicist J. Fontaine, *Les infiltrations protestantes
et l'exégèse du Nouveau Testament* Paris, 1905. See *Revue du clergé français*
41, 1905, 553.
[3] F. Dubois cited by G. Tyrrell, *Lex Orandi* London 1904.

The comparison was by no means easy, however. From the outset what appeared both to characterise and divide the two theologians was the appeal to religious experience. If it was possible to observe analogies between the two theories of religious knowledge it was necessary to examine why they implied a different idea of revelation and of dogma, and why they led to opposite conclusions concerning the economy of salvation and the Church. It was necessary to investigate the historical background of the two theologies. Although Sabatier never defined what he understood by 'religious experience', it was difficult to avoid the impression that it recalled the 'experience of the divine' of Schleiermacher, Ritschl, and German liberal theology. Such terminology raises questions for the Catholic theologian: does not religious experience conceal all the ambiguities of a world of religious indifferentism? Can it be an authentic expression of the Word of God and a manifestation of faith in the Gospel? For a solution of these various questions it was thought that Newman's philosophy could be called on to furnish useful comparisons.

To Sabatier, religious experience is the source of dogma; individual experience is thus set up as a permanent creative religious datum. He wrote:

> I am well aware that many Christians think that God has revealed dogmas to us in the Bible, and will accuse us, speaking as we do, of denying revelation. God forbid! We believe with all our soul in divine revelation and the special action of God in the soul of the prophets, the apostles and especially of Christ. But here it is a question of knowing if God's revelation consisted of doctrines and dogmatic formulas. No. God does nothing that is useless, and since these doctrines and formulas could have been conceived, and indeed were, by human intelligence, he has left to it their formulation. But God, entering into relationship and contact with a human soul, causes it to undergo a certain religious experience from which, subsequently, through reflection, dogma emerges. What constitutes revelation, therefore, what must be the rule of our life, is fruitful, creative religious experience as it occurred in the first place in the souls of the prophets, of Christ and of the apostles. We can set our minds at rest. As long as this redemptive and restorative experience continues and is renewed in Christian souls Christian

dogmas may well be modified, they will never run the risk of coming to an end.[1]

And he goes further: religious experience can be considered as a criterion, and even as the sole criterion of the truth:

> By what criterion would you recognize in the books you read and in what you are taught, an authentic revelation by God? Listen. One criterion alone is infallible and sufficient: every divine revelation, every religious experience that is really good for the nourishment and sustenance of your soul, must be able to be repeated and to be continued as an actual revelation and individual experience in your own conscience. What cannot enter thus, permanently and constituently, into the very texture of your spiritual life to enrich it, set it free and transform it into a higher life, cannot be a light for you nor, as a consequence, a divine revelation.[2]

Here is a whole religious philosophy taking shape. Sabatier, perceiving the difficult balance between knowledge and experience, idea and feeling, resolved it in accordance with the intuitive approach of Ritschl's theology. For him the fundamental element always remains primitive religious emotion; the concept is only its envelope, its vehicle, the means for incommunicable emotion to be transmitted, despite everything, in a religious community which does not live continuously in tune with manifestations of the divine:

> We can go a step further and analyse dogma in order clearly to separate the elements composing it. There are two of these elements: fundamentally, a mystical and practical element, the strictly religious element which comes from the experience or piety of the Church: this is the living and fruitful foundation of dogma; then an intellectual or theoretical element, a judgement of the mind, a philosophical proposition acting both as envelope and expression of the first. Now it is not an arbitrary relationship which unites and combines these two elements in dogma; it is an organic and necessary relationship. We can

---

[1] Auguste Sabatier, *Esquisse d'une philosophie de la religion, d'après la psychologie et l'histoire* Paris 1901, 307–8. (Authorised English translation by T. A. Seed, London 1897, republished in 1957. Since this translation sometimes substantially abbreviates the original, we have given our own rendering, though we have retained references to the translation for convenience. [Ed.])

[2] Sabatier, 58 (E.T. p. 62).

return for a moment to the origin of the religious phenomenon
and to the formation of the first and simplest doctrinal formulas.
Faced by one of the prodigious spectacles of nature man, feeling
his weakness and dependence in respect to the mysterious power
there revealed trembled with fear and hope. This trembling is
primitive religious emotion. But this emotion necessarily implies, for thought, a certain relationship between the subject
undergoing it and the object which caused it to be. Now
thought, once aroused, will necessarily express this relationship
by an intellectual judgement. . . . But it must be carefully noted
that intellectual notion and religious emotion remain essentially
different in nature. Of course, the intellectual notion by being
expressed and by means of the imagination can serve to renew
or strengthen the emotion, and the dogma serves to reawaken
piety, but the two are not to be confused. The notion is like an
algebraic expression representing ideally a given magnitude; it
is not the magnitude itself. This is what must be clearly understood to avoid disastrous confusions. In religion and in dogma
the intellectual element is therefore only the expression or the
envelope of the religious experience.[1]

Some passages in Sabatier can be deceptive and appear very close
to Newman's thought. For example there is one, certainly inspired
by the *Essay on the Development of Christian Doctrine*[2], in which
he describes what he called, using a word intentionally different
from Newman's, dogmatic evolution:

We shall be asked, perhaps, why keep dogmas? Why consent
any longer to this imperfect mixture of pure religious life with
fundamentally outworn philosophical notions? Let us have a
religion plain and unvarnished. Not so long ago a certain school
of theology, and certain Christian positivists were talking in this
way and calling for a religion without dogmas and, as a result,
without worship. Do you know what happens when you follow
this advice? By doing away with Christian dogma, you do away

---

[1] Sabatier, 304–5 (E.T. p. 246).
[2] Sabatier Book III, ch. 2, 'La vie des dogmes et leur évolution historique',
297–336. This chapter is a lecture given at the faculty of Protestant theology in
Paris in 1890. In the following years three Protestant theses on Newman appeared,
inspired by Auguste Sabatier: D. Joye, *La théorie de Newman sur le développement du dogme chrétien* Paris, 1906; A. Jöriman, *Exposé critique de la doctrine
de Newman* Geneva, 1904; R. Gout, *Du protestantisme au catholicisme: J. H.
Newman Montauban-Anduze*, 1904.

with Christianity; by leaving aside all religious teaching you destroy religion itself. . . . A religious life which was not given expression would neither be known nor communicated. So it is wholly irrational to talk of a religion without dogma or without worship. Orthodoxy is absolutely right when against rationalism or mysticism it proclaims the necessity for a church to formulate its faith in a doctrine without which religious consciences would remain confused and indistinguishable.

If therefore life must take shape in an organism, thought in language and religion in dogma, it is no less inevitable that this organism should change, that language should be modified and that dogma should evolve. This is another law of life, to which there is no exception in nature. The error of orthodoxy or its illusion, would be, in its turn, to deny or to desire to arrest this unceasing metamorphosis. The life of an organism is shown by the movement and perpetual exchange of the material elements which compose it. When languages receive no new elements they are dead. In the same way if dogmas remain immutable it means that there is no life in them.[1]

But let there be no mistake about it, the conception of religion and dogma was entirely different:

A Church, claiming infallibility, said of its dogmas what a general of the Jesuits said of his order: *sint ut sunt aut non sint*. It is an illusion. Stationary for a moment on one point, movement starts again on another. In one half of Christendom, and that one which is certainly the most alive, the critique of Christian dogma has been continuous since the sixteenth century. Even within the Catholic Church, her ablest advocates, like Möhler and Newman, unable to hide that Catholicism today is no longer what it was in the first centuries, have made this strange concession to history, applying to dogmas the theory of evolution. In Paris, in 1682, the dogma of the personal infallibility of the bishop of Rome would have been condemned as an error; the orthodoxy of those days has become since 1870 the most serious of heresies today. Despite these phenomena to be observed in history the idea of the unchangeableness of dogma has so taken hold of public opinion that we shall scandalize philosophers no less than Catholic Christians, and many Protestants with them, by showing it to be the obvious fiction it is;

[1] Sabatier, 308–9 (E.T. pp. 249–50).

since dogmas, like all other manifestations of life, undergo a process of evolution as natural as it is inevitable.[1]

The principal effect of this demonstration was thus to bring home how mistaken it is to confuse religion with the dogmas which are its expression, and how far the latter are from being its soul and essence;

> It is thought that it is dogmas which produce religion and that the effect disappears when the cause is abolished. The most obvious teaching of religious science is forgotten; from it we learn, on the contrary, that religion came before dogmas, just as language came before grammar and poetry before all the poetics in the world. Piety of the heart – that inmost emotion, arising spontaneously under the immediate influence of external events or inspired words – ; and prayer – springing forth from human anguish to the God whom the human mind is perhaps as yet unable to name – , constitute the life of religion to so high a degree, that when this interior piety no longer exists the best constructed dogmas and the most magnificent ceremonies are empty of all real religion.[2]

Despite the undoubted divergences, the comparison of Newman's work with Sabatier's was inevitable. It seemed feasible. L. Maisonneuve quoted these characteristic lines from Sabatier: 'God, entering into relationship and contact with the soul of man, caused him to undergo a certain religious experience. Then, subsequently, through reflection dogma emerged.' Maisonneuve added at once: 'The orator who at the University of Oxford preached those fifteen famous sermons which allowed his conversion to be foreseen would have had no difficulty in endorsing those words.'[3] Then, too, Ward's article which created something of a stir in France, set out the agreement of the two thinkers on the four following points:

1. Revelation sets before the human mind facts, acts, beings, supernatural principles, which produce impressions and images; reflection works upon these data to obtain from them and form successive and distinct judgements: these are dogmatic propositions.

---

[1] Sabatier, 298–9 (E.T. p. 245).
[2] Sabatier, 300. This paragraph is omitted in the English translation.
[3] L. Maisonneuve, 'Newman et Sabatier' in *Bulletin de littérature ecclésiastique* 3, 1901, 213.

2. These formulas, by which the inward religious idea proceeds from its spontaneous condition and implicit form to its reflective condition and explicit form, are not essential to the purity or perfection of religion: a truth can for centuries form the principle of life for millions of faithful souls without being formally expressed.

3. Dogmatic propositions, expressing truths such as the Trinity or the Incarnation, are only partial analyses of the impressions or the ideas which these truths produce in us, and are symbols of reality. They cannot exhaust their content, or be equal to their object; they put it before us in distinct propositions and as it were in fragmentary fashion, they do not penetrate right down to its mysterious depths and can never be its adequate expression.

4. Nonetheless dogmas are essential; 'By abolishing them Christianity is abolished. . . . A religious life which was not given expression would neither be known, nor communicated. It is therefore entirely irrational to talk of a religion without dogma and worship. . . . Without a doctrine religious consciences would remain indistinct and indistinguishable.'[1]

It is reasonable to examine the implication of these comparisons. Did Newman, for the same reason as Sabatier, appeal to religious experience? His French commentators, possibly on the strength of translations, felt able to assert it.[2] It was almost common form to quote in this sense the famous passage from the first chapter of the *Essay on the Development of Christian Doctrine*:

Thus in time it will have grown into an ethical code, or into a system of government, or into a theology, or into a ritual, according to its capabilities: and this body of thought, thus laboriously gained, will after all be little more than the proper representative of one idea, being in substance what the idea meant from the first, its complete image as seen in a combina-

[1] Sabatier, 309 (E.T. p. 250). This comparison of Newman and Sabatier by Wilfrid Ward is given by Maisonneuve, 213–14.

[2] The passage from Newman usually quoted (see below, note 30) has the word *trial*. Mme Boyeldieu d'Auvigny (Paris 1846, p. 35) had translated quite correctly by *examens*. L. Gondon, whose version, whatever may be said about it is no better than Mme Boyeldieu's, had translated the word by *expériences* (Paris 1848, p. 47). H. Bremond who in 1905 reprinted, generally speaking, the translation by Mme Boyeldieu d'Auvigny, revised it at this point and it is the idea of *expérience* that he has retained. Recent translators, M. Lacroix (Paris, 1964, p. 64) and L. Bérard (Paris 1964, p. 81) have both translated the word by *expérience*.

tion of diversified aspects, with the suggestions and corrections of many minds, and the illustration of many experiences.[1]

Yet, if it is likely that Newman's personalism implies a genuine religious experience, this experience is never shown by him as made up of subjective emotions or inexpressible thought[2], but rather as furnishing approximations of reality. For Newman it was always a matter of partial but *true* representations, of inadequate, imperfect but always *true* symbols. It is enough to quote this passage from the *Essay*:

> There is a truth then; ... there is one truth; ... religious error is in itself of an immoral nature. ... The principle indeed of Dogmatism develops into Councils in the course of time; but it was active, nay sovereign from the first, in every part of Christendom. A conviction that truth was one; that it was a gift from without, a sacred trust, an inestimable blessing; that it was to be reverenced, guarded, defended, transmitted; that its absence was a grievous want, and its loss an unutterable calamity. ...[3]

Quoting these words, L. Maisonneuve pointed out how far they were in opposition to the Protestant theologian's continuously repeated assertion that 'the real content of the creed is entirely subjective'.[4] Between Sabatier's conception of religious experience and Newman's cautious but constant references to it there are profound differences. For the former it constitutes the source and criterion of revelation; for the latter it must always be referred to revelation and brought into conformity with it, before it can be effectively understood. Sabatier's conception risks confusion with natural experience; whereas Newman's, directed as it is to God and attentive to his Word, emerges gradually in all its originality and distinctness to whoever seeks it where it is made manifest, namely in the life of the people of God.

Once these fundamental differences are acknowledged, and with these reservations, we may admit that revelation is not a mere

[1] *Essay on the Development of Christian Doctrine*, 1903 ed., ch. I, sect. IV 38. See especially H. Bremond's introduction to the French translation (Paris, 1906), p. 6.

[2] See H. F. Davis in *Downside Review* 76, 1958, 294–6, and in *Blackfriars* 39 (1958) 310–21.

[3] *Essay on the Development of Christian Doctrine*, 1845 edition, ch. VI, sect. ll, 2; 1903 edition, ch. VIII, sect. i, 357 and 360.

[4] Maisonneuve, 218.

manifestation of God to the intellect and involves an experience which causes the soul to recognise what is conveyed by the sacred books in images or more less perfect concepts. This idea was developed at some length by Fl. Dubois in a paper devoted to Sabatier in 1905[1] from which I shall quote, if I may, a passage of deep significance:

Knowledge of the original fall came to the first man not only from a divine revelation in the form of a curse, but from what he experienced. Of course, Adam could not be directly aware of the loss of original grace, any more than we are aware of the loss of the state of grace – the supernatural, as has been said, is not the subject of experience – but he experienced in his flesh the goad of concupiscence, the darkening of the mind which had previously abounded with clarity and light, the torments of pain from which his body had hitherto been free; at the same time he felt that his happy intimacy with God, that of a son, in which he lived with God, had given place to coldness and abandonment; and the contrast of his present state with what it had been gave him the feeling of his great downfall. At a later date theologians were to express in abstract formulas what had been thus experienced.

We, too, experience not the fall in itself, but the penal consequences of the fall: like our first father we are subject to ignorance, concupiscence and death; we feel a mysterious solidarity in suffering and punishment which calls on us to go back, as to its natural cause, to a solidarity in sin, and when faith tells us that this solidarity in sin exists, 'in whom we have all sinned' (Rom. 5 : 12), our reason cannot object to a solution of the problem of evil which safeguards the responsibility and justice of God.

The dogma of the Incarnation or of the divinity of Christ was not on his lips a metaphysical and abstract definition, but the expression of an inner experience. Christ was conscious of uniting in the person of the Word the two natures, of being truly the Son of God, in the metaphysical sense of this word, and this experience was expressed in intellectual judgements like 'I and the Father are one'. [Jn 10 : 30.]

Our divine adoptive sonship through grace, of which the Incarnation is the meritorious cause, affords a remote image of

[1] F. Dubois, 'Dogme et piété', in *Revue du clergé français* 42, 1905, 493–9.

the natural sonship of Christ: 'He gave power to become the children of God' (Jn 1 : 12). Through the inexpressible operation of the Holy Spirit we repeat, so far as we can, Christ's experience and, like him, we address God as, 'Our Father': 'You have received the spirit of sonship. When we cry, "Abba! Father!" it is the Spirit himself bearing witness with our spirit that we are children of God.' [Rom 8 : 15f.]

In the same way when St Paul said that the Church is the 'mystical body' of Christ he was not stating an abstract thesis, he was experiencing in himself the brotherly solidarity which by grace united among themselves and to Christ the members of the Church; he exclaimed, 'Who is weak and I am not weak? Who is made to fall, and I am not indignant?' [2 Cor 11 : 29f.] And this religious experience was expressed by the intelligible symbol of the union of members in the body. . . . [1 Cor 12 : 12.]

Even so abstract and metaphysical a dogma as that of the Trinity assumed in Christ's consciousness the form of an impression, of an actual experience. For Christ felt himself to be in closest union with the Father and the Holy Spirit, in the fellowship of the one essence which theologians have termed circumincession, and this interior experience he revealed in those formulas in the Gospel of St John which tradition has interpreted as the living and concrete expression of the dogma: 'That they may all be one; even as thou, Father, are in me, and I in thee.' [Jn 17 : 21.] 'I made known to them thy name, and I will make it known, that the love with which thou hast loved me may also be in them, and I in them.' [Jn 17 : 26.] Or again: 'But when the Counselor comes, whom I shall send to you from the Father, even the Spirit of truth, who proceeds from the Father, he will bear witness to me.' [Jn 15 : 26.]

So we can grant M. Sabatier that revelation in the soul of the prophet was not a simple doctrinal assertion, a form of abstract teaching, but that the intellectual element was usually accompanied by a religious experience, an emotion, a correlative feeling. We shall even go further; we concede that dogma in the strict sense of the word, as a truth of faith defined by the Church, is not deduced from abstract premises by a dialectical process, but that it is always nothing less than the expression of a collective religious experience, of the life of the Church. . . .

Having made this distinction we repeat that dogma is not the mere gathering together of logical concepts, but the expression of a living experience of the soul of the Church. In making definitions the Council Fathers and the Popes are not dialecticians, deducing from propositions previously revealed further propositions of faith by simple syllogistic inference; these definitions are the echo of the living consciousness of the Church, of the life of the Church, of tradition in short, in its various manifestations in books, the liturgy, monuments, institutions etc., they obey not the abstract logic of the schools, but the immanent logic of life which makes explicit the confused and unconscious motives guiding it and endows it with intelligible expression. They do not confine themselves to consulting like archeologists the monuments of primitive tradition, they scrutinize principally the present conscience of the Church, of which the bishops form the authorized mouthpieces[1], and, finally, what they express and define is the unanimous desire, however obscure, of the universal conscience. . . .[2]

And so we come back to Newman. . . . For it was he who explored thoroughly the idea of organic development that had already been put forward by Vincent of Lerins in the fifth century, and endowed Catholic theology with a theory of dogmatic progress wide enough to include all the facts of history, flexible enough to answer all objections. Our thesis here is that dogmas are implicitly contained within religious experience which is, chronologically, the primary Christian fact; and that dogmatic formulas are but its transposition and explicit formulation. This conception was very dear to Newman, and the Oxford University Sermons serve only to develop it. If it is borrowed from the philosophy of Schleiermacher, a point that we do not examine here, it can be said that Israel has grown rich on the spoils of Egypt and that never was an adaptation so fruitful in results for Catholic theology.

In comparing Newman's thought with a French and German theological trend to which it was alien, and by which it was unaffected, French authors have perhaps, though with the very best

---

[1] In a footnote L. Maisonneuve made it clear that 'we do not say that they are only this, but the *Ecclesia discens* prepares the definitions of the *Ecclesia docens*'.
[2] See Bull (*Ineffabilis Deus* of 8 December 1854) defining the Immaculate Conception, the section formerly in the Roman Breviary on 15 December.

of intentions, fostered an interpretation of his work which, however interesting, has in the long term proved prejudicial. Newman's work appeared to them to open the way to a dialogue with philosophical thought and also to broaden the horizons of theological reflection. That was certainly the declared intention of the best-known representatives of this school of Newman studies, Charles Denis, Ernest Dimnet, and Henri Bremond. Unlike Fathers de la Barre and Bainvel who, in formulating a theology of development, only alluded to Newman's religious philosophy, they intended to extract from Newman a whole system of thought. They considered that Newman had probably not himself foreseen what could be obtained from his own ideas on the theory of knowledge and that the time had come to reveal its fruits.

There thus arose a tendency, a whole trend of research, a group of authors, all gathered round the name of the great cardinal, which was soon given the name of *Newmanistes*.[1] But "Newmanism" never constituted a school. It has never even been defined, and it would probably be possible to distinguish two or even three "Newmanisms" which had different champions and to some extent succeeded each other. There was the school which emphasised the symbolism of Christian revelation, taking a line that could be compared with that of Auguste Sabatier and giving countenance on occasion to the view that Newman was a fideist; there was the school which, assimilating Newman's thought to the philosophy of Action, appealed to it in support of the doctrines of im-

---

[1] The word *newmanisme* in French was used mostly by the opponents of the revival founded on Newman's teaching: E. Michaud, 'Newman et newmanisme' in *Revue internationale de théologie* 13, 1905, 641–7; Th. Retaud, 'Newman et newmanisme' in *Revue augustinienne* 11, 1907, 161–72, 273–96; 12, 1908, 21–39. But the term was often used by Bremond himself (see *Revue pratique d'apologétique* 3, 1907, 655 note). Father Lebreton even went so far as to talk of *newmaniaques*, 'Chronique de théologie: Autour de Newman', in *Revue pratique d'apologétique* 3, 1907, 488–504. At the same time an anonymous article, probably by L. Batiffol, endeavoured to establish the necessary distinctions 'Can it not be said that there is Newmanism and Newmanism? This is not the first time that the *Bulletin* has tried to make this distinction. On the subject of a brilliant and somewhat disturbing book by M. Dimnet, the *Bulletin* (1906, pp. 29–30) pointed out the undesirable confusion that had arisen between Newman and the interpretation of his thought put forward by his posthumous followers, who are more less connected with symbolo-fidelism.' *Bulletin de litt. eccl.* 9, 1907, 80). See also L. de Grandmaison in *Etudes*, 104, 1905, 260 and J. Bainvel, *Revue de phil.* 6, 1905, 188.

manence.[1] Lastly, there was the school which, emphasising the psychological, historical, and moral elements of Christian doctrine, saw in Newman's work an antidote against the excesses of scholasticism and a theology based solely on metaphysical and ontological data.

This last form of "Newmanism", made famous by Bremond, is probably the best known. It made its way into England where for a time it was feared that it would do harm to Newman's memory.[2] But despite its limitations, its errors, and its imperfections, this last generation of scholars has given good service to Newman studies.[3] The time has come to give it the credit which is due. Its best representatives, F. Dubois, J. Bricout, V, Ermoni, Mgr Mignot, J. Guibert, and the editorial team of the *Revue du clergé française*, prepared the way for the contemporary renewal of Catholic theology far better than their opponents, E. Baudin, T. Retaud, and others of the *Ami du clergé* and the *Revue augustinienne*.

The controversy over Newman's theory of knowledge gave rise to a well-known episode in 1906, after the publication of Henri Bremond's book *Newman, Essai de biographie psychologique*. The work was much influenced by previous studies by Fairbairn,

---

[1] This interpretation put forward in the first place by Ch. Denis and O. Lemarié was repeated by H. Bremond, also in 1907: 'Had he been born sixty years later Newman would not have written the *University Sermons* or the *Grammar*, he would have written *L'Action*. We are blamed for falsifying and corrupting Newman's teaching by making this great man into the forerunner of the philosophy of action. The precise contrary is true. This philosophy provides Newman's thought with just those complementary features and explicit proofs which MM. Baudin and de Grandmaison have shown us that it needs. A scholastic would betray his own conscience by preaching Newmanism; a follower of Maurice Blondel has no scruple in publishing *Psychologie de la Foi* (*Revue pratique de l'apologétique* 3, 1907, 665 *n*.). Blondel had some acquaintance with Newman's work through the works of his own master L. Ollé-Laprune, but he only read Newman much later.

[2] See Wilfrid Ward, 'Newman through French Spectacles' in *The Tablet*, 21 July 1906, 86–9, and 11 August 1906, 215–16. It is surprising to find Ward denouncing a *rapprochement* between Newman's thought and French religious philosophy of this period, since he himself had shown the way to it in 1901.

[3] Subsequently there has even been an interpretation of Thomist philosophy inspired directly by Newman. This school, for which the intellectual nature of the act of faith belongs less to strict rationality than to the connaturality of the soul with God in faith, is connected with the name of Father Rousselot. See R. Aubert, *Le Problème de l'acte de foi* Louvain 1950, 452–69; L. Bouyer, 'Newman's Influence in France', in the *Dublin Review* 217, 1945, 185 and, especially, M. Nédoncelle, introduction to *Newman: Sermons universitaires* Paris 1955, 35–50.

Whyte, R. W. Church, and especially that by E. Abbott. It bears the mark of its period and can only be read with difficulty nowadays. But the epilogue, in which Bremond expressed his personal ideas, keeps a certain historical interest on account of the reactions which it provoked.[1] According to Bremond, Newman's religious thought can be summed up in these three principles: the primacy of conscience, the communion of saints, and integral dogmatism. This summary, as such, was excellent, but the accompanying explanation was summary and rapid. Taking Newman's remark about conscience in the *Letter to the Duke of Norfolk* out of its context, Bremond in some way transformed it into a principle of universal application. Without mentioning the many aspects under which Newman refers to conscience, Bremond presents it as a psychological and moral reality, distinct from the intellect and only occasionally related to it. Conscience seemed to have the power to intervene as a source of truth and to act as the regulator of dogma.

It was in these circumstances that the French Jesuits, represented by de Grandmaison and Lebreton, who had hitherto taken little part[2], entered the discussion. De Grandmaison, owing to the kind of university training he had received, was far removed from Newman. But he had made, nevertheless, a great effort to know him and was to be one of those who at the end of their lives could say sincerely what they owed to Newman. Father Tristram, who knew de Grandmaison, considered that there could be no doubt about his admiration and veneration for Newman. Nonetheless, this admiration went hand in hand with certain intellectual reservations which, at the outset, certainly prevailed over the interest he showed in Newman. In one of those humorous sallies that were habitual with him Bremond compared Father de Grandmaison to Balaam:

The hesitations, the fumblings, if I may be allowed the word, in the two admirable articles by M. de Grandmaison have something pathetic about them. Like Balaam, he came to curse and

---

[1] H. Bremond, *Newman, Essai de biographie psychologique* Paris 1906, 410–22; 8th edition, 1932, 323–51. 'An impertinent book', said Wilfrid Ward. 'A brilliant phantasy', H. Tristram in *Newman Centenary Essays* London, 1945, 241.

[2] During the years 1898–1905 Father Bainvel seems to have been careful not to mention the name of Newman. So, too, Father de la Barre, who had mentioned him in his book *La Vie du dogme catholique* Paris 1898. The latter became more favourable again to Newman after 1908.

yet he seems to murmur between the lines, 'How shall I curse him whom the Lord hath not cursed?'[1]

In one of his first articles Fr de Grandmaison was responsible for a judgement which was to prove far-reaching and to have many consequences. 'As a psychologist', he wrote, 'Newman will always remain among the masters of religious thought', but 'Newman is too original, too personal a thinker to be followed with safety.'[2] This estimate was to hang over Newman's work in France for some decades, and its repercussions have persisted into our own day: Newman a psychologist rather than a theologian, a master of the spiritual life rather than of doctrine. This distinction is certainly the origin of the idea, subsequently widespread, of the "psychologism" of Newman. The authors of this particular idea are to be sought at the beginning of this century; they are Bremond and de Grandmaison.

Father Lebreton, who went further, blamed Newman for a certain nominalism.[3] In reality, Fathers Lebreton and de Grandmaison, misdirected by Bremond, and somewhat concerned to cut short the latter's programme of reform, did not perceive the depth of Newman's appeal to the conscience. Their view of conscience was confined to its phychological and moral value. They did not see that Newman felt obliged to treat conscience as primarily religious, and as the voice of God himself.[4]

III

Nowadays we are witnessing a revival of Newman's influence which goes far beyond the issues debated at previous periods. Newman's personality is better known today thanks to works of high quality. The sources of his thought – the Fathers, the Anglican tradition, English philosophy – have been more closely studied.

---

[1] *Revue pratique d'apologétique* 3, 1907, 666 note.
[2] L. de Grandmaison, 'Newman considéré comme un maître' in *Etudes* 109, 1906–II, 721–50; 110, 1907–I, 39–69. In this article L. de Grandmaison discerned 'unequivocal traces of a state of mind bordering on that which sees in dogmatic statements only the authorized symbols of unknowable truths'. He mentioned the 'bitter fruits' of Newman's anti-intellectualism. At a later date, in collecting his articles devoted to the development of dogma in his book *Le Dogme chrétien* Paris 1928, Father de Grandmaison omitted this one.
[3] J. Lebreton, 'Le primat de la conscience d'après Newman', in *Revue pratique d'apologétique* 3, 1907, 667.
[4] See M. Nédoncelle, 'Reflections on the authority of Conscience', in *Problems of Authority*, ed. John M. Todd, London 1962, 192–3.

Of course, for a Frenchman of today, Newman remains a difficult author, remote in time and by reason of his turn of mind. He
suffers from the neglect of one century for another. To encounter
him a certain distance has to be covered. But this great voice
which was not heard in his own century, penetrates to ours. It
penetrates, not directly, but like the voice of a forerunner, like a
prophetic voice, for the ideas with which his name is bound up,
for which he fought all his life, are henceforth living ideas. These
inspiring ideas can be briefly summarized under three heads:

1. Newman contributes to contemporary Catholic theology *a certain idea of the Incarnation and of the economy of salvation*. In a
way remarkable for his period Newman had a vivid perception
of the historical character of God's plan of salvation. He owed this
view to constant study of the Bible and the Fathers, and to those
of Alexandria particularly. This passage from the *Apologia* has
sounded in the ears of all theologians:

> The broad philosophy of Clement and Origen carried me
> away. . . . Some portions of their teaching, magnificent in them-
> selves, came like music to my inward ear, as if the response to
> ideas, which, with little external to encourage them, I had
> cherished so long. These were based on the mystical or sacra-
> mental principle, and spoke of the various Economies or Dis-
> pensations of the Eternal. I understood these passages to mean
> that the exterior world, physical and historical, was but the
> manifestation to our senses of realities greater than itself. Nature
> was a parable: Scripture was an allegory: pagan literature,
> philosophy, and mythology, properly understood, were but a
> preparation for the Gospel. The Greek poets and sages were in
> a certain sense prophets; for 'thoughts beyond their thought to
> those high bards were given'.[1]

Quoting Clement of Alexandria Newman likewise wrote in his
Essays Critical and Historical:

> We maintain then, as we have already said, that Christianity,
> nor Christianity only, but all God's dealings with His creatures,
> have two aspects, one external, one internal. What one of the
> earliest Fathers says of its high ordinance, is true of it altogether,
> and of all other divine dispensations: they are twofold, 'having
> one part heavenly, and one part earthly'. . . . If then [God] is

[1] *Apologia*, Longmans' edition, London 1893, 26–7.

still actively present with His own work, present with nations and with individuals, He must be acting by means of its ordinary system, or by quickening or, as it were, stimulating the powers, or by superseding or interrupting it. ... This is the animating principle both of the Church's ritual and of Scripture interpretation; in the latter it is the basis of the theory of the double sense; in the former it makes ceremonies and observances to be signs, seals, means, and pledges of supernatural grace. It is the mystical principle in the one, it is the sacramental in the other.[1]

Newman's conception of the Church as both invisible and visible is connected with this view of the economy of salvation. For him the Church is not visible simply because she is a community and every society must be visible; she is visible because God manifests his plea of salvation to man in accordance with its own mode of action. Newman writes in the *Apologia*:

There had been a directly divine dispensation granted to the Jews; but there had been in some sense a dispensation carried on in favour of the Gentiles. He who had taken the seed of Jacob His elect people had not therefore cast the rest of mankind out His sight. In the fullness of time both Judaism and Paganism had come to nought; the outward framework, which concealed yet suggested the Living Truth, had never been intended to last, and it was dissolving under the beams of the Sun of Justice which shone behind it and through it. The process of change had been slow; it had been done not rashly, but by rule and measure, 'at sundry times and in divers manners,' first one disclosure and then another, till the whole evangelical doctrine was brought into full manifestation. And thus room was made for the anticipation of further and deeper disclosures, of truths still under the veil of the letter, and in their season to be revealed. The visible world still remains without its divine interpretation; Holy Church in her sacraments and her hierarchical appointments, will remain, even to the end of the world, after all but a symbol of those heavenly facts which fill eternity. Her mysteries are but the expression in human language of truths to which the human mind is unequal.[2]

---

[1] *Essays Critical and Historical* II, London 1901, 190–3.
[2] *Apologia*, Longmans' edition, London 1893, 26–7.

At a time when the Catholic Church is seeking to go beyond a too sociological view of the Church and no longer conceives herself merely by the analogy of the body but as primarily the 'great sacrament' of salvation, she invokes this idea of sacramental economy which Newman had learnt from the Fathers of the Church.

2. Newman provides help in the rediscovery of a fuller and more accurate idea of *tradition*. Here again there is no passage of Newman that can be quoted as having specially influenced Catholic thought. Newman did not write a book on tradition as is done nowadays, unless the *Prophetical Office* and the *Essay on the Development of Christian Doctrine* are included in this category. But Newman was concerned throughout his life and in all his work with the tradition of the Church. In his *Apostolical Tradition* Newman quotes this passage from John Kaye:

> If we mistake not the signs of the times, the period is not far distant when the whole controversy between the English and Roman Churches will be revived, and all the points in dispute again brought under review. Of those none is more important than the question respecting Tradition; and it is therefore most essential that they who would stand forth as the defenders of the Church of England should take *a correct and rational view* of the subject – the view, in short, *which was taken by our divines at the Reformation. Nothing was more remote from their intention than indiscriminately* to condemn all Tradition.[1]

Newman's idea of tradition was at first linked with that of the *consensus* of antiquity and with his interpretation, following Butler, of the canon of Vincent of Lérins. But subsequently Newman turned his attention to the 'prophetical tradition' and, in the *Essay on the Development of Christian Doctrine*, he understood that Scripture itself postulated tradition. For sacred Scripture initiates a series of developments which it leaves open, and does not finish. Consequently, the question is no longer so much one of knowing whether this or that doctrine is contained in Scripture, but rather of knowing whether it is the outcome of a series of developments begun by Scripture. From this time Newman's idea of tradition was closely bound up with that of the development of doctrine.

Newman nowhere says, at least to my knowledge, that tradi-

[1] *Essays Critical and Historical* i, London 1901, 119.

tion is the 'conscience of the Church'; but this idea which has become the very centre of the Catholic idea is quite in accordance with his thought. The expression, which is Möhler's, was quoted by Newman himself in his celebrated *Rambler* article in July 1859.[1] And it is remarkable to see how the authors who in the modern period have developed this idea of 'tradition, the conscience of the Church', Fathers de la Barre, Bainvel, and Lebreton did so with Newman as their authority.[2]

3. The final aspect, which we must refer to, if only briefly, is his religious philosophy. Here his influence on contemporary theological thought is more widespread, though less easy to pin down. But quite certainly it is the aspect of his influence which holds the most promise; it could inspire the renewal of contemporary theology.

Opportunely enough, Newman reminds theologians that belief, to be living, must always be linked with personal experience.[3] For this reason faith is in some way related to art and to the creative imagination – it includes something of the knowledge gained through images, and it cannot be reduced entirely to concepts. As an act of personal knowledge, the act of faith, as conceived by Newman, is the highest example of real assent. The *Grammar of Assent* is thus the grammar of a personalism that is both required and assumed by contemporary theological investigation. In 1938, in his introduction to the French translation of the *Apologia*, Mgr M. Nédoncelle hoped that the origination and development of this personalist philosophy would be inspired by Newman.[4] Perhaps the time is now ripe for this final development which might prove the most fruitful of all Newman's work in the Catholic Church.

[1] *On Consulting the Faith Matters of Doctrine* edited by J. Coulson, London 1961, 73; French translation in *Newman: Pensées sur l'Eglise* Paris 1956, 419. The expression is quoted by Newman from Perrone in French.

[2] See A. de la Barre, *La Vie du dogme catholique* Paris 1898; J. V. Bainvel, 'L'Histoire d'un dogme' in *Etudes* 101, 1905, 617–25; J. Lebreton, *L'Encyclique et la théologie moderniste* Paris 1908, 36–7. Previously J. B. Franzelin, *De divina traditione*, thesis XI, had spoken of tradition as *conscientia fidei*.

[3] The idea of spiritual experience is given expression for the first time in a conciliar text in the constitution *Dei Verbum* (Divine Revelation) of Vatican II, n. 8: *ex intima spiritualium rerum quam* experiuntur *intelligentia* (through their interior understanding of the spiritual realities which they experience). See Bishop Butler 'Newman and the Second Vatican Council', p. 238 below, for a further discussion of this point.

[4] See M. Nédoncelle, introduction to the French edition of the *Apologia*, translated by L. Michelin-Delimoges Paris 1939, p. lxxxi.

2
Newman's influence in Germany

Werner Becker

Writing in 1946 Gottfried Söhngen compared the unique importance of Newman for German-speaking Catholics with Shakespeare's place in literary Germany:

> Just as Shakespeare through perfect translations has become part of us, so Newman has become *our* religious thinker – a thinker who appeals to us Germans as if he were one of ourselves, and as if he had written specially for us, without diminishing his importance for Christians in England and throughout the world.[1]

Ever since Newman first became known as the leader of the Oxford Movement, Christians in Germany have taken a great interest in his struggle for truth and the renewal of the church.

In 1846 his essay on *The Development of Christian Doctrine* was translated into German[2], and until 1866 German translations appeared almost immediately after his books were published in England. In spite of a Newman renaissance after each of the two World Wars, his influence on theology in the German-speaking countries has, however, varied a great deal. The publication of his essay on *The Development of Christian Doctrine* was a promising beginning, but during the last third of the nineteenth-century Catholics in Germany became less interested; and, in particular, his importance as a theologian was no longer acknowledged. Today, we do not see it as an objection to the theological

---

[1] G. Söhngen, *J. H. Kardinal Newman, Sein Gottesgedanke und seine Denkergestalt* Bonn 1946, 9.
[2] Schaffhausen 1846, and (partly) Breslau 1847.

character of his writings that they are 'conversational', that they originate from a specific situation rather than from a systematic intention, and that he regarded them as no more than 'essays'. If in a letter Newman once said of himself, 'I am not a theologian', he had in mind a systematic conception of theology which we now think too narrow. Any speculative effort involving the whole person in engagement with the revelation of God – especially if this is made with a kerygmatic intention – is now held to be of a theological character.

(I) 1833–1866

Catholic Germany first became acquainted with Newman in the period 1833–1866, and chiefly but not solely because of what Henry Tristram called his 'catholic ethos'. The works of Newman, especially his *Apologia,* were then being widely read. Cheap editions were in nearly every parish library in Germany, and his thinking was becoming theologically influential. From the beginning of the nineteenth century a strong theological movement had been developing at Tübingen, where J. A. Möhler, his friends and his successors tried to reconcile the Enlightenment and the philosophy of German idealism with Catholic theology. Many passages from the work of Möhler, Johannes Kuhn, and others might be quoted which offer surprising parallels to the words of Newman. But they are only parallels, and no immediate influence is to be found, although the efforts to expel the rationalism which afflicted contemporary Catholic theology are very much in the spirit of Newman's insistence upon the need to 'realise' our assent.

Ignaz Döllinger in Munich was the only prominent German theologian who knew Newman personally. As an ecclesiastical historian Döllinger considered Newman 'the greatest living authority' on patristics, and he spoke of having read the *Lectures on Justification* twice: 'it is in my estimation one of the best theological books published in this century.'[1] In the sixties, however, Döllinger turned entirely to ecclesiastical politics, and his influence upon Catholic theology in Germany ended in 1871, the year of his excommunication. Newman's attitude towards Döllinger later on is known from letters to A. Plummer published

---

[1] W. Ward, *The Life of John Henry Newman* I, London 1912, 444.

by Professor F. L. Cross and translated into German by Professor Fries.[1]

During the period 1833–1866 only Friedrich Pilgram, to my knowledge, expressly acknowledged Newman's influence on his theological thinking. He remained a layman for life, and is now acknowledged to be one of the classical Catholic German theologians, on account of his book *Der Physiologie der Kirche* (Mainz 1860).[2] He read Newman's book on development immediately after the publication of the German translation in 1846 – the year of his conversion to the Catholic Church – and in his last years he spoke of the study of Newman as having been 'of great benefit to him'. In his discussion of the problem of knowledge, especially the perception of faith (*Glaubenserkenntnis*), the parallels to Newman are obvious. In one of his works he claims[3] that 'truth does not consist in the formal logical conformity (*Ubereinkunft*) of thinking, but in the conformity of man himself with the object'.

(II) 1866–1906

In Germany after 1866 neo-scholastic doctrines dominated the text-books, so that Newman's fertile thoughts could have no lasting influence. The influence of the Tübingen School also declined. The time of the great theologians had passed. Catholic theology became 'confined to narrow apologetics and to an intransigent dislike of science'.[4] German Catholicism lived in seclusion from historical and spiritual development in the non-Catholic world, and the so-called 'Catholic movement' fought for the freedom of the Church against the State by relying on the strong religious faith of the common people. In 1871 Newman himself remarked that there were hardly any intellectual Catholics to fill the gap that had been left by the departure of Döllinger and his friends. In such a situation Newman was disregarded. Neither the *Grammar of Assent* nor Newman's preface to the new edition of the *Essay on Development* in 1878 was translated

[1] See F. L. Cross, *J. H. Newman* London 1933, 16. H. Fries and W. Becker, *Newmanstudien*, Bd. I 1948, 68–76.

[2] In 1931 I drew the attention of the public to him again by my introduction to the new edition of his main work (Mainz 1931, ed. H. Getzeny).

[3] See *Controversen mit den Ungläubigen*, 1855 quoted by Bernhard Casper in *Die Einheit aller Wirklichkeit* Freiburg 1961, 109, 115.

[4] Paul Simon, 'Newman and German Catholicism' in *Dublin Review* 219, July 1946, 82.

into German. It was not Newman, but Cardinal Manning who was now esteemed; and Henry Tristram discovered more Newman quotations in Protestant publications of this period than in Catholic ones. In 1878 the German periodical *The Catholic* partly disavowed Newman's theology. It suggested that selected works only should be published, and then only 'with a good theological – or, to speak frankly – scholastic commentary'. The courage with which Newman had confronted some traditional forms of Catholic piety received the following comment: 'It is a pity that this unusual man could not sufficiently overcome himself to be rid of the last remainders of his Protestant past.'

The publication of the *Grammar of Assent*, his elevation to the Cardinalate, his quiet death in 1890 – none of these was noticed by German Catholics. There was only one important newspaper article in memory of Newman – that written by the ecclesiastical historian F. X. Kraus in collaboration with Lady Blennerhasset[1]; but even Kraus showed little insight into Newman's theological interests. When he had called on him in Birmingham he was looking not for a theological conversation, but for one on ecclesiastical policy; and he triumphantly reported afterwards that Newman agreed with him in rejecting the methods of the Roman Curia.

It is, of course, well known that the modernists at the turn of the century in England and France often referred to Newman, but it was to a Newman of their own invention. In Germany there was no modernist movement in this sense. Catholics concentrated on the practical aims of the 'Catholic movement' and 'Reform Catholicism'. In France, however, there was at this time a true Newman renaissance unconnected with modernism; but such a renaissance only came later in Germany. It was a man of letters, Karl Muth, who, soon after founding his periodical *Hochland* (1903), drew attention once again to Newman, and to the opportunities he provided for a freer and wider theology. After Newman's books had been out of print in Germany for decades, one volume of his sermons was published in 1907. It encouraged many readers to begin thinking theologically in new directions.

(III) 1906–1920

By 1906 Professor Josef Mausbach had presented in *Hochland* a very well-balanced theory of the development of dogma based on

[1] *J. H. Newman in memoriam* in *Deutsche Rundschau* 17, 1891, 40ff. and 190ff.

Newman's book, which was available to him in a new French translation.[1] Matthias Laros[2], a disciple of Hermann Schell (and an expert on Pascal) also began to write in favour of Newman. He saw in his writings 'a programme which combined the old with the new, the tradition of the primitive church with the modern progressive spirit'. But at the same time, following Bremond, he reproached him with playing down the role of reason in establishing faith. Christian Pesch, on the other hand, accepted Newman's distinction between difficulties and doubts in matters of faith, and defended him against the charge that he was content to accept mere probability as a sufficient ground for faith. In 1912 interest in Newman was promoted in Germany by Ward's biography; and Laros published in *Hochland* the first version of his own Newman biography. What is of even greater importance is that Daniel Feuling, the future professor of dogmatics at the Academy of the Benedictine Monks at Salzburg, began to write about Newman, whose ideas form the basis for Feuling's book on the doctrine of the Catholic faith.[3]

(IV) 1920–1940

Between 1920 and 1940 there took place among German Catholics a general spiritual and intellectual awakening. It was described by Guardini in 1921 as a 'Church movement' based on 'the awakening of the Church in souls'. Guardini insisted that mere concepts or dogmas should no longer be the objects of theology, but rather the realities they stood for. The importance of conscience was re-emphasised as the means by which we attain to an understanding of reality, and in particular of the personal reality of our fellow man (das Du). The neo-scholasticism, which had been officially promoted and protected by the Church authorities, was set aside; and a new philosophy of religion emerged, influenced by the phenomenology of Max Scheler, who commended Newman as 'a great authority'. This new orientation of theology had its long-term effects in Vatican Council II. There was so much to learn from Newman, especially the desire for 'a valid dogmatics' (*das Dogmatisch-Echte*) as Adolph Kolping has

---

[1] *Hochland* 3, 1906, Bd. 2, 406ff.
[2] M. Laros (d. 1964) was one of the leaders of the Una Sancta movement in Catholic Germany.
[3] *Katholische Glaubenslehre* Salzburg 1937.

described the spirit of this period.[1] In this atmosphere a real Newman renaissance arose. New German translations of his work
appeared. Laros gave his Newman lectures in many cities. At the
time of the Catholic movement seventy years before, Newman's
sermons and pamphlets had been the centre of interest. Now
interest centred on *The Development of Christian Doctrine* and
the *Grammar of Assent* translated by Theodor Haecker.[2] In 1922
Laros published the *Apologia* as the first in a projected ten-volume
edition of selected Newman texts. The five small volumes of the
Newman Synthesis published by the young Jesuits, Przywara and
Karrer, had a very large circulation. This Synthesis was intended
'both to help the Newman movement in Germany, and to make
explicit the system implicitly existing in Newman's work'.[3] Przywara's short introductory volume remains unsurpassed to this
day.[4]

Like Bremond, Haecker and Przywara now started a correspondence with Father Bacchus, Newman's trustee in Birmingham. Przywara wrote:

> Newman's thought will be readily understood and accepted by
> educated people in present-day Germany, because of recent
> philosophical developments. These have done away with the
> prejudices and arbitrary abstract constructions of a sceptical
> psychology, and now – thanks to the Logical Enquiries of
> Husserl – a more genuine investigation of spiritual experience
> is possible.[5]

At that time German Catholic youth showed a deep interest in
theology. Important annual meetings took place. After the Con-
gress at Ulm in 1923[6], which drew huge crowds of Catholic
students, to hear lectures by men such as Abbot Herwegen, Karl
Adam, Romano Guardini, and Erich Przywara, Przywara wrote
to Father Bacchus:

> I was astonished to learn at this Congress of the extent of the
> philosophical and religious movement that has sprung up among

---

[1] A. Kolping, *Katholische Theologie gestern und heute* Bremen 1964, ch. III,
'Die Wende zum Dogmatisch-Echten', 62ff.

[2] Munich 1921 and 1922.

[3] J. H. Newman, *Christentum. Ein Aufbau*, trans. and ed. Otto Karrer, Bd. 4.
Freiburg 1922.

[4] Letter to Father Bacchus (Birmingham Oratory Archives).

[5] English edition, London 1930.

[6] Organised by the Verband der Katholischen Akademikervereine.

7*

German Catholics. I devoted one evening to Newman, trying to combine a Thomistic philosophy of the object with Newman's philosophy of personality and his psychological account of faith.

In these lectures, published in 1923 as *The Divine Secret of the World*[1], Przywara presented his philosophy of polarity. In Newman he finds the conception of 'opposite virtues', rooted in all that is real.

> The objective, the logical and universally valid (*allgemeingültig*) in Thomas Aquinas has to be completed by realising the empirical and psychological growth of man in his soul and in history. . . . Newman's epistemological difficulties were the same as ours, he understood our historical situation and also what is going on in our hearts; and he discovered that account of reality for which we today are searching.

Behind the 'monumental brightness of Thomas Aquinas' Przywara detects a more personal emphasis; while behind Newman's 'personalist philosophy' he finds the object-centred philosophy of Thomas. He ends by saying: 'Not Thomas *or* Newman, but in faithfulness to Catholic polarity, Thomas *and* Newman' (p. 176). In the letter to Father Bacchus already quoted, he goes so far as to claim that Newman's books have the same significance for the present time as those of St Thomas had for his. Przywara stresses that Newman goes back to the Alexandrian Fathers and – like Aquinas – to Aristotle.

> Cognition of God is not a mere theoretical process (*Ereignis*), it means confessing God (*Sich-Bekennen zu Gott*); and in its ultimate religious sense it includes the will as a principle of conduct.

Przywara defends Newman's conception of development of doctrine by saying that this development exists for Newman only within revelation itself, without external additions, and always under the control of ecclesiastical teaching. In his book on Augustine's personal development, Przywara claims that in modern times 'the spirit of St Augustine is fully re-born only in Newman'.[2]

[1] *Gottgeheimnis der Welt* Munich 1923.
[2] *Augustinus, die Gestalt als Gefüge* Leipzig 1937, 61 and 66.

But one cannot say that the renewal of Catholic theology in Germany in the 1920s took Newman as its pattern. Newman was everywhere acknowledged to have anticipated many of the current questions and their solutions; but for the most part theologians were content with the lip-service of 'It is Newman who may be considered to have been the forerunner of this or that doctrine'. Przywara, who continued to plead Newman's importance was unfortunately regarded as an outsider, not because of his advocacy, but because of the peculiarities of his thought and style.[1]

In 1945, Father Tristram said somewhat pessimistically that all the hopes had been wrecked which, twenty-five years earlier, had been put in the German Newman movement. Newman was indeed frequently quoted, but rarely studied. The language barrier was, of course, a difficulty for German theologians. The projected translation of Newman's works in twenty-one volumes, planned in 1922 under the supervision of three professors of theology (Feuling, Przywara and Simon), ceased in 1928 after only two volumes had been published. The *Newman Synthesis* by Przywara was composed of excerpts too short to be convincing. Laros, who had been editing selected works of Newman since 1922, was unable to complete his series before the Second World War began; and the five 'constructive books' of Newman were missing, although part of the Oxford University Sermons came out in 1936 and 1940. In 1935 Laros had entrusted this translation to a Jewish layman as a protest against the Nazi persecution of the Jews, who himself told me: 'I was only able to translate literally because I do not share Newman's philosophical and theological views.' Most translations of the more difficult writings of Newman hindered rather than promoted his theological understanding by German readers.

Since the First World War, however, Newman experts in German theology have ceased to be an isolated group. Most of the theologians who were willing to seek a new understanding of St Thomas and prepared to go beyond him, did so largely under the influence of Newman. The Jewish convert, Edith Stein, for instance, edited works by St Thomas and at the same time translated Newman's letters.[2] As a student I was myself able to hear

[1] It is typical that the recent work on dogmatics *Mysterium Salutis* to which we shall refer later cites a French source (Aubert) for its judgement that Przywara was one of the first to oppose the influence of Cartesianism in theology.

[2] J. H. Kardinal Newman, *Briefe und Tagebücher bis zum Übertritt zur Kirche* Munich 1928.

lectures in Tübingen and Bonn on Newman and his relationship to the Tübingen school and to M. J. Scheeben. In his lectures on the history of dogma, Professor Bernhard Geyer drew his basic conception from Newman's work on development, and Professor Arnold Rademacher quoted Newman's ideas in his lectures on apologetics. In 1935 I was able to lecture regularly on Newman and his conception of realisation at Marburg University; and in his great work on dogmatics begun in 1937, but not concluded until 1958, Michael Schmaus dealt with Newman as a classic theologian comparable to the Fathers of the Church.

(V) *The Newman renaissance after 1945*

The greatest and most effective Newman renaissance was to arise in Germany only after the Second World War. The Nazis had not succeeded in keeping down the interest of German Catholics in Newman. When in 1941, I wrote a pamphlet on Newman's Sermons, it was censured as follows: 'If you can't do without foreign brainwork, then you'd better stop writing.' But they did not stop me or my friends! 'In Newman German Catholicism sees prefigured its own spiritual and religious renewal since the first world war', wrote Walter Lipgens.[1] No other great theologian of the past could have inspired this renewal or its programme.

I became part of this new phase of the Newman renaissance in the following way. After being released from a Russian prison camp I reached Cologne in October 1945 to find that the centenary of Newman's conversion was being celebrated amidst the ruins of that city by a university week, and that lectures were being given by M. Laros, R. Grosche, G. Söhngen, and Paul Simon. They described themselves as 'united in their devotion to Newman'.[2] From Cologne I proceeded to Tübingen, where I was introduced to the young Dr H. Fries who, during the war, had completed his thesis on Newman's philosophy of religion, under the guidance of Professor Rupert Geiselmann. Encouraged by the Cologne meeting, he conceived the plan of publishing *Newman Studien*. We set to work, and by 1948 the first of six volumes was published.

---

[1] J. H. Newman, *Summe des Christlichen Denkens* Freiburg 1965².
[2] G. Söhngen, the Dedication of his pamphlet on Newman (see p. 174 *n.* 1 above).

The Newman Curatorium was also established. Its aim was 'to publicise the theological work of Newman and to complete in our time the work he has left us to do'. In the preface to the first volume of *Newman-Studien* we wrote: 'We wish neither to create an artificial Newman cult, nor to cater for a merely historical interest. Our aim is theological as well as religious.' Dr Fries emphasised that 'our concern was not with the abstract notions of a theological system, but with the reality of man as he is in relation to the living God. This is the world of Newman's thought'.[1] The catastrophe of our time has forced us to a new understanding of human and Christian existence; and the theology we have had to build up anew in Germany has had to serve this understanding. To us Newman is the teacher of kerygmatic theology.[2] Like Thomas Aquinas, he tried to meet the great movements and thoughts of his own time and to bring them into a vivid relation with the Word of God and Christian life.[3]

Fries follows Przywara in pointing out that the problem of faith can be solved only by philosophy and theology working together. By founding faith on conscience, Newman steers a middle course between the extremes of a rationalistic apologetics and a blind, unthinking acceptance. Dr Fries writes:

What Newman has to say about the relation of natural religion to the religion of revelation, and about the arguments for revelation, is fundamental theology in its best sense.[4]

He goes on to demand that German theology should follow Newman when he tries to establish revelation as fundamentally historical in character, so that its laws and structures may be investigated in terms of a historical development.

By means of this understanding of the relation of revelation to history Fries is brought to Newman's view of the Church. Newman recognises in the unity of the Church the variety of its offices and functions, so that the *sensus fidelium* of the Christian people retains a fundamental significance. As Fries says:

For Newman the authority of conscience remains inviolable before the infallible authority of the teaching church and the Pope.[5]

[1] Bd. 1, 181.
[2] See the doctoral thesis of J. Mann, *Newman als Kerygmatiker* Leipzig 1965.
[3] *Newman Studien,* Bd. 1, 184.
[4] *Newman Studien,* Bd. 1, 181ff.
[5] *Newman Studien,* Bd. 1, 197.

But, it will be asked, how much of this programme has been realised in German theology today? Many hopes were frustrated by
the premature death of such leading theologians as Paul Simon
and Th. Steinbüchel. But we have already mentioned the work
of Schmaus, whose seven volumes of dogmatic theology were
published between 1938 and 1958. In them he refers not only to
the Fathers but to modern philosophers and men of letters, while
Newman himself is frequently quoted. In this work Schmaus
'breaks with the Latin tradition' of the dogmatic manuals[1], and
he no longer writes in the abstract but in the categories of the
history of salvation. In this Schmaus has been encouraged by Newman's example.

One of the best-known professors of fundamental theology of
Germany, G. Söhngen, was among the organisers of the 1945
Newman conference in Cologne. In his Cologne lecture, Söhngen
associated Newman with the Platonic manner of thinking and
with Augustine, Bonaventure and Möhler (pp. 17, 63). Comparing
Newman with St Augustine, Söhngen makes the critical remark:

> Newman finds his place, so to speak, in the prolegomena to dog-
> matics, he is far more a philosopher of religion and a funda-
> mental theologian than, in the strict sense, a dogmatist; and he
> is certainly not a speculative dogmatist. [p. 41.]

The influence of Newman upon Söhngen's work in general is
testified to by the editors of a publication in honour of Söhngen's
seventieth birthday[2]; and as will be shown below, Söhngen has
recently returned to his Newman studies.

In Switzerland in 1957 the professors of the seminary in Chur
published *Probleme der Theologie heute*, in which they pointed
out the influence of Newman on contemporary theology. As with
many other works of the same kind, no other author of the nineteenth century is quoted as frequently as Newman. In his contribution, Professor Trütsch commends Newman for emphasising
the personal character of faith which, at the beginning of the century, had succumbed to 'the dictates of system'.[3] But the author
deeply regrets the lack of any German-speaking theologian able
to mould the suggestion of Newman 'into a shape which would be

---

[1] Kolping, *op. cit*, 172f.
[2] J. Ratzinger, H. Fries (eds.), *Einsicht und Glaube* Freiburg 1962.
[3] *Probleme der Theologie heute*, 54.

systematically more satisfying and more in conformity with tradition'.[1] In the same book Otto Karrer adopts Newman's position that 'the entire revelation is contained in Holy Scripture'.

In 1959 the Newman expert H. Fries succeeded G. Söhngen in the chair of fundamental theology in Munich. Today he and Söhngen, together with Karl Rahner and the Swiss theologians Feiner and Trütsch, are the principal collaborators in a new dogmatic work, *Mysterium Salutis*, which is being prepared jointly by sixteen leading theologians. Only the first volume has so far been published; but even from the index one can gather that of all the authors of the nineteenth century, or even of the entire period since Thomas Aquinas, Newman is the most quoted. Trütsch remarks on a new aspect of Newman's influence on the theological thinking of today. He suggests that Newman

helped Catholics in France and in Germany to adopt and develop methods of thought which have appeared (in German philosophy especially) only *after* his death.

Everywhere in Germany theologians are busy with the new questions of historicity and personalism, above all in their application to apologetics; and if you look at any theological review in the German language you will find that these questions are nearly always answered in the spirit of Newman.

To return to *Mysterium Salutis*. In his essay on 'Revelation, God's acts and word in the history of salvation', Fries writes entirely in the spirit of Newman on the significance of the re-emergence of the personal in theology. In his extensive contribution 'The wisdom of theology through the way of science', Söhngen calls Newman 'a great prophet of God's hiddenness'. Newman's statement about God's absence from His own world is quoted: 'It is a silence which speaks; it is as if somebody else had taken possession of His work.' In the succeeding pages, when discussing the problem of analogy, Söhngen makes use of Newman's distinction between the 'notional' and the 'real', applying it to the reciprocity of dogma and kerygma:

All dogma transcends itself in the direction of the kerygma . . . in which it is realised and realisable.[2]

Karl Rahner and his collaborator Karl Lehmann contribute the chapter on the historicity of the transmission of revelation. In the

[1] *Probleme der Theologie heute*, 59.
[2] *Mysterium Salutis*, 933.

past Karl Rahner has taken as his starting-point the neo-Thomist position of Maréchal and Rousselot, the latter himself going back to Newman. Now, Rahner refers to Newman for the first time, 'for an adequate solution of the problem of the development of dogma'; and Newman's view of the development of Christian doctrine is comprehensively discussed. Rahner maintains that – like the Tübingen School – Newman broke through to an emphasis on the dynamic and historic in the events of revelation[1] although he was free from the Tübingen dependence on the traditions of the Enlightenment and German idealism. According to Rahner, the development of revealed truth proceeds 'by means of the Word and of the thing itself together'.[2] Rahner emphasises that all future attempts to interpret the development of dogma must be made along the lines suggested by Newman, especially where these are similar to the Tübingen school and to the thinking of Blondel.[3] Alternative solutions, Rahner continues, 'diminish the reality of revelation by their over-emphasis on formal logic, whereby essential theological features are neglected'. Only a theologian like Newman who deals first 'with the actual and historically recognisable cases of the history of dogma, is able to vindicate the evolution of dogma as the legitimate history of an unchanging faith'.[4] Revelation, says Rahner, is not a system of propositions but a saving event, and therefore a communication of 'truths'.[5] Rahner is completely in accord with Newman when he takes as his example the experience of human love, which can never reflect fully upon itself. He comments: 'Reflex knowledge is always rooted in an antecedent cognitive seizing of the thing itself'.[6] Although Rahner concludes that at present there is no generally accepted comprehensive and consistent Catholic "theory" of the evolution of dogma, his own view is now very close to that put forward by Newman.

In his discussion of the role of tradition, Rahner again refers to Newman. He speaks of a comprehensive tradition as the principle of that life which creates and preserves the Christian reality;

[1] *Mysterium Salutis*, 747.
[2] 'In Medium des Wortes und der Sache selbst in einem' in *Mysterium Salutis*, 757. See Coleridge on symbolism and Newman on the double function of religious propositions (Coulson, 'Newman on the Church', 126f. and 129 *n*. 2). [Ed.]
[3] *Mysterium Salutis*, 754.
[4] *Mysterium Salutis*, 756.
[5] *Mysterium Salutis*, 757.
[6] *Mysterium Salutis*, 761.

and he identifies this tradition with that Christian 'sense' (*phronema*) 'existing within the community of the faithful'. Citing modern theological literature Rahner suggests how we might develop Newman's doctrine of the significance of the testimony of the laity in matters of faith.

Among other German theologians who refer to Newman in their efforts to renew Catholic theology, there is, for instance, Hans Urs von Balthasar, a disciple of Przywara and de Lubac. In his book on Karl Barth he suggests that modern Catholic theology is characterised by an 'urgent desire to comprehend historicity in all its dimensions'. Balthasar speaks of the present break-through as having been prepared by Möhler and Newman. Von Balthasar regards Newman's life and doctrine as a test-case for German theology and for its ability to grasp that the 'immanent historicity of man' and the 'transcendent historicity of God's revelation in the world' (p. 346) are homogeneously related.

If you look at the long list of doctoral dissertations on Newman, you see that not only at Munich and Tübingen but also at Freiburg, Mainz, Bonn, and Trier – as well as at Erfurt, the only centre of Catholic theological research in East Germany – Newman's importance is being recognised. Many questions are considered in these dissertations – for example, the unity of the Church, the relation to it of the individual, 'personalism', kerygmatic theology, or the relation of revelation to tradition. Through these often very valuable studies by young theologians, Newman's contribution will from now on effectively influence theology in Germany.

In earlier times Newman's new and unusual views became known in Germany mainly through translations which were often inadequate, even faulty. This, too, is different today. Through the work of Otto Karrer, and more recently Johannes Artz, the translations of Newman's theological works are (for the first time) of an acceptable scholarly standard. As early as 1945, Otto Karrer produced in Switzerland his Newman Synthesis, which contains all the important Newman texts on the Church.[1] The Benedictines of Weingarten have translated Newman's *Parochial Sermons* in eleven volumes and rigidly adhered to Newman's texts.[2] Soon after the war Dr Laros entrusted to me the supervision and completion of his Newman selection, and between 1959 and 1964,

[1] J. H. Newman, *Die Kirche*, 2 vols, Einsiedeln 1945–1946.
[2] Stuttgart 1948–1962.

volumes IV to VII of this edition were published.[1] With the publication of volume VIII, *On the Development of Christian Doctrine*, an index volume produced by Johannes Artz will be added.

The German public has so far not yet realised what an exact German edition of the *Essay in Aid of a Grammar of Assent* will mean for the appreciation of Newman. Since Przywara, no one has so insisted that Newman's terminology must be interpreted theologically and has so laboured to have it translated into German as Johannes Artz has done. But now we can expect that in all faculties of fundamental theology in German-speaking countries the *Grammar of Assent* in this new translation will be the basis for teaching and research. German theology at present is concerned with the same questions which preoccupied Newman. It wants to help the Christian to see himself as God sees him; and – with Newman – it asks what are the grounds for our Christian belief. It considers the Church realistically as on pilgrimage, or as a diaspora in the pluralistic world of today. It no longer conceives grace and nature as two floors, one above the other, but as permeating each other. Like Newman – even if not always with the Englishman's sense of practical reality – German theology turns to the concrete, the individual, and the historical. It is not truth, but its understanding which is conditioned by the individual and by history.

At the end of the Council, in his famous sermon before the Orthodox and Evangelical observers on 4 December 1965, Pope Paul VI said: 'The whole Council was moving in your direction'; and those German theologians who wish to build up the future will have to be prepared, as many are, to move in that direction too. As the preface to *Mysterium Salutis* emphasises, modern dogmatic theology cannot disregard the

> existing open dialogue with other ecclesiastical communities, rather it must see itself as an ecumenical theology trying not only to limit and to distinguish, but also to unite and to bridge, without of course making concessions concerning the truth.[2]

---

[1] Vol. IV: *Polemical Writings: Letter to Pusey; Letter to the Duke of Norfolk; The Essay on Consulting the faithful in Matters of Doctrine*. Vol. V: *The Idea of a University*. Vol. VI: *The Oxford University Sermons* and other Newman texts on the problem of faith and reason. Vol. VII: *The Essay in Aid of a Grammar of Assent*.

[2] *Mysterium Salutis*, Preface, 36.

The number of leading theologians is increasing who recognise that in this task they may not disregard Newman's great example. Przywara and Laros, Grosche and Karrer, Lortz and I myself[1] have shown Newman to our fellow Catholics as an ecumenical figure. As a convert he never denied what he owed to Anglican tradition, including also its Evangelical form. And our leading German theologians will assure you that we, too, are prepared to learn more and more from your great Newman, the son of beautiful Oxford, encouraged in this by Pope John and his Council, which has been also the Council of John Henry Newman.

[1] W. Becker, 'Ökumenische Aspekte der Katholizität J. H. Newmans', *Festgabe Joseph Lortz*, ed. E. Iserloh and P. Manns, 1 Baden-Baden 1958, 481-506.

Newman in the Low Countries: a note

A. J. Boekraad, MHM

Newman's work was the fruit of a long life. When he died it looked insignificant to many. Yet it was destined to become a seed in many countries: at first a thing hardly worth noticing, but in time growing in shape and vigour, with a future that can hardly be foretold.

In the Low Countries – Belgium, Luxembourg, the Netherlands – we may describe the first stage of Newman studies as a period of mere preservation of the seed. People took an interest in him as a curious personality, stimulating in the events of his life and the originality of his views. It started with the short but fascinating study by the Protestant Pastor and scholar Dr A. Pierson, in which he tried to evaluate Newman's importance for Western culture and Catholicism, *Mannen van Beteekenis* (Men of Importance) The Hague 1890. This period was mainly confined to an interpretation of Newman's teaching in relation to modernism. The book by Charles Sarolea, a former Belgian Catholic (*Cardinal Newman* Edinburgh 1908) helped to create the myth that Newman was a leader of modernism by 'ingeniously misunderstanding him' (174); while the articles of Dr H. Ahaus – a Mill Hill Father – on 'Newman and the Modernists' in *De Nederlandsche Katholieke Stemmen* (a review comparable to the *Dublin* or *Clergy Review*) published in the same year offered a first defence of Newman. Dr J. V. de Groot devoted an appreciative chapter to Newman in his book *Denkers van onzen Tijd* (Modern Thinkers) Leiden 1910. There were incidental studies e.g. by the Belgian scholar Dr F. de Hovre on Newman's educational theories in *'T Katholicisme, zijn paedagogen, sijn paedagogiek* (Catholicism, its teachers and their theories) 's Hertogenbosch 1924, and biographies by two Protestant theologians Dr H. Stoel, *Kardinaal*

Newman Groningen 1914 and Dr J. H. Gunning J.Hz., *John Henry Kardinaal Newman* Amsterdam 1933. This latter work was intended to be both for Protestants and Catholics and so affords a first sign of the appreciation of Newman as an ecumenical figure.

Though the works of this period are of limited importance, they helped to preserve the seed by keeping interest in Newman alive and preparing the way for a more scholarly approach.

In Belgium this new approach was achieved by Professor P. Sobry of Louvain in his book *Newman en zijn Idea of a University* (Antwerp, n.d., probably 1934). It is a penetrating study of Newman's style in relation to his distinctive consciousness and way of thinking. Although it is chiefly concerned with *The Idea of a University*, it is by no means restricted to this aspect of Newman's work, but makes a real effort to gain a better understanding of the man as a whole by correlating his life, style, and ideas. In the Netherlands the first two works that show this new approach are by two theologians, who, at the time when they wrote these books, were both non-Catholics. They each took a specific theme and in its examination treated Newman as their master and guiding light. Dr W. H. van de Pol considered the idea of the Church as a guiding principle in Newman's theology, *De Kerk in het leven en denken van Newman* (The Church in the life and thought of Newman) Nijkerk 1936, whilst Dr C. J. de Vogel wrote a valuable work on Newman's teaching on Justification: *Newmans gedachten over de Rechtvaardiging* Wageningen 1939. Both works are characterised by a great fidelity to Newman's mind and by a constant effort on the part of the authors to assimilate the 'philosophical temper' proper to him. All three authors, by listening to Newman himself, succeeded in entering into his secret so that the "myth" vanishes and the true "mystery" of this great thinker rises before us. The seed has started to grow, struck root, and promises a good harvest.

At the same time a different but parallel trend of thought was operative in Newman studies: it took the form of an objective explanation and defence of Newman on the part of more traditional thinkers, generally from a Thomist standpoint. The two most important authors of this type were J. G. M. Willebrands and Dr Zeno, OFMcap.[1] They did extremely useful and valuable work in

---

[1] Archbishop Willebrands played a very important part in Vatican II as secretary of the Secretariat for Christian Unity. [Ed.]

the investigation and objective portrayal of the true Newman, but their concern to bring him into harmony with accepted Thomist doctrines was to some extent a barrier to a full appreciation of the distinctive richness, value – sometimes – originality of Newman's own theology or philosophy. They contributed greatly to discarding the earlier "myth". Willebrands wrote a series of important articles: 'Het Christlijk Platonisme van Kardinaal Newman' (The Christian Platonism of Cardinal Newman) in *Studia Catholica* 1941, and 'De persoonlijke aard van het denken' (The personal nature of human thinking) *Studia Catholica*; 'De natuurlijke Godskennis als Probleem bij Newman' (The problem of the natural knowledge of God according to Newman) in *Theological Essays* Utrecht 1944; 'De ontwikkeling der Idee volgens Newman vergeleken met Hegel' (The development of an idea. The views of Newman and Hegel compared) in *Bijdragen* 1946, No. 1. From the very themes of these articles it is obvious that the author was not afraid to tackle the most difficult problems, and in spite of a somewhat Thomist approach, he was a real inspiration to many other students of Newman. Dr Zeno has published numerous articles and books. He is a great protagonist of Newman's cause, and has worked tirelessly to make it better known, writing in newspapers and periodicals, producing pamphlets and books. His most important works are: *Newman's leer over het menselijke denken* Nijmegen 1943, later translated into English: *Newman, our way to certitude* Leiden 1957; *John Henry Newman, zijn geestelijk leven* (John Henry Newman, his spiritual life) Hilversum 1960; *Zekerheid* (a translation of the *Grammar of Assent*) Hilversum 1963. In all these works he remains consistently faithful to the texts of Newman; and their merit is that they give us the seed preserved and purified from all non-genuine elements, so that it may be ready to develop into the full grown plant it is destined to be.

Dr J. H. Walgrave OP was the first who combined the methods both of objective description and inner penetration in two important articles in *The Periodical for Philosophy* (*Tijdschrift voor Philosophie*) of 1939 and 1943. The first entitled: 'Newman's beschrijving en verantwoording van het werkelijke derken' is an excellent introduction to 'a synthetic view of Newman's teaching on human cognition as seen against the background of Western philosophy'. Especially emphasised were the kinship with phenomenology – though this originated so much later in Germany with Husserl – and the importance of analogy. The second article: 'De ontwikkeling van de kennis volgens John Henry Newman' (The Development of knowledge according to John Henry Newman) constituted a fine completion of the first. Dr Walgrave, who shows great sympathy for Newman as a thinker, brings out the originality of his views and principles and stresses the psychological aspects of his work. This article was the forerunner of his first great work: *Kardinaal Newman's theorie over de ontwikkeling van het dogma in het licht van zijn kennisleer en apologetiek* (Newman's theory on the development of dogma seen in the light of his theory of knowledge and his apologetics) Antwerp 1944. In 1957 the same author published a magisterial work: *Newman, Le developpement du dogme* Tournai–Paris, which was translated into English.[1] Father Boekraad's two works: *The Personal Conquest of Truth according to J. H. Newman* Louvain 1955 and – in collaboration with Father H. Tristram of the Oratory, *The Argument from Conscience to the Existence of God* Louvain 1961 belong to this group. He tries to show that Newman's work – particularly that on the subjective aspects of knowledge – constitutes a decisive contribution to Western philosophy. In this connection he discusses Newman's emphasis upon the function of personal and historical factors in knowledge, and the role of conscience and intuition.

There have also been numerous translations of Newman's works into Dutch by Father A. Pompen OFM, including *The Apologia, The Development of Christian Doctrine,* and *The Present Position of Catholics* Bussum 1947.

Much of the work of the authors mentioned above would never have had its full effect and recognition had it not been that in the smallest of the three countries concerned, a crucial work was undertaken by the Abbé Nicholas Theis. In 1944 he had written a study of Newman's philosophy of higher education, in which he gratefully acknowledges the guidance of Professor P. Frieden, later Minister of Education of Luxembourg, but his zeal and enthusiasm were not satisfied with that. He conceived the bold plan of bringing together as many students and admirers of Newman as possible. The First International Newman conference, held in Luxembourg from 23 July till 28 July 1956 was the result of his generous and untiring efforts. The Abbé Theis must have felt very gratified when he noticed the happy atmosphere in which this

[1] *Newman the Theologian* London 1960.

first meeting of Newmanists from all over the world was celebrated. It proved a source of new inspiration to many; the converging tendency of different lines of Newman research became
clear, and the conviction that Newman had a message for our own
times was strongly felt. The German Newman Circle undertook
to publish the lectures given at this conference in one of the
volumes of the *Newman Studien*[1], a concrete sign of this new international co-operation. Thus a second conference was planned,
once again to be held in Luxembourg, and 1961 brought us again
together from 24 July to 29 July. This time the meeting was devoted to the consideration of the theory of the development of
Christian Doctrine. The international character was even more
marked by the presence of some young American scholars and a
member of the Gregorian University in Rome Professor de
Achaval. The third conference followed in May 1964, in com-
memoration of the first centenary of the *Apologia*. This time the
conference had a definite ecumenical aspect[2], and its success made
it clear that the next conference should if possible take place in
England. The present Oxford Newman symposium is the result.

Thanks to the vision and constant enthusiasm of the Abbé
Theis Luxembourg had done what only Luxembourg could do:
unite the many independent efforts of European scholars. England has now begun to do, what only England can do: to provide
the background of scholarship and atmosphere proper to Newman's works, so that the character and originality of his thought
may be fully appreciated.

[1] See Becker, p. 182 above.
[2] The results of this conference are discussed in the Introduction, and the
English contribution was published as *Newman – a Portrait Restored*, John
Coulson and A. M. Allchin, London 1965.

3
Newman through nonconformist eyes

Gordon Rupp

I live by admiration, hope and love, and Newman has always inspired me with all those feelings toward himself and many of his works. So much so that I intend this little essay of mine to be more of a nature of an acknowledgment and a tribute than anything else: an acknowledgment, that is, of what I owe of enlargement and enrichment of heart to this great Author.[1]

That John Henry Newman cast a spell over minds far beyond the bounds of the Church of England and the Church of Rome has long been recognised. He was on any showing a great man in a century of giants and, like Abraham Lincoln and David Livingstone, had admirers of many creeds. Indeed, I do not doubt it would be possible to compose a paper on 'Newman and unbelievers' and to bring the tributes of many of no faith at all in that age of half belief and unbelief who in his debt. A great man – a great man of letters ('guardian angel of the English language', one admirer called him) – a saint. Do these things explain it? To press the inquiry to its deepest levels the witnesses from Victorian nonconformity are relevant.

In the complex pattern of Victorian society, the nonconformists were important. Though not entirely freed from the repressions and exclusions of a century and a half of persecution and social ostracism, they were prosperous, independent, and self-confident: important enough for government to take notice of them, especially the Tapers and the Tadpoles at the time of a general election: 'The Wesleyans – don't forget the Wesleyans' cries some-

[1] A. Whyte, *Newman on Appreciation* Edinburgh 1901, 11.

body in Disraeli's *Sybil*. Sharing the good fortunes of a prosperous section of the middle class of which they came near to being an establishment, with their new buildings, their crowded congregations, their great pulpiteers, they were by reason of these things still to some extent self-contained. Bigger than the older Dissenting Churches put together, in the first half of the century the Methodists held a middle position. They called themselves, and were not then offended when others called them "the Body", and in the great matter of disestablishment it is important that as a whole the Methodists would not throw their weight against the Established Church. But it was the Catholic revival which very rapidly flung the Wesleyans and the older nonconformists into the Free Churches and formed the formidable nonconformist alliance of the last half of the nineteenth century.

This increases the puzzle of Newman. It is easy to account for nonconformist indifference, hostility, and prejudice, but the intriguing question is to account for the appreciation and admiring affection. They did not read him for his English alone – nor yet for his moralism – as they also read their Carlyle and their Ruskin. Somewhere deep below the ecclesiastical and cultural differences, deep called unto deep and heart spoke to heart. But let us begin with the fact, of which Father Ryder wrote:

> It is wonderful the extent to which of late years all sorts of persons with religious difficulties have had recourse to him. Members, often ministers of various religious bodies, Methodists, Presbyterians, etc., with no sort of leaning towards the Church have sought his guidance and sympathy ... indeed now and again one came across something which looked like a cultus of Cardinal Newman outside the Church.[1]

And he goes on to tell how in a large manufacturing town a Baptist minister had preached for three Sundays on Cardinal Newman as a model of Christian virtue and used as his text an exposition of 'Lead, kindly light ...'.

I propose to give you the testimonies of four eminent nonconformist divines for and against Newman, and then to look at those elements in Newman's life and thought which to a surprising degree speak to the heart of Evangelical Protestantism.

The Rev Dr James Rigg (1821–1909) was a Worthy of nineteenth-century Wesleyan Methodism. He was twice President of

---

[1] W. G. Ward, *Life of Cardinal Newman* II, London 1912, 358.

the Conference and, as first principal of Westminster Training College for Teachers (recently and happily translated to Oxford), he was much occupied in educational affairs. Not only did he know all the leading figures in the nonconformist world, but his pious biographer informs us that 'he enjoyed the confidence of four successive Archbishops of Canterbury'. As Mr Gladstone said in 1875, to coin a phrase, 'That Rigg is an able man . . . one of the ablest men I have met in committee'. In the light of what I am going to say it should be said that he was not of the straitest sect of the Evangelicals, and that in the matter of Church and educa- tion he refused to take the nonconformist line but remained true to the old high Wesleyan tradition. All the same, intellectually the mid-Victorian Methodists were an undistinguished lot – in contrast with the generation of Watson, Clarke, and Bunting.

Rigg was the author of several books. His most considerable work, written at the age of thirty-six, was *Modern Anglican Theo- logy*, an all-out attack on the theology of Frederick Denison Maurice and his circle, whom he accused of poisoning the pure waters of Evangelical doctrine with a neo-Platonism deriving from Coleridge. Its chief value today is that it is a vast armoury of quotations not only from Maurice, but also from Kingsley, Julius Hare and Jowett.

In later life, Dr Rigg (and not least after the appearance of the *Apologia*) came to think more highly of Kingsley with whom he corresponded, and he struck up a friendship with his neighbour at Westminster, Dean Stanley. Now Kingsley was a great man, or at least Maurice-Kingsley made a great man like Chester-Belloc, and we lose the poignancy of the great debate if we play down Kingsley's great qualities and virtues or dismiss him simply as a second-rate thinker and writer, as the chief exponent of "mus- cular Christianity". But that cult did exist, and how very grisly it could be, we find when we turn to the writings about the Catho- lic revival of Dr Rigg.

It was in the 1880s that Rigg turned his literary attention to the Oxford Movement. By this time he had become the spokesman of a self-confident, self-conscious Wesleyanism, deriding openly the idea of reunion with the Church of England in terms of absorp- tion. But the sharpest edge of his mind, which perhaps was no Wilkinson sword blade at that, was towards the reviving of Popery. He led the group which induced the Methodist Church to draw up a new service of baptism in the 1880s, the express purpose of which was to exclude baptismal regeneration. Though one of the moderate Evangelicals he found himself in deep agreement with the Protestant underworld's best seller, Walsh's *Secret History of the Oxford Movement*, and, though his own *Oxford High Anglicanism* was more restrained and less sensational, he sold enough copies to be able to publish an enlarged edition four years later in which he deplored that 'Romanising neo-Anglicanism which would . . . have sorely changed for the worse the morality and manly virtue of our nation'.

His writings against Maurice and Newman and their friends are a sad, because entirely unconscious, revelation of the extent to which the English Evangelical tradition stood itself in need of refreshment. I need not enter into the rigidities of its doctrine, but turn at once to what he has to say about Newman.

The curious key of his criticism is found in a note to page thirteen on 'The feminine vein in Newman's character'. 'Newman', says Rigg, 'was not indeed effeminate; but he seems to have been without any specially masculine tastes, pursuits or passions. . . . He was addicted to no specially manly exercises. He was not an athlete, he had no tastes in that direction . . .'[1], and this is a common quality, he thinks, of the pioneers of the Oxford Movement . . .'the friendships of Newman and his circle were passionately deep and warm . . . more like those of women who live aloof from the world in the seclusion of mutual intimacy. . . .'[2]

> Newman's was a characteristically feminine nature: it was feminine in the quickness and subtlety of his instincts, in affection and the caprices of affection . . . in a gift of statement and grace of phrase which find their analogies in the conversation, in the public addresses and even in the written style of gifted women. He was wanting in virility, in manly strength, and we cannot easily accept as a great man anyone who is not a truly manly man.[3]

> With Newman, as with people of a commoner sort, feelings, prepossessions, prejudices determined the creed: his logic was ever an after thought and a mere instrument of defence or persuasion . . . a characteristically feminine mind, poetic, impressible, receptive and reproductive, rather than original and com-

[1] J. H. Rigg, *Oxford High Anglicanism* London 1895, 32.
[2] Rigg, 109.
[3] Rigg, 132.

manding; and with the feminine mind was joined a feminine temperament.[1]

One feels that Dr Rigg might at least have considered the possibility of considering Newman, if not as the Grand Old Man, at least as the Grand Old Woman of the nineteenth century, and to have placed him with Jane Austen, Harriet Martineau, and Miss Nightingale and the Brontës, as fit to rank at least in some immortal Parthenon.

Another point for Rigg was Newman's worldliness. Were not cricket and other games played in the Oratory School at Birmingham on Sunday with noises offensive to pious nonconformist ears? And then there were violins, and other music.

> He was diligent in reading his *Times* daily, following with keen curiosity public affairs... editing Latin plays for the Oratory boys and acting as theatrical manager of costumes and scenery ... he was also a diligent novel reader.[2]

Influential as Rigg was, and representative as he was of one section, and not the narrowest of Victorian Evangelical opinion, the next generation of Methodists, of Hugh Price Hughes and John Scott Lidgett were of a more catholic temper. Lidgett succeeded Rigg in the field of educational statesmanship, and though a leader in the Free Church partnership, was an architect of Methodist Union, and a founding father of the Ecumenical Movement. As a young divine, he refused even to read Rigg's attack on his hero, Frederick Denison Maurice, and I suspect he had as little patience with Rigg's *Oxford High Anglicanism*. He himself embodied what we must now call the 'holy worldliness' which Rigg had so deplored in Newman: for he became Vice-Chancellor of London University, Chairman of the LCC, and founder of the Bermondsey settlement, very proud to be the first Methodist minister to be licensed to sell tobacco and run a billiard saloon. At the heart of Lidgett's religion was the Nicene Faith. And in his memoirs he tells how deep upon him was the influence of Newman's writings, especially his writings about the Early Church.[3]

Alexander Whyte spoke for others who shared this debt when he wrote:

> No one can feel the full force of Newman's great sermons on

---

[1] Rigg, 155.   [2] Rigg, 157–8.

[3] For a more critical estimate of Newman, see Lidgett's 'John Wesley and John Newman' in *God, Christ and the Church* London 1908.

'The Incarnation' and on 'The Atoning Death of God the Son' who has not gone with Newman ... up to the sources of the sermons in Athanasius, and in Basil, and in Cyril. The greatest and the most sure to be lasting of Newman's sermons are just his rich Athanasian Christology, poured into the mould of his incomparable homiletic. ...[1]

And in contrast with Pearson on the Creed, Whyte adds:

Newman delivers all his readers ever after from a cold, dry, notional, technical, catechetical mind, he so makes every article of the Creed a very fountain of life and power and beauty. He so lifts up his own superb imagination to its noblest use that he makes first himself and then makes us to see, the Divine Persons and their Divine relations and operations, as never before. Till all our Creeds and Confessions and Catechisms become clothed with a majesty, and instinct with a beauty, and welling over with personal applications and comforts, new, and unexpected, and ever abiding.[2]

But however much the Victorians rejoiced in the light, whether of reason or of faith, they were all to some degree conscious of the encircling gloom. We need always to remember the polarities of optimism and pessimism, of belief and unbelief and half belief, the corrosion of older certainties in minds like Carlyle and Froude and Ruskin, the muted trumpets of 'In Memoriam'. From some of this the nonconformist world was isolated and insulated, still to an extent a 'garden walled around', still confident in an earlier rational apologetic, of Butler and Paley. I would not exaggerate this, but I think it is true that Victorian Evangelicalism knew little of that razor edge between faith and unbelief, the long tradition of *Anfechtung* from Luther to Kierkegaard. It was natural for such to find in Newman an incomprehensible surrender of the intellect. One who in controversy and argument showed a mind so keen, sensitive beyond most, aware of the subtlest inferences – from this to the Holy Coat of Treves and the sacred House at Loreto, and to many of them, the hardly more reputable notions of Infallibility and the Mariological dogmas, this seemed indeed a surrender.

Moreover, Newman had a drastic way with half-way houses, not only in regard to the paper defences of a *Via Media*, but, as

---

[1] Whyte, 125.   [2] Whyte, 126-7.

he explicitly stated in his essay on John Keble, that the alteratives might in the end be Rome, or rationalism. If for Luther reason was the devil's whore, Frau Hulda, Newman was almost as trenchant in his description of reason as the instrument of the world, of what St Paul called the wisdom of this world.

These things explain the superficial plausibility of the charge of scepticism brought against Newman in 1885 by the Congregationalist divine, Andrew Fairbairn.[1] He was a scholar of growing distinction, at this time the Principal Designate of the new Mansfield College, Oxford, one who helped greatly in forming theological faculties in the Universities of Manchester and Wales. As a scholar, he was not to be despised. He was a considerable theologian, a Free Churchman with the blood of the Scottish Covenanters in his veins. But he was also a fine teacher, to whom many students owed their souls, and a preacher of whom some Methodist fishermen once said, 'He did talk to we like an angel'.

For him the traditional proofs of the existence of God, and notably the argument from design were of great importance, and it was particularly this proof about which Newman had reservations which he never abandoned. So that Fairbairn's mind was puzzled and affronted by the *Grammar of Assent*. In an article in the *Contemporary Review*, March 1885, he asserted that the *Grammar* 'was pervaded by the intensest philosophical scepticism'. Newman's philosophy he asserted may be described as 'empirical and sceptical, qualified by a peculiar religious experience'. 'He has a deep distrust of the intellect ... he dare not trust his own, for he does not know where it might lead him, and he will not trust any other man's.' To what he called Fairbairn's 'vehement rhetoric', Newman replied in an article in the same review in October, with politeness, if you discount the evident fact that Newman had not the slightest interest in Fairbairn or his opinions, but was only concerned with what his own friends might think. In December, Fairbairn returned to the charge that 'to conceive reason as Dr Newman does is to deny it the knowledge of God, and so to save faith by the help of a deeper unbelief'.[2]

Newman consulted his friends about writing anything further in public admitting that 'it would take a very brilliant knock down answer to Dr Fairbairn to justify my giving up my place as an "emeritus miles" and going down into the arena with a younger

[1] W. B. Selbie, *The Life of A. M. Fairbairn* London 1914, 203ff.
[2] Selbie, 203ff. Ward, *Life of Cardinal Newman* II, 505ff.

man'. What he did was to publish privately some footnotes, which appeared as the third part of *Stray Essays on Controversial Points*, short, pointed, luminous paragraphs.[1]

He had no difficulty in disposing of the charge, which in fact Dr Fairbairn had no notion of preferring, that he was a 'hidden sceptic' – 'for a long seventy years amid mental trials sharp and heavy, I can in my place and in my measure adopt the words of St Polycarp before his martyrdom'. He also made plain the sense in which he spoke of the faculty of reason, and the reason for his denunciation of it when it became what St Paul calls 'the wisdom of this world'.

It is plain that there was genuine misunderstanding. It is also, I think, plain that Newman's answer is not completely convincing. But Fairbairn's biographer, Dr Selbie, is surely right when he says that 'the two men were working on different planes and using language each in a way that was hardly intelligible to the other'.

Perhaps the best footnote is to remember that in the course of this controversy, Fairbairn paid the following tribute to his adversary:

> It costs a very peculiar kind of suffering to conduct a controversy, after his personal intervention, with the one man in all England on whose lips the words of the dying Polycarp sit with equal truth and grace. Not that Cardinal Newman has been either a hesitant or soft-speaking controversialist. He has been a man of war from his youth, who has conquered many adversaries. . . . He has, as scarcely any other teacher of our age, made us feel the meaning of life, the evil of sin, the dignity of obedience, the beauty of holiness: and his power has been due to the degree in which men have been constrained to believe that his words, where sublimest, have been but the dim and imperfect mirrors of his own exalted spirit. . . . He has greatly and variously enriched the religious life of our people and he lives in our imagination as the last at once of the Fathers and of the Saints.[2]

So far, I have spoken of nonconformists who were admirers of Newman. In Alexander Whyte, Newman had, in Kierkegaard's

[1] *Stray Essays on Controversial Points* private 1890, 69ff. I am indebted to the Rev D. Pailin for permission to read his as yet unpublished MA thesis on the *Grammar of Assent* (Manchester 1965).

[2] Selbie, 208.

phrase, a lover. Alexander Whyte (1836–1921) was one of the really great figures of the Scottish Church in the nineteenth century, and his life by G. F. Barbour, an outstanding biography, the reading of which must have been for many a theological student, as for me, a climacteric event. Whyte was born in J. M. Barrie's 'Thrums', the little Forfarshire town of Kirriemuir, a kind of Victorian Tannochbrae, but one where doctors of divinity counted for more than men of medicine and where the tensions between Drs Cameron, Finlay, and the egregious Dr Snoddy were as nothing compared with the suspicious rivalries of Auld Licht, Wee Frees, and Episcopalians. From this unpromising and unecumenical setting, Alexander Whyte went forth to become in due season Principal of New College of Edinburgh; but his real fame was as a preacher, as the famous minister of St George's, Edinburgh.

It was as a preacher that he was drawn to Newman, and as a preacher he understood him, so that his little book on Newman has insights into Newman missed by Father Bouyer. Whyte's generation did not despise its inherited Reformed Calvinism, but there was an opening up to new influences, Hegel in philosophy, and in theology the Greek Fathers. And then Whyte came from that part of north-east Scotland where in the seventh as in the seventeenth century theology and mysticism have ever blended. The lectures, which over many years he delivered to his people of Edinburgh, covered a wide range of Protestant and Catholic spirituality, Dante and Tauler being especially beloved. From unpromising beginnings Whyte grew to a true Catholicity, and thus he defined the true Catholic:

> How rich such men are . . . for all things are theirs. All men, and all books, and all churches. Whether Paul, or John, or Augustine, or Athanasius, or Dante, or Behmen, or Luther, or Calvin, or Hooker, or Taylor, or Knox, or Rutherford, or Bunyan, or Butler, or Edwards, or Chalmers, or Newman, or Spurgeon. And we have not a few of such Catholic Evangelicals in our pulpits, and among our people, in Scotland, and they are multiplying among us every day.[1]

There were three points of personal contact between Whyte and Newman. The first was the visit which, with two friends, Dr Marcus Dods and Dr Thomason, he paid to the Oratory.

[1] Whyte, 65–6.

8

'In those days of entrenched Protestantism it needed no small courage for three Free Churchmen, who were still young in the ministry, to go on a pilgrimage to the Oratory'. Shyly they entered, though they did not fail to notice the large violincello propped against the wall. 'He received us with all that captivating urbanity which has become proverbial; . . . the old saint treating us in all that with a frankness and with a confidence as if we were old friends of his, as indeed we were.'[1]

When Whyte was married in 1881, his wife gave him a portrait of Newman and wrote asking Newman for his autograph. Newman replied thanking her:

> for what you say about the interest which Dr. Whyte takes in my writings, which suggests the hope and trust that, in spite of the sad divisions of Christendom, a great work is going on in the hearts of serious men tending towards the restoration of the scattered members of Christ, even though not in our day, yet in the future, in the 'times and seasons which He has appointed'.[2]

Newman enclosed four autographs and a few days later wrote to ask whether what he had sent would do. Barbour asked 'could the fine gold of Christian courtesy be further refined than this?' Henceforth his portrait hung in a place of honour in Whyte's study, between pictures of Carlyle and Herschel (as one has hung in my own study for thirty years – between Luther and Karl Barth!).

In 1883 Whyte published a short commentary on the Catechism, and sent a copy to Newman. Newman replied courteously, but took exception to Whyte's assertion that the doctrine of transubstantiation meant that 'all communicants literally and physically eat the flesh and drink the blood of Christ'. Newman asserted that 'not the most ignorant or stupid Catholic thinks that he eats physically the body of Our Lord'. Whyte at once accepted Newman's explanation and asked him to draft a line which appeared to state the correct Catholic view, and when Newman expanded his objection in a further letter, he offered to print the letter itself in a further edition. To this last suggestion Newman demurred on the ground that 'it would be a poor return on my part to your

[1] Barbour, 194–5.
[2] Barbour, 241.

courteous treatment of me in your book, to turn your Catechism
into a controversy'.

Whyte's sentence, amended to the judgement of Newman,
appeared in the new form in the second edition. But the last word
was a letter from Newman, whose conscience had been troubled
as he had himself been disarmed, by Whyte's charitable handling,
to say that it was very likely that the framers of the Catechism
had in mind 'extreme notions of the multitude who were in many
places superstitious and sadly in want of instruction'.[1]

Here in 1884 is the very spirit of *De Ecumenismo* and a reminder that we who like to think of ourselves as the pioneers of
ecumenicity are in fact the epigoni of men like Lidgett and Alexander Whyte.

Whyte had read every printed syllable of Newman's writings.
He had, for example, read and reread all the *Tracts for the Times*.
He spoke with approval of an old Scottish carpenter who was
wont, as a devotional exercise, simply to read through the titles
of the *Parochial and Plain Sermons*, and he himself wrote to a
young student:

> Take a volume of first-rate sermons – Newman, or Robertson,
> or Parker, or Spurgeon etc. – and enter the texts of a whole
> volume.[2]

To another he wrote:

> I am better pleased with your teaching than with your style.
> You should re-write this discourse, and ask as you write – would
> Newman have used this and that expression in a sermon?[3]

In his seventieth year he wrote to one of his children:

> I wrote my last forenoon sermon three times over. And that is
> the only thing in which I resemble Newman. He wrote *all* his
> sermons as often as I wrote mine last week.[4]

But it was not just as a craftsman that he was drawn to Newman
as a master. It was, says Barbour:

> Newman's constant and all-pervading conviction of the presence
> of God in the life of man, his awed sense of the insignificance

---

[1] Barbour, 241ff.
[2] Barbour, 290.
[3] Barbour, 294.
[4] Barbour, 295.

of all earthly interests in comparison with the moral and religious issues which reach out into eternity: his delicate but
searching analysis of the hidden processes of good and evil in
the heart, his reverence of spirit and the quiet perfection of his
English style[1]

which effected an effortless mastery over an ear and conscience so
sensitively attuned as those of Alexander Whyte.

Whyte's criticisms of Newman are trenchant, and were only
published after Newman's death, but they are to be taken seriously
against the background of his admiration and his love. His criticism of the sermons is that they are under the Law.

> Looked at as pure literature, Newman's St. Mary's sermons
> are not far from absolute perfection; but looked at as pulpit
> works, as preaching the Gospel, they are full of the most serious,
> and even fatal, defects. With all their genius they are not pro-
> perly speaking New Testament preaching at all.... As an
> analysis of the heart of man, and as a penetrating criticism of
> human life, their equal is nowhere to be found. But ... they
> lack the one all-essential element of true preaching, the message
> to sinful man concerning the free grace of God.
>
> That message was the one thing that differentiated the
> Apostle's preaching from all the other so-called preaching of his
> day. And that one thing which has been the touchstone of all
> true preaching ever since the Apostle's day, and will be to the
> end of the world, that is all but totally lacking in Newman's
> sermons.[2]

> Moses was never dressed up in such ornaments before....
> The old lawgiver would not know himself, he is so beautified
> and bedecked by Newman's style. But, all the time, he is
> Moses. All the time, with all his ornaments, he still carries his
> whip of scorpions hidden away among his beautiful garments.
> Do and live! Disobey and die! and he draws his sword on me
> as he says it.

> I have given not a few of Newman's books to young men in
> other circumstances and at other stages ... but never one of his
> beautiful books to a broken-hearted and inconsolable sinner. I
> have often given to men in dead earnest, books of the heart and

---

[1] Barbour, 194.
[2] Whyte, 90f.

soul that Newman and his Tractarian school would scowl to name.[1]

And Whyte gives a list of Puritan and Evangelical classics of devotion from Bunyan down to Spurgeon and Ryle. And he goes on to say that, while he has often and gladly recommended Newman's writings, he could never recommend either his *Lectures on Justification* or the *Sermons* to a penitent whose sins had found him out.

Newman was the Rembrandt of a Tractarian school at the heart of which was theological chiaroscuro. The darkness was Protestantism, the errors of the Reformers, and to compare Newman with John Adam Möhler is to feel that Anglo-Catholic polemic had, in this regard, obtusenesses and blind spots and rigidities beyond those of the Church of Rome. Whyte, with his love of Puritan and Protestant divinity, could not but be constantly wounded by Newman's deadly ironies and his occasional devastating contempt. Recalling how, in 1843, Newman had issued a formal retractation of all the hard things which he had said against the Church of Rome, he wished that in 1890 Newman had retracted all his 'slings and scoffs . . . at men whose shoe lachet he should have said he was not worthy to unloose . . . such men of God as Luther and Calvin and the Anglican Reformers, as well as Bunyan and Newton and Wesley, men to whom their Master will yet say, "Well done, good and faithful servant" and that, too, in Newman's hearing'.[2] Well, it is blessedly true that:

> And sometimes even beneath the moon,
> The Saviour gives a gracious boon,
> When reconciled Christians meet[3]

But Whyte perhaps asked too much of the nineteenth-century sublunary pieties. We remember how in Dante's *Paradiso* those who were unreconciled, theological enemies on earth go out of their way to do honour to their former adversaries. And if, in the light of glory, St Thomas can lead forward Siger of Brabant, then we may expect Newman in the forefront of such heavenly ecumenicities.

That, in my study, Newman's portrait should rest between those

[1] Whyte, 97–8.
[2] Whyte, 66–7.
[3] John Keble quoted by Alexander Whyte, 31.

of Luther and Karl Barth may seem offensive to pious eyes, I know. My own copy of the *Lectures of Justification* I have underscored and annotated on every page and almost every paragraph, and question and exclamation marks abound. But the testimonies I have brought forward point to a common Christian core, that fundamental unity in Christ which is the starting point rather than the goal of the search for visible unity.

Then there is the well known fact of the deep continuities in the religion of Newman himself, from his Evangelical upbringing through his Anglican ministry to the Church of Rome. To the end of his life he continued to republish those Oxford sermons; so little did he need to repudiate, so that the recent Catholic anthology *The Heart of Newman* draws its most splendid passages from this pre-Roman source. Let us forget for a moment the polemic and ponder one or two remarkable similarities.

Here is a University movement; its core a group of younger scholars and teachers. It is involved in a crisis in which a whole contemporary culture is concerned, so that it is at once a protest against the present, and a bid for the allegiance of a coming age. At its nerve centre is one man, head and shoulders above his fellows, a man, like Shaw's St. Joan, in love with religion, over whose life might be inscribed the text, 'The zeal of thine house has eaten me up'. It is he who pens one after another their manifestoes, and upon whose head the disapproval of authority descends. And this, unlooked for; for he is the most unwilling, the most obedient of rebels, and in his protest had hoped for and looked for the support of his ecclesiastical superiors. But one by one they fail, until at last, disowned and discredited by those leaders from whom he hoped so much – he takes the final, fatal step of rebellion: he steps outside his Church.

Every word of that paragraph applied equally to Martin Luther and to John Henry Newman, and I would there were time to bring dozens of citations from the writings of both men during the critical, fateful months of their development, to show the rapidity of their mental growth, their anguished hypersensitivity and sometimes perhaps a theological arrogance, the more terrible because so impersonal, so free from pride and personal vanity, to demonstrate all the intricate similarities between the utterances of the one between 1517 and 1521 and the other between 1841 and 1845. Both men stand for the opposite of what is now called 'religionless Christianity' as reminders that, despite all the gravity of divine judgement, God never disavows His People, that for their renewal he ever sends His champions, and that they are almost without exception those to whom He has given the terrible and beautiful calling of being religious men, ecclesiastics, and theologians.

Luther and Newman were preachers, of each of whom it could be said that the pulpit was their throne, the secret of their ascendancy over the minds of men, and their writings but powerful extensions of their sermons. Of both it might be said, as Karl Holl said about Luther, that theirs was above all a religion of conscience.

Who between Luther and Newman, and apart from them, could ground the Priesthood of Believers here and not in ecclesiology:

> Conscience [said Newman] is the aboriginal Vicar of Christ, a prophet in its informations, a monarch in its peremptories, a priest in its blessings and anathemas: and even though the eternal priesthood throughout the Church should cease to be, in it the sacerdotal principle would remain and would have a sway.[1]

Both mastered words to the point of genius and did so because both were poets, and indeed musicians. Both were great polemic divines, writing as occasion moved them, so that Whyte speaks for Luther as well as Newman when he comments on the way in which:

> his passions largely decide and fix his standing-ground for the time; and then how his imagination, ... and his argumentative talents – all come in to fortify, and to defend and to make warlike and aggressive every present position of his.[2]

Poor Kingsley! Poor Erasmus!

And then, Luther was a much gentler person than most people dream, or than you would gather from his polemic, and I think there may be this speck of truth in what Rigg's essay says about Newman having a feminine mind though, if so, it is also true of Luther, that both think with their imaginations, and teem with beautiful and profound intuitions, and it is these, rather than

[1] J. H. Newman, *Letter to the Duke of Norfolk*, 164.
[2] Whyte, 118.

their logic, which hold us – seven times out of ten wonderfully right – and then in the next breath utterly and disastrously wrong with the other three (a quality of our late and beloved Gregory Dix).

Nineteenth-century Evangelicalism was further from Calvin than it knew, and its Calvin something infected by its passage from the age of William Perkins through the eighteenth-century Evangelical tradition – as any comparison between Karl Barth and modern Evangelicalism reveals.

But it is Calvin's lucid clarities in French and Latin which come nearer to Newman than Luther, and both share, perhaps even one inherited from another, two fundamentals of their theology. You remember Newman's famous statement of how in his youth his mind came to rest in:

> the thought of two, and two only, supremely and luminously self evident beings, myself and my Creator –[1]

so close to the magnificent opening of Calvin's masterpiece:

> The whole sum in a manner of all our wisdom, which only ought to be accounted true and perfect wisdom consisteth in two parts, that is to say, the knowledge of God and of our-selves.[2]

And the hall mark of both great divines is their reverence for God:

> If we begin to raise up our thoughts unto God, and to weigh what a one He is, and how exact is His righteousness and power, after the rule of which we ought to be framed....[3]

How like the passage in the Grammar of Assent where Newman also bids us:

> Contemplate the God of our conscience as a Living Being, as one object and reality ... we must patiently rest in the thought of the Eternal Omnipresent and all knowing....[4]

And perhaps Newman's youthful conversion was nearer to Calvin than that of the Evangelicals, like John Wesley.

I may not stay to draw parallels, which you might think even

[1] *Apologia* 1881, 4.
[2] J. Calvin, *The Institution of the Christian Religion* (Thos. Norton's translation), Bk. 1, ch. 1.
[3] Calvin, *Institution*, Bk. 1.
[4] *Grammar of Assent*. See 'The Heart of Newman', 1963, 11.

more forced and outrageous between Newman and Zwingli – for there is a most interesting point at which Zwingli's hymn, 'The Plague' written during an almost fatal illness recalls Newman's 'Lead, Kindly Light' – both coming through to a trust in Providence: Zwingli's 'Lord I am thy vessel – make me or break me – ' and 'So long thy power hath blessed me....' And then John Wesley – though it might seem that all they had in common was that both were divines and Oxford dons – there might be some virtue in that 'all', beside the interesting junction which puts Alexander Knox halfway between them both, for both were theologically linked with the Father of Irish Ecumenicity.

I myself would distinguish rather sharply between the doctrines of the Reformers and what nineteenth-century Protestants conceived to be the Principles of the Reformation. But when modern German and French Catholic scholars stress the individualism of Newman, they have in mind surely such passages as this in which Newman puts what many Protestants conceive to be the real meaning of the Priesthood of all Believers, the fact that none may stand between the soul and God:

> This I know full well, that the Catholic Church allows no image of any sort, material or immaterial, no dogmatic symbol, no rite, no sacrament, no saint, not even the Blessed Virgin herself, to come between the soul and its Creator. It is face to face, 'solus cum solo', in all matters between man and his God.[1]

In a well-known essay, G. K. Chesterton contrasted Bunyan's *Pilgrim's Progress* with *Canterbury Tales*, and criticised the loneliness of Pilgrim's way with the happy band of Canterbury Pilgrims. But the real comparison is between *Pilgrim's Progress* and the 'Dream of Gerontius', and the shuddering loneliness of Newman, which I am bound to say recalls for me the criticism of Alexander Whyte of Newman's sermons, at least at the point of death, when the encircling gloom is almost overpowering, and where the 'Dies Irae' prevails over *tantus labor non sit cassus*. I am not forgetting 'Praise to the Holiest' either, but I wonder whether it isn't Elgar in the end who saves the Christian balance? And then Newman's defence of Private Judgement – not in his polemical essay on the subject, but in places in the *Apologia* where he asserts there is an awful never-dying duel in the Church between Authority and Private Judgement – 'alternately advancing

[1] *Apologia* 1881, 195

and retreating as the ebb and flow of the tide' – which if it irre-
sistibly recalls the Mock Turtle and the Gryphon in *Alice* – 'will
you, won't you, will you, won't you' – defends perhaps all that
Protestants ought ever to have defended, apart from the grave
questions of religious liberty and the duty to obey one's conscience.

I hope these are not forced parallels, a magnification of accidental resemblances. They seem to me some of the evidence for an
ecumenical norm, a core of unity, stemming from our unity in
baptism, from which in our time a dialogue might well begin.
For there are these deep continuities in Newman himself, and
they are not simply that, in spite of all temptations to belong to
other nations, and perhaps Eye-talian – above all Eye-talian, he
remained an Englishman. On the Continent let Hans Küng talk
it out with Karl Barth, but in England let us begin with Newman
and not the Bishop of Woolwich. Begin with the *Lectures on the
Prophetical Office of the Church*, and go on to the *Development*
and the *Reply* to Pusey.

There is a story; it may be apocryphal, but it was told me by the
grandson of one of the two concerned. Some time in the 1880s,
two men sat side by side on a park bench in Birmingham. One
was an old Methodist minister, a supernumerary, the other
Cardinal Newman. They talked about the Church, and Newman
took an umbrella and drew a circle in the dust. 'I think', he said,
'it is important to get the circumference right.' 'Ah', said the
Methodist, taking the umbrella and poking a hole in the centre
of the circle, 'we think that all that matters is the centre. Get that
right and the circumference will come right too.' Well, in these
days we must begin with the centre, with the Living Word of
God from whom the Church is born. But the circumference
matters too. *Securus judicat orbis terrarum*. And it is He, the
Saviour of Mankind, who sits on the circumference of the earth,
with all mankind compassed within the orbit of redeeming love.

Like the other Protestant observers at the Vatican, I as less than
the least, gratefully marvelled at the place of honour, where we
sat, but most appropriately of all, as it seemed to me, that we sat
where day after day we could not but stare and ponder at one text
of the many inscribed in gold high up in the nave – for I think it
may be the key text for our ecumenical dialogue, heart searching
but inspiring in promise, glossing our thought of *aggiornamento*
with the thought of *Ecclesia semper reformanda* – 'When thou
art converted, strengthen thy brethren'.

Note on the Free Church attitude to Newman

H. Cunliffe-Jones

I want to add this further word on the Free Church attitude to Newman. I was brought up in colleges in the A. M. Fairbairn tradition, and I am not conscious that it is from this tradition that I have gained my present appreciation of Newman as a great Catholic theologian, who has brought not only deepening, enrichment and transformation to his own Roman Catholic Church, but also is a great teacher for every Christian communion.

Though I owe a widening of my outlook to my own Principal, Dr Nathaniel Micklem, I am not conscious that to him I owe my approach to Newman; I would ascribe it rather to Father Martin D'Arcy's introducing me through his *The Nature of Belief*, when he was Master of Campion Hall, Oxford, to Newman's *Grammar of Assent*: to Dr Alexander Whyte's Catholicity of spirituality: and to my own delighted appraisal of Newman at first hand.

In saying that he is for me a great Catholic theologian, I am not wanting in the least to deny that he carried into the Church for which he was destined not only his own genius, but that Evangelical experience which was the foundation of his own spirituality, and also his long wrestle with the possible true Catholicity of the Church of England, and all he learnt from his friends there – not repudiating the past but only coming to change the previous anti-Roman element into a positive pro-Romanism. But it is out of his final destiny, which brought peace to his troubled, questing mind, whatever his discomforts with the ecclesiastical institution, that he speaks to the world.

In the nineteenth century, and partly still in the twentieth,

Newman was understood as the chief architect of the Oxford Movement, who so unfortunately and so mistakenly left it. There was little attempt to appraise the work of his whole life.

A. M. Fairbairn, as Professor Rupp has reminded us, criticised Newman for the 'scepticism' of his thought. The criticism for what it is worth is quite true; but the question at issue is whether this 'scepticism' is not the surest foundation for Christian thought. Newman was not sceptical in the sense of being an unbeliever; but like other great theologians – Karl Barth is a twentieth-century illustration – he was sceptical of the pretensions of reason in relation to the truth of God. Reason, he thought, functioned truly when, at the apex of its thinking, it accepted with gratitude God's revelation as a gift from God which it was not competent to judge, but only to start from as the basis of confidence. Fairbairn's ebullient unrestricted Hegelian confidence in reason hardly wins an enthusiastic loyalty from the twentieth-century Free Churchman: by comparison Newman's 'scepticism' is at least much nearer the truth.

The main obstacles which prevented nineteenth-century Free Churchmen from making a fair appraisal of Newman seem to me to be three. First, they said in effect: Here is a man who dismisses summarily, and apparently with contempt, those who to us are our great spiritual guides. This seems such a shocking misjudgement that we can have little confidence that he has anything of any importance to say to us. The fact that Newman had never encountered those spiritual guides at first hand was apparently hidden from them; and also the fact that some of his searching analyses of the defects of popular Protestantism might help Protestantism to recover from some of the unworthy habits of thought and action into which it had fallen. But there is no doubt that his dismissal of Protestantism was a very great barrier to their learning from him.

Then, too, the 'no-popery' atmosphere of the century, from which Newman himself extricated his own thinking and feeling with difficulty and which had a field day at the time of the Vatican Council of 1870, expressed itself intellectually in a profound hostility to the conception of 'infallibility'. Newman had come to accept the infallibility of the Church: for them this was treason to the thinking mind. This was an effective barrier to exploring the riches of his thought which he poured out from within the support of this dogma, whether true or false, and dis-

covering and appropriating much insight into the factors affect-
ing belief and the witness of Christian laymen. Today we ought
to recognise that all Christian believers are committed to some
belief in infallibility and explore together the different, if overlapping places, where we find it.

The third obstacle was his book on *Development*. Professor
Owen Chadwick in his book *From Bossuet to Newman* has shown
how little Catholic theology was willing to recognise the fact of
development; Protestant theology was similarly inhibited.
Ex hypothesi, a Protestant ascribed no value to tradition not even
to his own. He might in fact, but at least he kept his theory pure.
The method of combating the enemy which nineteenth-century
Free Churchmen took was to concentrate on the details of Newman's theory, and hide from themselves the broader issue on
which Newman has been the great teacher of Catholic and
Protestant alike. But things have changed. I myself have been a
member of a Congregationalist commission, in which for the
first time in a Declaration of Faith we have openly acknowledged
our indebtedness to tradition in the Church. This, I believe, is
due to the slow influence of Newman.

Newman's services to the Oxford Movement must always be
recognised, and also its formative influence upon his thinking.
But the characteristic Anglican representatives of the Oxford
Movement are, undoubtedly, Keble and Pusey. Newman found
his true home in the Roman Catholic Church. In his life as a
whole, he emerges not only as a great teacher of that Church,
but also as a great teacher of all twentieth-century Christians.

4
Newman's influence in England

H. Francis Davis

It would be gratifying to be able to say that Newman has had an influence on the course and character of British theology. Yet it would be unrealistic to see this influence in any province but that of a certain dated Church of England ecclesiology. Clearly his Anglican defence of the Oxford Movement, and his theory of Anglo-Catholicism did have a great influence in his time, and during the following half-century. Probably one could say that that influence has never died out. Perhaps even modern Anglo-Catholicism continues to owe a great deal to Newman's ecclesiology before 1840. But, beyond this, it would be unrealistic to say that he has ever yet been an important influence in dogmatic theology, especially in our universities. Of course, there is a sphere, that of the philosophy of education, where his influence in both England and Ireland, as well as in all English-speaking countries has been immense. It goes without saying that he has always had, and will always have, a place in English literature. His theory of informal reasoning is known and examined in schools of philosophy and psychology. Finally, his part in the Church history of the nineteenth century has been studied exhaustively.

During the nineteenth century, there was of course much polemical theology centred round his name. Immediately after his conversion, his *Essay on the Development of Christian Doctrine* provoked many replies of a polemical nature. Later, at the time of the modernist crisis, the name of Newman was quoted with approval here as in France by both Catholic and Protestant modernists, who hoped they could be justified in quoting his views of doctrinal development in support of their own evolutionary understanding of Christianity. George Tyrrell certainly saw Newman as a forerunner of his own particular views; and Tyrrell was not the only one to maintain that, when modernism was condemned, Newman was condemned with it.

In all these polemics, Newman had his apologists. Bishop Dwyer of Limerick defended him against the modernist attack. From the time of Bishop Dwyer's defence and the translation of the German Jesuit Father Przywara's great work[1], Newman came for a period to be looked upon as virtually a traditional – almost scholastic – theologian, who mediated in a more vague, less exact, but far more attractive idiom what had been put so much more clearly by St Thomas.

But Newman remained hardly noticed in the theology departments of our universities. As the century has proceeded, Newman is still studied almost exclusively as one of the great figures in nineteenth-century British religious history. It would not, however, be true to say that the English universities are unaware of his growing reputation on the continent and in America in the fields of theology and philosophy of religion. More and more he is being accepted in England as a fit subject for research degrees. Lately I have heard of one British university that wishes to introduce a course on Newman as a philosopher of religion.

One factor accounting for the lack of Newman study and research in the field of dogmatic theology has been a fairly widespread neglect of such theology altogether. English university tradition has not encouraged this study. It is indeed studied almost exclusively in theological colleges distinctive of certain definite theological traditions. We are indeed still widely under the influence of nineteenth-century denominationalism, which could only think of doctrine in terms of the special theories characteristic of someone's particular churchmanship. The Scriptures have usually succeeded in being regarded as exact studies worthy of university standing, while dogmatics would come under the classification of Church history.

As a result of this, while there have been certain important monographs on biblical theology, there has been on the whole a certain poverty in the field of doctrinal study and research. There are signs that this may be changing, owing perhaps chiefly to the growing interest in modern continental and American dogmatic

---

[1] E. Przywara, *A Newman Synthesis* 1930. See E. Przywara, *Christentum: ein Aufbau*, vol. 4.

theology. Up to date, this interest has been largely centred on a special group of theologians, whose work was first widely popularised by Bishop Robinson. The success of this new school appears to be due in no small measure to the poverty of any general deep or scientific understanding of dogmatic theology in our educated public. As Mr Coulson has reminded us, Newman in his Introduction to the Catholic edition of the *Via Media*, speaks of theology as 'the fundamental and regulating principle of the whole Church system'.[1] If this is true, it is understandable that a neglect in the field of theology will weaken the whole Church system, and leave it open to attacks from without or within.

In view of the fact, as stated above, that Newman has been up to now neglected in the study of dogmatic theology in England, and especially in our British universities, it seems that it might be more fruitful to use the opportunity given by this paper to look forward to the future. I would like to consider one field in which Newman might have some special value in our British university theological studies in our own time. At the moment there is a wave of theological secularism which threatens to undermine confidence in traditional theology. This phenomenon is not really so new in the British scene as our contemporaries are apt to think. It existed in Newman's day. He himself prophesied that it would grow in strength, and in its challenge to Christian theology.[2] The study of Newman is valuable in this context both as a direct antidote, and as supplying a life to the ancient teachings, which alone will give them strength to resist the present tide of doctrinal liberalism. With regard to the latter point, Father Stephen Dessain has already shown us the possibilities of Newman's living and dynamic scriptural theology.[3] It is, however, chiefly the former matter – Newman's anticipated answer to the secular challenge – that I would like to treat here.

The new secular theology, as popularised in England, starts out from the point of view of linguistic analysis. The beginnings of the English modern preoccupation with this approach seems to be the movement mainly associated with Professor Ayer's book on *Language, Truth and Logic*, published for the first time some

---

[1] Coulson, 'Newman on the Church – his final view, its origin and influence', p. 135 above.

[2] C. S. Dessain (ed.), The Catholic Sermons of Cardinal Newman, German 9, 'The Infidelity of the Future', 117–33.

[3] Dessain, 'The biblical basis of Newman's ecumenical theology'.

thirty years ago, and reprinted some fourteen or more times since. It was a book written with some passion, indeed Professor Ayer today is much more moderate in his attitude. But, as is so often the case with epoch-making books, people are influenced far more by the original eloquence and passion than by the later modifications. In another sphere, it could be said that Karl Barth's *Commentary on the Romans* still exercises an immense influence, while Barth himself in his later books speaks with a moderation that a reader of the original book would hardly have thought possible. The case is similar with *Language, Truth and Logic*. Distinctive of this book was the contention that the word 'God' and other theological terms were meaningless to modern man, since they corresponded to nothing in human experience, and were unverifiable by scientific observation.[1]

The logic of the linguistic analysis shook the faith of many undergraduates of our universities on its first appearance. It created a soil well prepared, through its general distrust of traditional theology, for the German demythologisers, and the secular theologies of Bonhoeffer, Tillich, and Van Buren. These theologians, as is well known from their published sermons, were men of deep religious feeling, who gave promise of supplying an explanation of, and a justification for the claims of, religious experience, without the need for answering the rationalist attacks on dogmatic theology. This new outlook has been popularised in English by Bishop Robinson, whose works have had a wide influence through translations into many of the world languages, including even Italian. Where the original attack of Ayer and Flew had excluded all theology as meaningless to modern man, the new theologians, while denying, or by-passing completely all forms of transcendence, have brought back theology under the qualification of 'secular', a theology on principle confined to the world that is empirically knowable. The new theology in this way meets the objections of the linguistic philosophers. Some of these redefine 'God' as the depth of reality in this world, man's ultimate

---

[1] In a broadcast talk (*The Listener*, 4 November 1965) Professor Ayer has said: 'I am still working on the epistemological problems which I thought I should solve so easily thirty years ago'; but he goes on to claim that in one respect he is unrepentant; although the achievements of the movement 'were mainly negative', 'the dust we swept away will not easily settle again'. And it is this change from asserting *positively* that theological assertions are meaningless to *negatively* asserting the objections which they must be shown to take into account which is already beginning to liberate much philosophical discussion of religion. (Ed.)

concern in this world. Others go so far as to exclude even the word 'God' from their 'theology'. It follows, therefore, that the Incarnation, Resurrection, or the Trinity, for example, cannot be understood or entertained in their traditional sense.

Professor Mascall has perhaps given us the most comprehensive and well-reasoned reply to the chief of these theologians. Many theologians, on the other hand, have shrugged their shoulders and continued as before on the ground that this new challenge will pass by, widely ineffective, when the novelty has worn off. Alternatively, they have hoped that the very absurdity and emptiness of a theology without God will turn out to be its own refutation. However, since a careful reading of Newman shows us that the new secularism is new only in name, existed in the last century, and will probably return under a different name in the next, it may be valuable to study the lines on which Newman might have dealt with it. When Newman was dealing with the forerunner of this modern theology, he saw that its success depended on psychological arguments even more than on pure reason. He saw three aspects in the last century which contributed to its success, which certainly are still operative.

The first psychological motive for a new theology was then, as it doubtless is still, that traditional theology deals with the unattainable and irrelevant. The second psychological motive was, and we find this still operative, that the realisation of this fact brings a sense of liberation and enrichment. The third motive is that a new theology is required for this present age of man's maturity. Those who cling to the traditional theology – like those who believe in Father Christmas – have failed to keep pace spiritually with their maturity in other sciences.

With regard to the first point, that theology deals with the unattainable or irrelevant, because it is divorced from human experience, an immediate reaction on our part would be to ask how far the modern movement for *ressourcement* in Catholic theology springs from a conscious or semi-conscious desire to rebut this charge. For this latter theology acts consciously on the assumption that theology, like natural science, has its genuine sources of religious knowledge; and (b) that it is a fully scientific and mature study of these sources, worthy of cultured man; and (c) that it can bring its own sense of expansion and enrichment.

To return to Newman, it might be interesting to take the last point first. Newman, in his customary breadth of view and sense of fairness, is the first to admit that not only Christianity, but often enough the attacks on Christianity, can bring with them a sense of enrichment and expansion. It is well known how strongly influenced Newman confesses he had been at the age of fifteen by the writings of Voltaire. We know how strongly impressed he was by the historian Gibbon; and Huxley recognised Newman's great ability to think himself into the mind of the unbelievers. In a sermon preached in St Mary's pulpit, Oxford, Newman expands on the psychological fact that any great opening out of human experience, any deep exercise of the human mind or carefully planned achievement of research brings with it a certain sense of enlargement.

> When a person [Newman said] for the first time hears the arguments and speculations of unbelievers, and feels what a very novel light they cast upon what he has hitherto accounted most sacred, it cannot be denied that, unless he is shocked and closes his ears and heart to them, he will have a sense of expansion and elevation.[1]

This, he continues, is especially the case when a person will often have a vivid sense of enlargement, and will feel they have gained something, as becoming aware of doctrines, opinions, trains of thought, principles, aims to which hitherto they have been strangers.[2] Not only can it happen through any university course of studies, Newman added, but also through travel, and even through a person's first introduction into the world of sin. Indeed any deepening and heightening of human experience will give a sense of liberation, if only because of the sense of truth attained and possessed it brings with it.

Hence one of the reasons why Newman vindicated the claims of the non-professional theologian to study theology was in order to enable him to gain that far more authentic enrichment that can only come from a deeper understanding and experience of the living Word of God.

> It is often remarked [Newman preached at Whitsun, 1841] of uneducated persons, who hitherto have lived without seriousness, that on their turning to God, looking into themselves, regulating their conduct, and studying the inspired Word, they

[1] *University Sermons*, 284.
[2] *University Sermons*, 285.

seem to become, in point of intellect, different beings from what they were before. Before, they took things as they came, and thought no more of one thing than of another. But now every event has a meaning; they form their own estimate of whatever occurs; they recollect times and seasons; and the world, instead of being like the stream which the countrymen gazed on, ever in motion and never in progress, is a various and complicated drama, with parts and with an object.[1]

About the accusation of immaturity, we are tempted to smile at the suggestion that our twenty centuries of Christian learning, filling the shelves of our ancient libraries, are but the fairy tales of mankind's childhood. However, Newman recognised in it some plausibility. Supposing those ancient libraries were filled with ancient works of natural science, there is a sense in which we might be forgiven for regarding them as immature compared with a modern Harvard or Heidelberg or Oxbridge. In science, at least, as Newman said, 'we begin where they ended; thus things progress, and each successive age knows more than the preceding'.[2] But can we honestly say that this is true of religion? In this field, on the contrary, said Newman, 'each must begin, go on, and end, for himself'. With perhaps some rhetorical exaggeration, he added:

> The religious history of each individual is as solitary and complete as the history of the world.[3]

Of course, considered as a body of learning, theology is like natural science and history, and we begin where our predecessors ended. We today have the advantage of all the learning of a St Thomas, a Newman, and of all the scholars of every age. But in the matter of theological wisdom and faith and real knowledge of God, do we not always begin as children, and can we say today we are wiser than St Thomas because we are born later in history? There is, indeed, one passage in Newman, where he seems to suggest probably ironically, a golden age of the future when mankind might reach spiritual maturity. He writes:

> When children cease to be born children, because they are born late in the world's history, when we can reckon the world's past

[1] *University Sermons*, 285.
[2] *Parochial and Plain Sermons* VII, 248.
[3] *Parochial and Plain Sermons* VII, 248.

centuries for the age of this generation, then only can the world increase in real excellence and truth as it grows older.[1]

But, if such an age will ever come, it will not come as the new theology would have it, by overthrowing its past, but by growing up in it to an adulthood where it will still be true that the child is the father of the man.

However, the most serious of the three reasons for overthrowing traditional theology is that it consumes people's valuable lives in the study of what we know to be meaningless. Newman thus enunciated the objection of the predecessors in 1850 of our logical analysts in 1950.

> Christianity [he quotes them as then saying] has been the bane of true knowledge, for it has turned the intellect away from what it can know, and occupied it with what it cannot. Differences of opinion crop up and multiply themselves, in proportion to the difficulty of deciding them; and the unfruitfulness of theology has been, in matter of fact, the very reason, not for seeking better food, but for feeding on nothing else. Truth has been sought in the wrong direction, and the attainable has been put aside for the visionary.[2]

The hope of this 1850 school of rationalists was to discredit theology, 'not by shutting its schools, but by emptying them; not by disputing its tenets, but by the superior worth and persuasiveness of their own'.[3] They relied on the immense counter-attraction of the physical sciences; the strong effect of these sciences on man's imagination, and the absorbing interest attached to these subjects from their marvellous results. For, they were convinced,

> Sciences which deal with tangible facts, practical results, ever growing discoveries, and perpetual novelties, which feed curiosity, sustain attention, and stimulate expectation, require, they consider, but a fair stage and no favour to distance that Ancient Truth, which never changes and but cautiously advances, in the race for popularity and power.[4]

Newman saw the seriousness of the challenge as much as Bishop Robinson sees it today. '*Supposing*, indeed,' said Newman, 're-

---

[1] *Parochial and Plain Sermons* VII, 248.
[2] J. H. Newman, *Idea of a University* London 1925, 389.
[3] *Idea of a University*, 403.
[4] *Idea of a University*, 403.

ligious truth cannot be ascertained, *then*, of course, it is not only idle, but mischievous, to attempt to do so; *then*, of course, arguments do but increase the mistake of attempting it.'[1] In other words, arguments from our sources will not help if our sources are not reliable, and give no real knowledge.

Newman's first answer to the nineteenth-century attack on theology was to point to the great volume of Catholic and Protestant theological literature, and say that, if this new school denied its claim to have attained to any truth about God, the *onus probandi* 'plainly lies with those who are introducing into the world what the whole world feels to be a paradox'.[2]

But this was not the whole of Newman's answer. All his life he had been defending, and to the end he would defend the claim of Christianity and its theology to possess an authentic source of religious truth, as authentic as that of the sciences. One objection of the unbeliever was and is that, while everyone accepts the evidence of the senses, not everyone accepts our witnesses to God and Christianity. There is nothing new in this objection. It was well known from the earliest time that God spoke through the prophets. The blessedness of those who believe, but have not seen, is never as universal as the confidence of sight. Walking by faith has always been a virtue leading into a realm of truth closed to those who have no other capacity than to walk by sight, but still a grace and not everyone had the grace to accept it. It was not only in the province of faith, but in many others, where human freedom and creativity enter into the search, that men can rise above the limits of the five senses. We have no right, said Newman, to take the universal reception of a source of truth as a criterion of its authenticity.

This is perhaps the point where we might introduce ourselves to Newman's positive account of the sources of religious knowledge. It should first be emphasised that Newman never wavered in his conviction that our sources of religious knowledge are both nature and revelation. He would not, therefore, accept the taunt that traditional theology is concerned with the so-called 'sacred' to the neglect of the 'secular'. For Newman both nature and revelation were sacred; and the theology which has both as its sources has both as its field of application.

The statement just made sounds as though Newman were to be

[1] *Idea of a University*, 390.
[2] *Idea of a University*, 390.

classified with traditional Catholic theology in making philosophy the handmaid of theology. But this would be to misunderstand the originality of Newman's approach. Nature, in this context, refers pre-eminently to human nature, to the human mind and heart and conscience, and only in a very secondary sense to inanimate nature. Further, he rarely uses the word "nature" in its abstract sense as excluding divine helps. He speaks of nature in the concrete. In speaking of nature as our first source of religious knowledge he writes:

> How far this initial religious knowledge comes from without, and how far from within, how much is natural, how much implies a special divine aid which is above nature, we have no means of determining, nor is it necessary for my present purpose to determine.[1]

Nature, I said, refers to the human mind. Newman does indeed admit two other approaches to God (1) from cosmology (2) from the common opinion of mankind. But he could not convince himself that the cosmological arguments actually and psychologically led people to a knowledge of God. Convincing to the believer, they would normally not occur to the unbeliever. When brought to the latter's notice, they often failed to convince, because impersonal. The truth is that the system of nature is just as much connected with religion where minds are not religious, as a watch or a steam-carriage. Physical philosophers are ever inquiring whence things are, not *why*; referring them to nature, not to mind, and thus they tend to make a system a substitute for a God.

However, every man is led to a knowledge of God in his own heart from early childhood through his conscience. If you ask for a proof that this is so, Newman answered that we might as well ask for a proof that other men have reason or a memory of a sense of the beautiful. Some things have to be assumed, as a basis to further reasoning. This is fundamental to our nature. Incidentally, Newman is careful to point out that he does not understand conscience here in its secondary sense as equivalent to the moral sense or judgement of what is right and what is wrong. He uses it in its deepest sense of a sanction, a dictate, a conviction that we must do what we think right and must avoid what we believe to be

---

[1] *Grammar of Assent*, 115. Newman does not really enter into the Baian controversy, for which see *Emares du Baly*, 1595; Denzinger, *Enchiridion Symbolorum*, nn. 1005ff.

wrong. He believes that this dictate is always associated with emotion, because it always is conscious of a relation to a person external to itself. Where the sense of the beautiful is normally related to *things*, whether they are beautiful or ugly, the conscience is related to *personal actions* whether they are approvable to an external person or blameworthy. Hence it gives us an indirect awareness or knowledge of a Person, absolutely wise and good, who sees our actions. It is interesting to note that this aspect of conscience has been pointed out, apparently quite independently, by the English philosopher, A. E. Taylor.[1]

Newman, as stated above, never wavered in his assertion that this was a fact of human experience.

> That such a spontaneous reception of religious truths is common with children, I shall take for granted, till I am convinced that I am wrong in so doing. The child keenly understands that there is a difference between right and wrong; and when he has done what he believes to be wrong, he is conscious that he is offending One to whom he is amenable, whom he does not see, who sees him. His mind reaches forward with a strong presentiment to the thought of a Moral Governor, sovereign over him, mindful and just. It comes to him like an impulse of nature to entertain it.[2]

If it is fideism to accept this, it is fideism, Newman would say, to accept other people's memory, reasoning, imagination, or sense of beauty.

Newman is not claiming that we have an intuition or direct vision of God. On the contrary we still have to reach forward with our mind to recognise the source of this voice in our heart. He makes Callista, the pagan in his novel of early Christianity, say to her pagan lover:

> You may tell me this dictate is a mere law of my nature, as it is to joy or to grieve. I cannot understand this. No, it is the echo of a person speaking to me. Nothing shall persuade me that it does not ultimately proceed from a person external to me. It carries with it its proof of its divine origin.[3]

It is still a proof of God by reasoning; but one intimately bound up with my own person, and leading directly to a personal God.

---

[1] *The Faith of a Moralist* 1930, I, Sect. v, 163–211.
[2] *Grammar of Assent*, 112.
[3] *Callista*, p. 314.

However, Newman in his Oxford days thought that there was something akin to faith in recognising this voice, since conscientiousness was always seen as a virtue and its force could be dammed by disobedience. He said in 1830 'all obedience to it (this voice in our conscience) is of the nature of faith'.[1] Yet he did not confuse this with Christian faith and obedience which, in the same sermon, he said are some way beyond it.

At various times of his life from 1830 to 1870, Newman refers to this conscience in such terms as 'the essential principle and sanction of religion in the mind', 'God's word', 'The echo of the living Word', 'The echo of a person speaking to me', 'our great internal teacher of religion'.[2] And in his *Meditations and Devotions*[3] he writes:

> By nature and by grace Thou art in me. I see Thee not in the material world except dimly, but I recognize Thy voice in my own intimate consciousness. I turn round and say Rabboni. One ever thus with me.

This no doubt sheds a new light on the often quoted dictum of Newman, almost identical with passages in St Teresa of Avila and St John of the Cross. 'Sublime, unlooked-for doctrine, yet most true! To everyone of us there are but two beings in the whole world, himself and God.' 'From a boy I had been led to consider that my Maker and I, His creature, were the two beings luminously such, in rerum natura.'[4]

> As the sunshine implies that the sun is in the heavens, though we may not see it, as a knocking at our doors at night implies the presence of someone outside in the dark who asks for admittance, so this Word within us, not only instructs us up to a certain point, but necessarily raises our minds to the idea of a Teacher, an unseen Teacher, and in proportion as we listen to that Word, and use it, not only do we learn more from it, not only do its dictates become clearer, and its lessons broader, and

---

[1] *University Sermons*, 19.

[2] It is interesting to notice how close to Newman's language is the section on conscience in the Constitution on the Church and the Modern World of the Second Vatican Council: 'Conscience is the most secret core and sanctuary of a man. There he is alone with God, whose voice echoes in his depths' (sec. 16).

[3] *Meditations and Devotions*, 496 (ed. 1893).

[4] *Parochial and Plain Sermons* I, 20; *Apologia*, 195.

9*

its principles more consistent, but its very tone is louder and more authoritative and constraining.[1]

One can now see the way in which Newman saw nature – the nature of our conscience – the echo of the living word of God within us as the divinely ordained way leading us to the patriarchs and prophets and to Christ Himself. Newman finds innumerable Scripture exhortations to illustrate his conviction. 'I will stand upon my watch and set me upon the tower, and will watch to see what he will say to me.'[2] Through nature and grace God 'speaks to us'. 'I am the good shepherd, and know mine as mine know me. My sheep hear my voice.'

Those who become Christians, he said once, are always crypto-Christians beforehand. He that hath ears to hear, let him hear. No one can come to me, unless the Father draw him.

In other words: (a) preparation of mind is necessary; (b) a highly important part of this preparation is the expectation that the God we know in our conscience will find a way to speak to us and give us further knowledge and helps; (c) Christianity fulfils all the aspiration, needs, and foreshadowings of natural faith and devotion; (d) hence the nature of Christian revelation will not be essentially different from God's way of revealing himself in our conscience.

I will now merely suggest to you the way in which this natural knowledge of God leads to God revealing – to the way in which, in God's providence, this original belief, vision, faith in the good, just God who commands us to do what is right and avoid what is wrong – how this prepared the Jews to recognise God leading them, speaking to them, redeeming them through the history of the Chosen People. There was here a kind of corporate conscience of a people listening to the God of their Fathers, of Abraham, Isaac, and Jacob, for whom the good Jew was always waiting, hoping, expecting.

Eventually this God of Abraham, Isaac, and Jacob who had spoken through his prophets to the religious conscience of his People, appeared personally in his Son Jesus Christ. Just as conscience was not a multitude of prohibitions but the echo of God's living word, so Christianity is not a multitude of statements and commandments but the living Word Himself.

[1] *Sermons Preached on Various Occasions* 1900, 65.
[2] *University Sermons*, 303.

... we recognize this central Image as the vivifying idea both of the Christian body and of individuals in it. . . . It was the Thought of Christ, not a corporate body or a doctrine, which inspired that zeal which the historian [Gibbon] so poorly comprehends; and it was the Thought of Christ which gave a life to the promise of that eternity, which without Him would be, in any soul, nothing short of an intolerable burden.[1]

This is where the *Hand* of God is shown that this 'new idea, one and the same', could 'enter at once into myriads of men, women, and children of all ranks, especially the lower, and have power to wean them from their indulgences and sins, and to nerve them against the most cruel tortures . . .'.[2] This idea or image of Christ has been the source of theology and the inspiration of Christian living through the centuries. It is called the Christian Idea by Newman in his *Essay on the Development of Christian Doctrine*, and the Divine Fact in his sermon on the same subject.[3] Yet its richness, truth, and beauty can never be adequately expressed; since, as Newman reminds us, far from being able to define Christ, we are unable to define even natural reality: 'It were as easy to create what is real as to define it'[4] – how much more difficult then to describe in the language of men 'the thoughts, ways, and works of God'.

This manifest inadequacy of language is the reason why we can never describe a single reality adequately with a single word, or even with a single proposition. The deeper the reality the truer this is. Indeed, the deeper the reality, the greater ultimately is its fundamental unity. And this leads to the paradox that the deeper the basic unity, the greater the multitude of propositions we need to describe it. The deepest unity of all is that of the Godhead, and the real meaning of this inner unity can never be exhausted, even though we multiply our propositions for a lifetime. All Scripture is an attempt to describe the Godhead in his activity with men. All the New Testament is a description of the Godhead made man in his redeeming activity: the mind which is habituated to the thought of God, of Christ, of the Holy Spirit, naturally turns, as I have said, with a devout curiosity to the contemplation of the

---

[1] *Grammar of Assent*, 465.
[2] *Grammar of Assent*, 463.
[3] *University Sermons*, Sermon 15.
[4] *University Sermons*, 330.

Object of its adoration, and begins to form statements concerning him.

In spite of this inadequacy of language, Newman was convinced that one of the purposes of the manifold propositions is to generate in our minds what he sometimes calls the Christian *idea*, what at other times he calls the *image* of Christ. Just as a long description in many words and propositions will generate in us the image of one human individual, so all the words of Scripture and statements of councils and explanations of tradition convey to us the Image of the One Christ.

> As definitions are not intended to go beyond their subject, but to be adequate to it, so the dogmatic statements of the Divine Nature used in our confessions, however multiplied, cannot say more than is implied in the original idea, considered in its completeness, without risk of heresy. Creeds and dogmas live in the one idea which they are designed to express, and which alone is substantive; and are necessary only because the human mind cannot reflect upon that idea, except piecemeal, cannot use it in its oneness and entireness, nor without resolving it into a series of aspects and relations.[1]

So, if we are to get right back to the source of our theology, we cannot stop at any one or two or three or ten or a hundred or any number of propositions, though all of them are important. With the skill of our minds and the help of the Holy Spirit, we must be always endeavouring to get through to the one Idea, which in our minds is forever being developed to express with more understanding the divine fact, of which from the beginning it has been the image or idea.

Theology is a search for God who has come to us in Person. It is an attempt to hear all that this Person tells of himself, so that with his help and our poor words we may have a less inadequate understanding of what he tells of himself. The history of this search is the history of theological development:

> All our attempts to delineate our impression of him go to bring out not one idea, not two or three or four; not a philosophy, but an individual idea in its separate aspects.[2]

For though the development of an idea is a deduction of proposition from proposition, these propositions are ever formed in

[1] *University Sermons*, 331–3.
[2] *University Sermons*, 330.

and around the idea itself (so to speak), and are in fact one and all only aspects of it.[1]

Because of his grasp of the historical nature of our religious understanding, Newman was one of the first theologians in the nineteenth century to affirm the essentially historical nature of Christian belief. For him the source of Christian theology is not in cosmological or ontological arguments, but in the word of God in conscience and revelation, which 'speaks to us one by one ... as the counterpart, so to say, of ourselves, and is real as we are real'.[2]

If our dogmas were but words or propositions, then the objections of logical analysis would be irrefutable; but these dogmas are verifiable through our possession of Christ in our hearts; they bear fruit in our lives, and will be eternally verifiable when Christ is all in all, and presents us as his Kingdom to the Father:

> He who worships Christ and works for Him, is acting out that doctrine which another does but enunciate; his worship and his works are acts of faith, and avail to his salvation, because he does not do them *as* availing.[3]

I have spoken critically of certain contemporary philosophers and theologians because I believe they have misjudged the true sources of Christian theology. These are to be found not in cosmological, epistemological, or sociological arguments but in our personal acquaintance with God through conscience; and Newman's importance for the study of theology today is that he places the emphasis where it ought to be.

Theology in Newman's sense is expressive not only of the inner reality of our lives and of God's revelation to them through Christ, but also of the daily living and worship of those lives:

> Consider the services for Christmas or Epiphany; for Easter, Ascension, and (I may say) pre-eminently Corpus Christi; what are these great festivals but comments on the words, 'The Son is God'? Yet who will say that they have the subtlety, the aridity, the coldness of mere scholastic science? ... Why is it that personally we often find ourselves so ill-fitted to take part in them, except that we are not good enough, that in our case the dogma is far too much a theological notion, far too little

---

[1] *University Sermons*, 334.
[2] *A Grammar of Assent* 1909, 492.
[3] *Lectures on Justification*, 339.

an image living within us? And so again, as to the Divinity of the Holy Ghost: consider the breviary offices for Pentecost and its Octave, the grandest, perhaps in the whole year; are they created out of mere abstractions and inferences, or what are sometimes called metaphysical distinctions, or has not the categorical proposition of St Athanasius, 'The Holy Ghost is God', such a place in the imagination and the heart, as suffices to give birth to the noble hymns, *Veni Creator* and *Veni Sancte Spiritus.*[1]

In 1841 Newman wrote these words:

Let us ever make it our prayer and our endeavour, that we may know the whole counsel of God, and grow unto the measure of the stature of the fulness of Christ; that all prejudice, and self-confidence, and hollowness, and unreality, and positiveness, and partisanship, may be put away from us under the light of Wisdom, and the fire of Faith and Love; till we see things as God sees them, with the judgment of His Spirit, and according to the mind of Christ.[2]

I dedicate this prayer to the ecumenical development of theology and doctrine, as we grow towards one.

[1] *Grammar of Assent*, 139–40.
[2] *University Sermons*, 311.

Part IV

Newman and the Second Vatican Council

Newman and the Second Vatican Council

B. C. Butler, OSB

The idea of making Newman a bishop had been abandoned long before the First Vatican Council, and he would not consent to attend it in the capacity of an advising theologian. It is hardly likely that he would have felt at home in the atmosphere of a Council where Italian and Neo-Ultramontane influences were, together, so predominant, and where the official theology was the scholasticism of days before Leo XIII initiated the revival of Thomism. It says much for the moderation of the Council itself and for Newman too that, four years after the definition of papal infallibility, he was writing his open *Letter to the Duke of Norfolk*, defending the new decisions on the papacy against the attacks of his old friend Gladstone.

Newman's was a voice in the wilderness in the English Catholicism of his day. Some may have realised already that it was a prophetic voice; and we may claim that the Second Vatican Council has proved the fact. It is too early to give a final judgement on the work and significance of this Council; but it is already possible to draw attention to some of its dominant motifs and to compare them with positions held a century ago by Newman.[1]

1. A determined and partially successful effort was made in the Second Vatican Council to recover a more biblical theology. It may sound strange today that such an effort should have been necessary. St Thomas Aquinas himself grounded his theology on biblical data. But in modern times the practice had grown up of

---

[1] I gladly acknowledge my debt to Heinrich Fries, 'Newman im Licht des Konzils', a lecture which, so far as I know, has not yet been published.

making scriptural study and dogmatic theology into two separate disciplines, and of giving priority to the latter whenever disputes arose between them. Appeals to Scripture were of course not absent from the treatises of dogmatic theology, but they were not always such as scriptural scholarship would approve. During the Council itself the biblical experts have had to keep an eye on the use of Scripture, to prevent the dogmatists from 'proving' positions by the quotation of texts which do not really bear the meaning required for the proof.

Perhaps the shortest way to satisfy oneself that this Council really tried to be genuinely biblical is to examine one of its key documents, the Constitution *Lumen Gentium* on the Church. The first chapter of this constitution deals with the Church as a mystery, and it illustrates this mystery by a variety of biblical images: the Church as God's flock, as his vineyard, his field; the Church as the Body of Christ. No mystery can be adequately conceptualised, and it is as though, in this chapter, the Council were saying to us: meditate on these biblical images; remember that they are images, not arguments, and that they cannot be directly synthesised into a sort of super-image or a concept.[1] But, if you take them together, you may catch through them an insight which will be worth more than any concept and be more convincing than any argument.[2]

The same biblical approach is carried over into the second chapter of the Constitution, where however the Church is more closely examined under the single image of the People of God. But the biblical tension of the chapter appears already in its first paragraph, in which God's plan of universal human salvation through the association of all men in this People is set over against the biblical assurance that the one sufficient ground of acceptance with God is – not membership of God's people, but – that one should 'fear God and work justice'. Such fidelity to the Bible leads on to a doctrine of 'belonging to the Church' which, though it is nowhere fully elaborated in the Constitution, is yet very much richer and more plastic than the rather rigid doctrine of Church membership emphasised by Pius XII.

It is hardly necessary to remind ourselves that Newman's theo-

[1] That this, too, was Newman's method is demonstrated by Mgr Davis, 'Newman's influence on England', pp. 229–30 above.

[2] Contrast Pius XII's great Encyclical on the Church, *Mystici Corporis*, which picks out *one* image of the Church, that of the Body of Christ, treats it as a concept, and draws out a whole body of logical consequences from this concept.

logy was based almost uniquely on the Bible. Its real foundations emerge in the *Parochial and Plain Sermons* and the *University Sermons* of his Oxford days, which embody a dialectical progress from the rather narrow biblicism of traditional Protestantism to that evolutionary vision which comes to light in the last *University Sermon*, on the 'Principle of Development'.

Precisely in the great work which marked Newman's move from the Church of England to the communion of the Roman See occurs a remarkable statement of his view of the Bible:

> It is in point to notice also the structure and style of Scripture, a structure so unsystematic and various, and a style so figurative and indirect, that no one would presume at first sight to say what is in it and what is not. It cannot, as it were, be mapped, or its contents catalogued; but after all our diligence, to the end of our lives and to the end of the Church, it must be an unexplored and unsubdued land, with heights and valleys, forests and streams, on the right and left of our path and close about us, full of concealed wonders and choice treasures. Of no doctrine whatever, which does not actually contradict what has been delivered, can it be peremptorily asserted that it is not in Scripture; of no reader, whatever be his study of it, can it be said that he has mastered every doctrine which it contains.[1]

Such was Newman's position about Scripture just before he had decided to become a Roman Catholic. Nearly twenty years later, we find him arguing against Pusey that a Catholic is not bound to hold that the extent of revealed doctrine is greater than the real – as distinct from the discovered – extent of that doctrine as contained in Scripture; he suggests that the function of tradition is to guide and enlighten us in our understanding of the inspired word.

The issue of the material sufficiency of Scripture was hotly contested in the Council. One of the reasons for the rejection of the original draft document on the 'Sources of Revelation' was, that it seemed to wish to commit the Church to the view that Scripture is materially insufficient as regards doctrine. Repeatedly, in the ensuing three years, the attempt was made to secure that the substituted document should not fail to carry this implication. The attempts were successfully resisted, if we may presume that even

---

[1] J. H. Newman, *Essay on the Development of Christian Doctrine* London 1800, 71.

Newman would not object to the statement that it is through tradition that we know the extent of the biblical canon.

The dispute is thus not over, since the Constitution on Revelation has been equally careful not to affirm the *sufficiency* of Scripture. Newman, had he been alive, would surely have welcomed this conciliar respect for living theological discussion.

2. I have referred to the *Essay on Development*. I think Newman might have been equally pleased with the following passage from the Constitution on Revelation:

> The Tradition which comes from the Apostles thrives under the assistance of the Holy Ghost in the Church: the understanding of the things and words handed down grows, through the contemplation and study of believers, who compare these things in their heart (cf. Luc. 2, 19 and 51), and through their interior understanding of the spiritual realities which they experience. The Church, we may say, as the ages pass, tends continually towards the fullness of divine truth, till the words of God are consummated in her. [art. 8.]

Very manifest in this passage is the notion that the Church's understanding of revelation is a progressive one, never complete during her earthly pilgrimage. But some may find more in it than that. The official reporter of the Doctrinal Commission, in presenting this chapter of the Constitution to the Council, took up the word 'thrives' (proficit), here applied not to the Church's understanding of her tradition, but to the Tradition itself. What does this mean? According to this spokesman, representing, however, it must be remembered, not the Council itself but the Doctrinal Commission, it means, not indeed that there can be any substantial addition to the contents of the Deposit of Faith, but that the Sacred Tradition is subject to a law of internal progress, like any other living reality, a progress which does not change its substance and yet really adds a perfection to the living reality. The increased understanding of the things and words handed down does not remain extraneous to them, but rather becomes a proper element of them. One can almost hear the echo of Newman's words:

> [A great idea] in time enters upon strange territory; points of controversy alter their bearing; parties rise and fall around it; dangers and hopes appear in new relations; and the old prin-

ciples appear in new forms. It changes with them in order to remain the same. In a higher world it is otherwise, but here below
to live is to change, and to be perfect is to have changed often.[1]

3. How does the development of doctrine, and the evolution of
theology, in fact proceed? The question brings us to one of the
most important contributions made by Newman to Christian
thinking, and it was a contribution made easier by the fact that
he had not been educated himself in the contemporary Roman
Catholic seminary system. Since the days at least of Aristotle, it
has been held in the West that the natural development of our
human grasp of truth is from data supplied by the senses through
rational judgement to rational inference and rigorously logical
conclusions. The description Newman gives of the development
of an idea is widely different. Like the traditionalists, he starts off,
indeed, from given data. But the development which he foresees
for the idea to which the data give rise is far more historically
conditioned than guided by *a priori* logic. The initial idea itself
is not reducible, in his view, to a single proposition. As he says:[2]

> With all our intimate knowledge of animal life and of the struc-
> ture of particular animals, we have not arrived at a true defini-
> tion of any one of them, but are forced to enumerate properties
> and accidents by way of description.

And he remarks, with some irony, that

> the attempt to determine the 'leading idea', as it has been called,
> of Christianity [is] an ambitious essay as employed on a super-
> natural work, when, even as regards the visible creation and
> the inventions of man, such a task is beyond us.

This being its initial nature and condition, the idea is carried forward through the lives of those who accept it and its evolution
is shaped by a thousand circumstances that are accidental to its
intrinsic nature. This notion of the life of an idea, with its implied
depreciation of formal logical process as dominant in the real
history of the human mind, is the major theme of the *Grammar
of Assent*, where the resultant 'real assent' is contrasted with the
conclusions of purely logical inference.

[1] *Essay on the Development of Christian Doctrine*, 40.
[2] *Essay on the Development of Christian Doctrine*, 35.

The drama of the Second Vatican Council may be said to have been in large measure governed by the challenge of logical inference to the demands of historical development. It has been suggested that the Council was a trial of strength between essentialism and existentialism.[1] There is much to be said for this view, but one may remark that the implied opposition is at the level of philosophy, not of theology strictly so-called. Again it has been suggested[2] that the conflict was between the notions of an Open Church on the one hand and of Non-historical Orthodoxy on the other. This analysis is certainly confirmed by the experience of the conciliar debates. What in effect the Council did was to open up the Church, to turn her eyes and desires outwards from a somewhat unhealthy introspection to the challenge and the needs of a world tremendously alive and in a phase of incalculable swift evolution. As one listened to some able theological discourses from conservative speakers in the debates, one was overtaken by the sense that they were giving admirable answers to questions which had long ceased to be relevant; but as regards the real questions of contemporary man they were dumb oracles.

I venture, however, to suggest that one of the deepest currents in the Council was immanently directed towards the substitution, as basically relevant categories for Christian thinking, of the principles of history and historical appreciation for those of Greek idealism. Two features mark the thought of modern man: natural science, and the sense of history or of duration. Although we are usually told that we are living in a scientific age, I am not sure that the latter insight, the sense of duration, is not more deeply and comprehensively operative than the former. It is to the everlasting honour of St Thomas Aquinas that, in the face of much ecclesiastical opposition, he met the revived Aristotelianism of his age not with condemnation but with welcome, showing that all its legitimate demands could be met by the Gospel and could in fact be made ancillary to the preaching of the Gospel. The Second Vatican Council has largely sanctioned the efforts of a number of modern theologians to meet the demands of the historical outlook with a similar welcome. Indeed it can be argued that historical categories are more apt for a religion of incarnation than are those of Greek idealism.[3] In adopting this attitude, the Council has in

[1] E. Schillebeeckx, *Vatican II: The Real Achievement* London 1967, 7ff.
[2] Novak, *The Open Church* London 1964.
[3] See Laberthonnière, *L'Idéalisme Grec et le Réalisme Chrétien.*

fact endorsed the general viewpoint which inspired Newman's thinking from the days of the Oxford Sermons to the publication of the *Grammar of Assent*, the one great work which he wrote in answer less to the immediate challenge of circumstances than to an inner need to express himself and his deepest intuitions, in a working of abiding significance.

4. It is characteristic of 'real assent' that, whereas the conclusions of logical inference have a universality which is also impersonal, real assent is a fully personal commitment within a unique and incommunicable vital situation. Some men seem incapable of locating truth elsewhere than in the impersonal conclusions of a strict logic. One of the ablest opponents of the Council's declaration on the Jews has argued that it is legitimate to speak objectively, 'in the external forum', of the Jews as guilty of deicide, while leaving their possible subjective ignorance of their crime to the judgment of God (Bishop Luigi Carli, in *La palestro del Clero*). The argument is clear and the ideas are distinct. We know, on the authority of the Council of Ephesus, that Jesus is God. We know, on the authority of St Paul, that the Jews killed Jesus. Ergo. But I imagine that I am not the only one who feels personally quite uncommitted by this example of inference.

Christianity has two poles: the objective, once-for-all, redemption of mankind accomplished in the Paschal event; and the act and habit of faith. Faith, as the Council has emphasised[1], is precisely a fully personal commitment made in responsible freedom, or with free responsibility. Among the fairly small group of conciliar speeches which really got to the heart of the Council's basic motivation was one by Bishop Ancel, auxiliary of Lyons, on the declaration on religious freedom. He argued that we should see not freedom but responsibility as the fundamental notion in this area. It is because man is responsible that he must be, and is, free. It is rewarding to examine the Council Acts and to see how pervasive is the concern which they express for responsible freedom, a concern which goes back to the insistence, found for instance in the decree on The Church in the World of Today, on the dignity of the human person and the respect which is owing to it. Such respect gives rise to the Christian courtesy, a part of charity, that assumes that those who differ from us are yet men of good will and good faith. It may be illustrated by the avoidance of the

[1] *Dei Verbum*, art. 5.

words 'heretic' and 'schismatic' and the refusal to impute blame in the Decree on Ecumenism; or by the determination in the Declaration on non-Christian religions to consider not their errors but whatever is good and noble in them. It explains the religious freedom which the Council claims from the State both for the Church and for all other respectable religious groups, and the suggestion that civil authority should make reasonable provision for conscientious objectors. It may have had something to do with the observation that proper freedom of thought and expression should be granted not only to laymen but to clergy who engage in scholarly or scientific work.

The *locus classicus* in Newman for the primacy of conscience is, I suppose, the great passage in the open *Letter to the Duke of Norfolk*, in which he says that he will join with the best of you in drinking the health of the Pope – but of conscience first; a passage most appropriately cited by the English Cardinal in his fourth-session speech on religious freedom.

5. Newman suffered years of misunderstanding and official distrust during his Roman Catholic days as a consequence of his essay *On Consulting the Faithful*. He had, it seemed, dared to suggest that when the episcopate failed in its God-given role of guarding the true faith, its work might be done by the laity. A century later, the Second Vatican Council has acknowledged the evidential value of the 'sense of faith' of the universal People of God, and has virtually compared it with the infallibility of the Pope. It has also, in its paragraph on charismatic gifts (*Lumen Gentium*, art. 8), indicated the whole People of God, in the persons of the baptised, irrespective of their hierarchical status or lack of it, as the recipient of those motions or inspirations of the Holy Ghost which constitute, if one may paraphrase the Constitution, the dynamic element in the Church over against the static element which is the hierarchy as such. It is hardly necessary to remark that this Constitution devotes a whole chapter to the laity, and that for the first time in Church history a Council has now published a decree[1] wholly concerned with the laity's part in the Church's mission. The Council's teaching on the laity, on the People of God as a whole, on the ministerial character of the hierarchy and the ordained priesthood, and on charismatic gifts should lead to a new burst of initiative from below. The Council

[1] *Apostolicam Actuositatem.*

does not, of course, forget the guiding role of the bishops, but it is significant that our Fathers in God are reminded that they should not 'quench the Spirit'.

6. It is greatly to be hoped that this teaching, together with the new emphasis on freedom, including scholarly freedom, will help theology in two connected ways. The Roman Catholic Church has for too long been dominated by a single theological tradition, broadly to be described as scholastic, and more particularly as Thomistic. One may be a fervent admirer, even disciple, of St Thomas Aquinas, without selling one's soul to those who are called Thomists.[1] One of the most valuable fruits of membership of the Council for me has been the *realisation* – if I may use this word in Newman's sense – that the scholastic theological tradition is not co-extensive with Catholic theology; that the Eastern Rites, which have full *droit de cité* in the Church, are not merely complexes of liturgical, not to say rubrical, usage, but are also theological traditions. It may be that, as a result of the Council – and partly perhaps in consequence of its recognition that clerical formation must be adapted to the various localities in which the Church lives – there will be a gradual return to something of the theological pluralism which Newman admired in the schools of the Middle Ages and which would be a natural outcome of putting into practice his own ideas about university education.

The second theological benefit which might reasonably be expected to proceed from the Council's teaching on the People of God, on the laity, and on charismatic gifts, is a great increase in the number, and an improvement in the quality, of lay theologians.

[As a result of the breach in modern times between culture and theology] the actual functions in the people of God – the clergy and the laity – took shape in a simple relation of subordination of the latter to the former; the state of discipleship (*docibles*) became more and more assimilated to that of subjects. . . . Theology was changed into a peculiar training of the clergy. . . . [It] developed its own technical language, more and more remote from the mind, the intelligence, and the cultural life of the generality.[2]

[1] See a remarkable conciliar speech by the new Archbishop of Turin.
[2] Quoted from an Italian newspaper's article on *The Rediscovery of Theology* (L'avvenire d'Italia, 4 November 1965).

From the evils of this divorce between theology and culture it may be the special task of lay theologians to deliver us. And should this come about, not only will it be in full harmony with the dominant motifs of the Second Vatican Council, but it will fulfil a hope which was undoubtedly dear to the heart of Newman, however far he may have thought it to be from the possibility of early realisation. Things, he held, would have to get worse before they could get better.[1]

7. If one stands back from the details of the comparison which has been attempted here, and takes a broad look at Newman on the one hand and the Council on the other, what does one see? In Newman, as I have already remarked, one sees a voice crying in the wilderness. There were, of course, other such voices on the continent of Europe. There was Döllinger in Germany. There were the opponents in the First Vatican Council of a definition of papal infallibility, with Dupanloup and some great German and central European prelates among them. But the strains and stresses to which Catholicism was subject in the revolutionary and liberal nineteenth century had thrown up a neo-Ultramontane type of Catholic protest and defiance which identified loyalty to the Church with extremist *esprit de corps*. And especially in the decade which culminated in the fall of the papal temporal power this 'aggressive and insolent faction', as Newman called it, seemed to be the very spokesman of genuine Catholicism. The threat to the temporal power was viewed as an attack on the person of an aging, politically enfeebled pontiff, and party fanaticism was allied with something like a personality cult. In England itself, the Archbishop of Westminster was a champion of advanced infalli-bilism. And the greatest Catholic mind after Newman himself, W. G. Ward, was using *The Dublin Review* as a platform for neo-Ultramontane theology; every papal Encyclical, every papal Bull, almost every Brief, must be held to be an infallible document, and those who denied this view were only to be excused from heresy on the grounds of invincible ignorance (like the Jews who 'killed God'). To stand apart from this powerful party required courage and faith.

Now after a hundred years, we have had another Council,

---

[1] For a fuller discussion of these issues and their implications see John Coulson (ed.), *Theology and the University: An Ecumenical Investigation* London 1964.

marked like the first by the emergence of two broadly contrasting wings of opinion and aim. But this time, it is those who can be considered the heirs of the neo-Ultramontanes who have constituted the minority, and have been forced back on their defences – though they have had, on the other hand, the immense advantage of strong curial support, not to say leadership—which, however, has been insufficient to bring victory to their cause. The tide has been turned, and a first, immensely important, step has been taken towards the vindication of all the main theological, religious, and cultural positions of the former Fellow of Oriel.

Such a reversal could hardly have occurred if the conclusions of the First Vatican Council had been such as to ratify the full demands of the neo-Ultramontanes; but an ecumenical council, despite appearances, is not a democratic parliament in which one party may win total victory over the other. A believer may be allowed to hold that above the contending factions in a Council there is the overruling guidance of the Holy Ghost – whose presence at the Second Vatican Council was at times almost palpable. After 1870, dialogue within the Church was still possible; and so it is after the Second Vatican Council. Largely through the persistent, patient, and gentle vigilance of the bishop who now sits in the place of Pius ix, the two wings of opinion retain their right to exist, after the Council as before, and the dialogue can continue. Newman, I think, would have approved of this result. And how warmly would he have approved of the other result of the Council: the fact that the Roman Catholic Church is now able to invite those outside her visible allegiance to a similar dialogue, based – as regards our fellow Christians, on fraternal respect for those who are our brothers in basic belief and usually in a common baptism; based, as regards the rest of mankind, on a common recognition of the dignity of the human person and respect for responsible freedom – a recognition which, for ourselves, is reinforced by our faith that all men are potentially members of the People of God, the mystical body of Christ.

The question whether Newman's thought influenced the Second Vatican Council in any discernible way merits an investigation of which I am not capable. My impression is, that such influence cannot be found to have been deep or determinative. But if this is so, it perhaps strengthens the case for regarding Newman as possessing a sort of prophetic charisma, as one who, because he knew of only two absolutely luminous realities, God and his own soul, was able not only to diagnose the evils of his own day but to see beyond them to the abiding purposes of the God of our salvation. *Cor ad cor loquitur* – not only, nor primarily, the heart of the religious man to the heart of God, but the heart of God to the heart of his faithful servant. This was Newman's motto; if ecumenical councils were given mottoes, this is the motto which I would propose for the Second Vatican Council. Cor ad cor loquitur: the heart of God to the heart of his Church; the heart of the Church to the heart of her God, and therefore to the hearts of all men of good will.

The Newman Symposium

Speakers
The Most Revd Dr A. M. Ramsey, Archbishop of Canterbury
The Right Revd Dom B. C. Butler osʙ, Abbot of Downside (now
    Auxiliary Bishop of Westminster)
The Revd A. M. Allchin, Pusey House, Oxford
The Revd Dr W. Becker, of the Leipzig Oratory
Professor J. M. Cameron, Leeds University (now of the University
    of Kent)
Mr John Coulson, Downside Centre of Religious Studies
The Very Revd Mgr H. F. Davis, Birmingham University
The Revd C. S. Dessain, of the Birmingham Oratory
The Revd B. D. Dupuy oᴘ, Le Saulchoir, Paris
Mr David Newsome, Emmanuel College, Cambridge
The Revd Dr T. M. Parker, University College, Oxford
The Revd Professor E. G. Rupp, Manchester University (now
    President-elect of the Methodist Conference)

Chairman
The Revd Canon F. W. Dillistone, Oriel College, Oxford

Bursar
Dr D. W. F. Forrester, Keble College, Oxford

Members
The Most Revd H. E. Cardinale, Apostolic Delegate to Great
    Britain
The Most Revd G. P. Dwyer, Archbishop of Birmingham
Mr K. C. Turpin, Provost of Oriel College, Oxford
The Revd Canon J. N. D. Kelly, Principal of St Edmund Hall,
    Oxford
The Revd Dr Johannes Artz, Bonn
The Revd A. J. Boekraad, St Bonifatius Missiehuis, Hoorn,
    Netherlands
The Revd R. Breen, Roman Catholic Chaplain, McGill University
The Revd Bede Bailey oᴘ, Prior of Blackfriars, Oxford
Miss Nina Burgis
The Revd Laurence Bright oᴘ

The Very Revd Mgr J. L. Carson
The Revd Dr V. Conzemius, University College, Dublin
The Revd D. Cousins
The Revd Dr H. Cunliffe-Jones, Manchester University
Mr D. DeLaura, Associate Professor of English, University of Texas
Mr Alexander Dru
The Revd W. G. Fallows, Principal of Ripon Hall, Oxford
Miss Hilda Graef
The Revd M. Hollings, Roman Catholic Chaplain, Oxford University
The Revd J. D. Holmes, of the Birmingham Oratory
The Revd L. Houlden, Chaplain of Trinity College, Oxford
Mr A. N. Jenkins, University College, Dublin
Mr M. McCann
The Revd Professor D. McElrath OFM, Washington
The Revd B. Mahoney
Mr Neil Middleton, Sheed & Ward Ltd
The Revd Professor R. Murray SJ, Heythrop College
The Very Revd Mgr M. Nédoncelle, Dean of Strasbourg University
The Revd G. O'Collins SJ, Pembroke College, Cambridge
The Revd D. A. Pailin, Manchester University
The Revd M. Perry, S.P.C.K.
Mr D. P. Pym, Exeter College, Oxford
Mr C. Rigby, St John's College, Oxford
Mr G. Rowell, Corpus Christi College, Cambridge
Dr H. G. Schenk, University College, Oxford
The Revd D. Sparrow
The Revd A. M. G. Stephenson, Vice-Principal of Ripon Hall, Oxford
Miss Joyce Sugg
Mr J. Sullivan
The Revd Nicholas Theis
Miss Meriol Trevor
The Revd V. de Waal, Anglican Chaplain, Nottingham University
The Revd Dr J. Walgrave OP, Louvain
The Revd G. Wamsley, Superior of the Birmingham Oratory
Mr A. R. R. Watkinson, Pembroke College, Cambridge
Mr B. Wicker, Birmingham University

Index